A MANUAL OF FALCONRY

The author casting off a Peregrine Tiercel.

A MANUAL OF FALCONRY

BY

MICHAEL WOODFORD

WITH CHAPTERS ON
ROOK HAWKING AND GAME HAWKING

BY J. G. MAVROGORDATO, C.M.G.

AND MAJOR S. E. ALLEN, M.C.

AND A FOREWORD BY
LORD PORTAL OF HUNGERFORD

Second Edition

ADAM & CHARLES BLACK
LONDON

FIRST PUBLISHED 1960
REPRINTED 1961
SECOND EDITION 1966
REPRINTED WITH MINOR CORRECTIONS 1967
REPRINTED 1970, 1971 AND 1972

BY A. AND C. BLACK LTD
4, 5 AND 6 SOHO SQUARE, LONDON, WIV 6AD

ISBN 0 7136 0736 X

DEDICATION

I dedicate this book to my wife, without
whose unceasing co-operation I could never
have become a falconer.

"Ye ffalconer right makes well his flight,
And maladies can cure,
And eke at night with swoote delight,
Can call his lasse to lure." *Anon.*

PRINTED BY Unwin Brothers Limited
THE GRESHAM PRESS
OLD WOKING SURREY ENGLAND

CONTENTS

PREFACE TO THE FIRST EDITION

IN writing this book I am well aware of the imperfections in my experience upon which I have had to draw. I consider myself extremely fortunate in having been able to persuade two such eminent falconers as J. G. Mavrogordato and Major S. E. Allen to write for me two of the most important practical chapters. There is a precedent for such a policy. Major Allen has told me that many years ago E. B. Michell confessed to him that of his famous book only the chapters on Merlins were actually written by him. The rest of the book was written by co-authors.

It may seem to the reader that I have laid too much stress upon the long-winged hawks at a time when so few people can hope to do them justice. I have done this because the hawk taken as the beginner's bird is the Kestrel and the Kestrel is a long-wing. The basic training of both short- and long-wings is the same in principle, differing only in detail. The flying techniques of the two groups of trained hawks vary greatly and these have been discussed in detail.

Like Blaine, I have used the term "falcon" and "hawk" indiscriminately, "hawk" being the comprehensive term for all the birds employed in falconry and hawking. Similarly, I have used the word "falconer" comprehensively except where "austringer" alone is intended. I have referred to all hawks and falcons in the feminine gender except in those instances where the male or tiercel is referred to specifically.

I make no excuse for reprinting at the end of this book Harting's Glossary of Falconry and Polyglot Vocabulary. These very useful items appear at the end of *Bibliotheca Accipitraria* by J. E. Harting, published in 1891, which is now a rare and expensive collector's piece. In these days of improved communication it is of great importance to be able to converse with foreign falconers and to be able to express oneself in the correct terms.

I should like to take this opportunity of thanking Roger Upton, who executed the line drawings for this volume, and all those falconers, both in this country and abroad, who have so freely availed me of their advice and experience over the years. I am sure that my readers will excuse me if on account of the need for economy in words my presentation of the facts has taken precedence over literary style.

Summer Lodge,
Evershot,
Dorset.
January 1960.

PREFACE TO THE SECOND EDITION

SINCE the publication of this handbook in 1960 there have been changes in the status of British and foreign birds of prey and in the law relating to them. As a result of the catastrophic decline, especially in East Anglia, of the Kestrel and Sparrowhawk, due, it is thought to the use of persistent chlorinated hydrocarbons as insecticides in agriculture, the latter has been placed on the protected list (November 1963), and few licences have been issued for the former. All British birds of prey, and Owls, are now afforded full legal protection under the provisions of the Protection of Birds Act, 1954.

The Peregrine, too, has become almost extinct as a breeding species in England and Wales, while suffering a serious decline in Scotland. British falconers have therefore decided that there is no longer any justification for taking peregrines from any of the North European countries for the decline seems to be almost world-wide.

In 1964 an international conference on birds of prey was held at Caen in Normandy. This conference was well attended by falconers from most European falconers' clubs. A resolution was passed calling on the governments of the participating countries to overhaul their protective legislation in the light of modern biological knowledge. This is now being done and any falconer who entertains ideas of importing a hawk or falcon from any foreign country should first ensure that the country concerned has not recently passed legislation protecting the species and prohibiting its export.

It is not recommended that hawks be purchased from pet shops or animal dealers. As a result of their long period of captivity these birds are extremely difficult to train and are often in a very battered condition. A further consideration is that many of the species offered for sale by these agencies are quite unsuitable for any of the quarry that is available in Britain.

At present the future seems black especially for the beginner for whom there is no suitable easily obtained hawk upon which he may try his "prentice hand". But there are chinks of light in that the Ministry of Agriculture has placed a ban on the most persistent of the farm chemicals which were contaminating the environment so insidiously. It is to be hoped that our birds of prey, which after all occupy the same position in the food chain as we do, will be able to rid themselves of these accumulated toxic agents and find their fertility restored. Meanwhile we must all temper our demands for what amount to endangered species, with restraint.

At the time of writing this preface a Bill to amend the Protection of Birds Act, 1954 has been debated in the House of Lords. This Bill which has passed the Committee Stage, contains an amendment which, if agreed by the House of Commons, will empower the Home Secretary to grant licences for falconers to fly their hawks at specified natural quarry species in specified areas. If this Bill passes onto the Statute Book falconers will be able to apply to the Home Secretary for a licence to hawk such traditional quarries as the blackbird and skylark with the sparrowhawk and merlin respectively. The reader is in consequence advised to check on the latest provisions of the Protection of Birds Act before embarking on the training of the species mentioned above.

ILLUSTRATIONS

IN THE TEXT

"I have bought me a hawk, and a hood, and bells and all, and lack nothing but a book to keep it by."

Every Man in his Humour.

FOREWORD

MR. WOODFORD's kind invitation to me to write a foreword for his book brings back to me a flood of happy memories from the days, more than fifty years ago, when I had my first glimpse of what must have been the golden age of modern falconry. I had been enchanted since the age of eight by the descriptions of hawking in the books on chivalry, but had no idea that hawks were still flown in this country. As a Winchester schoolboy I was motoring home with my father one September day in 1907 from a rifle-shooting expedition to the Churn range on the Berkshire downs. Suddenly we saw under the lee of a rick beside the track a cadgeful of falcons and tiercels. The owner, Captain Gilbert Blaine, was coming towards us carrying a falcon feeding on a partridge she had just taken. I can still feel today the thrill of wonder and delight which passed through me that afternoon and was renewed at each of the many days of glorious sport at partridges and larks which Blaine's kindness allowed me to share with him then and in later years. How lucky to have, as one's very first sight of falconry, such splendid hawks so perfectly trained and managed —and yet, how hard to have to be content for many years with results so far below those one had seen with one's own eyes! In the long struggle for success I read and knew almost by heart the hawking books of those days—by Freeman, Salvin, Fisher, Harting, Michell and Lascelles—now, alas, as Mr. Woodford says, hard to find and expensive to buy (and also in many ways much out of date). For this present revival of the sport, marked by the appearance of many new experts, by the founding of a flourishing club of which Mr. Woodford is secretary, and by a good deal of excellent publicity, is really the opening of a new phase in the history of British falconry for which a new book was very much to be desired.

Recent legislation has given the genuine falconer a charter for the taking and keeping of his hawks, but conditions for practising the sport in the field have greatly changed and not for the better. One of the wild birds that gave former generations the finest of flights at the least expense, the abundant and lovely skylark, is now banned by law as a quarry: partridge land in open country is much more difficult to find and myxomatosis has largely removed the best quarry for the Goshawk. Moreover, the wider distribution of money has greatly increased the number of casual gunners who emerge from the towns at week-ends ostensibly to shoot "vermin." These people, who in practice seem to loose off at anything they see, must add tremendously to the risks of hacking or flying hawks in any but inaccessible country. For all these reasons it must be very difficult indeed today for any but the most fortunate owners to achieve the success in the field that was possible even twenty or thirty years ago. It cannot be said too often that enjoyment of the sport is not dependent on the size of the bag but on the quality of the flights obtained, but I think it is undeniable that only by making successful flights in the right country day after day for a period of weeks at least can an eyas hawk achieve first-class style, and that whoever flies a really first-class hawk well in good country is bound to make a good bag which, if not the measure of enjoyment, is certainly the measure of success.

Mr. Woodford's book will be specially valuable to the beginner in at least three respects. First, the author has a deep professional knowledge of the physiology and pathology of the birds of prey. Whereas fifty years ago the young falconer daily felt breastbones and pinched wing and leg muscles in an attempt to assess the condition of his charges, today he can learn from Mr. Woodford to get essential information from a weighing machine and to use antibiotics and other modern drugs instead of the rhubarb, Cockles's pills and other home-remedies on which earlier generations were advised to depend.

Secondly, the author has taken immense pains to explain in the fullest detail the successive steps in manning, managing and training both long-winged and short-winged hawks—too many earlier writers have tended to take for granted the reader's knowledge of elementary problems which in fact puzzle many beginners and, if not solved for them, may easily cause early discouragement.

Another virtue of this book is that the author does not minimize difficulties, nor hold out false hope of success to people who live in the wrong country or have not enough time to do a hawk justice. Hawking is the most difficult of all sports for the man without much leisure, and anyone who disregards Mr. Woodford's warning is likely to involve himself in disappointment and financial loss and the sport itself in some discredit among the uninstructed.

A further useful service to falconry is that this book, published so

Lanner (Passage), Saker (Haggard), Peregrine (Haggard).

Lanner (Passage), Saker (Haggard), Peregrine (Haggard).

soon after the recent changes in the laws relating to the protection of birds, gives essential information as to the rights and duties of the falconer towards both hawks and quarry. We can all gladly accept the licensing regulations in return for the protection of the Peregrine and Merlin, though some of us may regret that it was necessary to protect the skylark against the almost infinitesimal extra risk of having to fly for his life against one of his natural enemies trained and helped by man. I would guess that hundreds of thousands of skylarks stand to be harmed by modern developments in agriculture for every one likely to be hurt by a trained Merlin, but such things are not decided by logic and I suppose we must be thankful in these days that any field sport at all is left to us.

Major Stanley Allen's contribution on game-hawking brings back my fondest memories, as it was with him that I enjoyed wonderful partridge-hawking on Salisbury Plain in the early twenties. He mentions Sibella, the best hawk I ever owned, and it may encourage some readers (not unjustifiably, I hope) to learn that this falcon during her training was a violent screamer and a sufferer from croaks. After killing her first partridge she never looked back and took over a hundred and sixty "to her own foot" in the season of 1922. For the falconer with the means and the leisure to fly the Peregrine at partridges or rooks in good country there could be no better adviser than Major Stanley Allen.

Mr. Mavrogordato's descriptions of the characters and capabilities of foreign hawks are deeply interesting and this section will be of great practical value to any reader who may have the opportunity to take up the sport abroad. His chapter on rook-hawking must be one of the best ever written on this subject.

It is with the greatest diffidence, after all these years, that I dare to make two suggestions not contained in this book but derived from my own experience many years ago. The first is that since lark-hawking has been made illegal, wild-caught Merlins might provide flights of very high quality against starlings in suitable country. When at school at Winchester I had a haggard hen Merlin which adopted against a flock of starlings exactly the brilliant tactics which Mr. Mavrogordato describes so well in the passage on the "Adenese Haggard" in his chapter on rook-hawking. Once the rudiments of hawking have been mastered the true falconer is for ever seeking "quality" in his flights and, as the author says, the wild-caught hawk is often an incomparable "stylist" though the experienced eyas specialist may be a cleverer tactician, as my own Merlins sometimes showed when joined by wild ones in a flight at a skylark.

My other suggestion is that much fun might be had with both male and female Goshawks at rats in ricks, clamps and round farm buildings. Good small ferrets are necessary and the hawks soon learn to treat them as allies. A Gos will snatch a rat like a flash from the top or side of a rick or from a hedge bottom or a pig-sty, and I never knew even a male Gos to be bitten by the largest of rats. The actual flight, of course, cannot be compared with a good one at a rabbit, but it is great fun and the hawks get very keen on it.

I am sure that any reader who may have done me the honour of reading this foreword so far must by now be impatient to read the book itself, so I will conclude by thanking the author for his valuable work and wishing those who follow his instructions every possible success in the field and the mews.

PORTAL OF HUNGERFORD

CHAPTER I

CHOICE OF HAWK

I⊤ would seem from the volume of correspondence that is received at the office of the British Falconers' Club that interest in the ancient sport of falconry is being maintained in modern times. Most enquirers ask for the title of a book from which they may glean the elements of the management, training and flying of hawks at quarry. It is unfortunate that many of the books published in the last hundred years are now out of print and in many cases are expensive collector's pieces. Also the proud possessor of one of these volumes is often disappointed by the fact that the author usually assumes that the reader has some knowledge of the subject and so does not "begin at the beginning." A further point is that these books were all written by "experts," men of advanced years who had been hawking for many seasons. They had forgotten what it was like to be a complete beginner and they had no real idea of the sort of problems that confound the tyro. Times, too, have changed and what was commonplace before the First World War is no longer so. The public attitude to Field Sports has changed, and many practices which were acceptable fifty years ago would now offend. Legislation, in the form of the Protection of Birds Act of 1954, has a profound effect upon what British bird of prey may be taken and trained and what quarry may be legally pursued. It is with these considerations in mind that I have compiled this manual.

The aspiring falconer must first decide upon the type of hawk which he proposes to keep. This will depend upon several factors. The sort of country in which he lives, or at any rate has access to for sporting purposes, has a profound effect upon the species of hawk chosen for training. If the country is at all enclosed, that is, broken into small fields with occasional woods and spinneys with few large open spaces, then he must make his choice from the two short-winged true hawks, the Sparrowhawk and the Goshawk. These two are birds of woodland and overcome their quarry in a short sharp dash. They rarely fly high or far and so do not usually kill out of sight. They are trained to the fist. The Sparrowhawk, no longer common as a result of indirect poisoning by toxic agricultural chemicals, is now afforded legal protection and a licence is required before it can be taken for falconry. The Goshawk is not resident in the United Kingdom and so must be obtained from the Continent.

The Kestrel, which is protected and so requires a licence, is a true long-winged falcon. It is easily obtained from the nest and many falconers consider that it is a suitable subject upon which the beginner may try his hand. It is easily tamed and flies prettily to the lure. But only exceptionally will it take quarry for its owner. Its natural instinct is not rapacious enough and its food consists of such small beer as mice, beetles, grasshoppers, etc., which it captures by hovering in the wind above its hunting ground. Occasionally it may take a small bird and in spring it undoubtedly catches inexperienced newly fledged nestlings. But these habits do not commend the Kestrel to the serious falconer. In spite of the above the Kestrel does, in some cases, provide a suitable introduction to the sport, and to assist those who do obtain one the British Falconers' Club have published a booklet by W. Ruttledge which describes the training and management of the Kestrel.

Another relatively easily obtained hawk, the training of which is a useful introduction for those who later intend to train Goshawks, is the Buzzard. This bird is protected and a licence must be obtained from the Home Office before it may legally be taken and trained. The Buzzard is a slow flyer in level flight, and although easily tamed it is barely capable of catching anything more than the occasional moorhen or young rabbit. In its natural state, of course, the Buzzard is a superb soarer. It rides on the upsurging thermals and with its primaries spread like fingers it soars round in vast circles, gaining height with each revolution until it is a mere speck in the sky. Like the Kestrel it is a humble feeder, eating carrion, beetles, earthworms and any small bird or mammal that it can catch. Before myxomatosis decimated the rabbit population Buzzards lived largely upon rabbit, but now they have had to develop other tastes and there are many reports of them taking such diverse quarries as grey squirrels and seagulls. These last are caught in winter by Buzzards that sit in hedgerow trees. The Buzzard waits until the gull, which feeds on the insects which congregate under cow pats, is within range and then drops suddenly upon it.

If the young falconer lives in truly open country such as is found on the moors of the North of England and Scotland or in the arable or downland country of Salisbury Plain and East Anglia, he may consider that he should choose a long-winged falcon like the Merlin or Peregrine. Both of these are, of course, protected and licences are required. The Merlin is a beautiful little falcon which nests on the ground on the moors in the North of England. In olden times it was the Ladies' Hawk, and it was flown almost exclusively at the skylark. It is not by accident that the lark was chosen as the quarry. The flight of a trained Merlin at a lark on the open downs in August and September was a very well-matched contest. The lark often sang as it ringed up into the sky and the whole spectacle was one of the most engaging that falconry could produce. Now that larks are protected the modern falconer who trains a Merlin must look for other quarry. Attempts have been made recently to fly at starlings when these can be found far enough from cover, and snipe have occasionally been taken.

The Merlin is very easily tamed and can be trained to stoop beautifully to the lure; in many ways it is a suitable second hawk for the beginner to train after he has served his apprenticeship on a Kestrel or Buzzard.

The Peregrine is the most spectacular bird to be employed in falconry. Unfortunately, those who can do justice to this superb bird of prey are extremely few. One only has to consider what is required for an even modest chance of success to realize that unless one's circumstances are exceptional, it is advisable to give the Peregrine a wide berth. It is not so much that the Peregrine is difficult to obtain or train. The difficulty comes in locating suitable quarry in a suitable place and finding the time, dogs, helpers and other essential ingredients to success. Peregrines are flown at game—partridge and grouse—and at rooks. The two flights are very different and require very different preparation and technique. To fly successfully at grouse or partridge, one must have a minimum of two (known as a "cast") trained falcons or tiercels—the female is called the falcon and is best adapted to the flight at grouse, and the male, called the "tiercel" because he is smaller by one-third, is best for partridges—and regular access to 3,000 acres of flat moorland or 1,000 acres of open farmland reasonably heavily populated with game. The services of a steady pointer or setter are essential for grouse hawking and may be necessary for partridge, too, if there is any amount of cover in the form of roots. I emphasize "regular access" because odd days on land belonging to or rented by a shooting friend are not good enough. In order that the falcon may attain the physical condition and technical skill to outfly and strike down her quarry she must be flown *every possible day* throughout the season. Week-ends are not enough and nor is a concentrated fortnight coincident with the falconer's annual holiday. It is essential that the falcon (or tiercel) be entered at the chosen quarry early in the season when the quarry are still young and inexperienced. It is also necessary that the falcon be flown at the chosen quarry as often as possible throughout the entire season. To do otherwise results in what is to my mind a travesty of a noble sport. In falconry style is everything. The bag is purely secondary. Peregrines that are not flown often enough have neither the skill which is so stylish nor the physical condition to allow them to approach their fast-flying quarry.

The flight at the rook is somewhat easier to engineer. But again regular flying results in a fit hawk (and falconer), and more style and success will attend the hawk that is flown every day. No dogs are needed for rook-hawking but to obtain any style at all the country must be very open, devoid of all cover in the form of woods, trees, or even telephone posts and wires. In the old days before barbed wire reached Salisbury Plain it was customary to ride to rook hawks and the flights obtained were not only of the highest quality, ringing high into the sky, but took horses and riders several miles across country. Rooks can be caught in relatively enclosed country by Peregrines— especially falcons—but the flight so obtained has not much to commend it, being little more than a rat hunt. Falconers who indulge in flying Peregrines in such country may kill many rooks but the flights lack the style so essential to good class falconry.

To summarize this chapter suffice it to say that the Kestrel and Buzzard are suitable subjects for the beginner to train as they are easy to tame and are relatively expendable. When he has had some success at disciplining himself to the daily task of looking after one of these humble species he may then aspire to a hawk from the two main groups—the short-winged Sparrowhawk and Goshawk which are trained "to the fist" and the long-winged Merlin and Peregrine which are trained "to the lure." His final choice will depend entirely upon his circumstances, the quarry available and the type of flying ground to which he has access.

Throughout this book I frequently use the term "hawk" loosely to mean both hawks and falcons. I refer, too, to "small hawks," meaning Merlin, Kestrel and Sparrowhawk, and to "large hawks," meaning Peregrines, Goshawks and Buzzards. I trust the reader will bear with these generalizations.

CHAPTER II

FURNITURE AND APPLIANCES

THE trappings of falconry are known as "furniture." In the main they are made of basic materials—leather, brass and wood. Only rarely have the designs been changed in the past 500 years. Modern materials, such as plastics and other synthetics, may have a small place in the falconer's workshop. All the items of furniture and equipment are of supreme importance to the falconer and it behoves him to take great care that they are of the best materials obtainable and that they are kept in good condition. Neglect of this may result in the loss and often the death of the hawk.

THE MEWS

Naturally, the accommodation which the falconer is able to make available for housing his hawks is going to vary enormously. What follows is meant as a guide to what is considered essential. The room or shed chosen should be well ventilated, draught free and dry. If possible it should have an insulated roof so that it is neither very cold in winter nor very hot in summer. Hawks can stand cold but it must be remembered that they are forced to sit where they are put and they have no opportunity to move if they find themselves in a draught. Damp is fatal. If the floor is of wood it is advisable to lay down a broad strip of roofing felt (heavy grade) underneath the screen perch and to sprinkle sand or sawdust upon this. It is essential that the mews can be blacked out and it is an advantage if the door can be double especially if hawks are at any time to be left loose. Dimensions will vary but 10 feet × 8 feet × 7 feet high would be able to house at least three hawks on a screen running its full length of 10 feet. It is an advantage to have a skeleton door composed of vertical wooden battens so that the maximum amount of sun and air can enter and yet cats and stray dogs are excluded. The window must be barred with vertical bamboos or dowelling set firmly in a frame 1½ inches apart. It is permissible to put wire netting *outside* this as a safety precaution. If possible, there should be no beams or projections above the level of the perch. Hawks always try to fly to a higher level to better survey the scene below. If there is a beam or ledge high in the roof they will always be trying to leave their perch to attain it. If such beams cannot be removed then they must be shielded from the hawk's sight with hessian stretched taut. The inside of the mews should be painted a dull matt colour and there should be as few distracting objects in sight of the screen perch as possible.

THE SCREEN PERCH

The hawks will spend many hours on this perch so the falconer must make it as comfortable as possible.

The requirements of the long-winged hawks vary somewhat from those of the short-winged.

The screen perch of long-winged hawks should consist of a beam of wood running the full length or width of the mews. It must be securely fixed to the wall at each end, should be about 4 feet from the floor and 3 feet from the back wall. The dimensions of the beam are important. Long-winged hawks like a flat wide perch so that their weight is taken by their entire foot and not just by the ball. They also like to balance themselves with their short stiff tails. To this end the top of the perch must be flat and about 4 inches across. Failure to provide a wide enough perch may result in the weight all being taken on the ball of the foot with the risk of swollen feet and corn formation. If Peregrines are left loose in a shed with the choice of a pole-like perch or a 6-inch shelf attached to the wall to perch on, they will always go to the shelf. This must provide conditions nearest to the rocky ledge upon which they perch in the wild.

The top of the perch should be covered with thick hessian or an old carpet with the pile side downwards. The best way to do this is to hang the hessian or carpet over the beam—secure it with roofing felt studs on each side and join the two dependent ends 3 feet below the perch so that the whole thing hangs like a roller towel. Iron rods or similar weights can then be inserted in the loop so that the screen hangs rigid. The screen has a two-fold function. Firstly, it provides a suitable foothold for the hawk to climb up to regain her perch should she bate off, and, secondly, it prevents the hawk from regaining the wrong side of the perch after a bate. Were she able to do this she would quickly wind her jesses round the perch. The method of attaching the screen material to the perch described above is better than having a single thickness of material attached to the lower side of the beam because in such cases the hawk has the right-angled ledge formed by the screen and perch to negotiate after a bate. After fixing the free ends of the screen to the wall below the perch to hold the whole thing taut there only remains to cut the holes below the beam through which the leash is passed. These holes are best bound if the material used is hessian because it tends to fray. The distances apart of the holes will depend upon the size and species of hawk kept. Small hawks (Merlins and Sparrowhawks) must be 2 feet from the wall and 3 feet apart and large hawks (Peregrines and Goshawks) must be 3 feet from the wall and 4 feet apart on the perch. There must be no possibility of hawks reaching one another on the screen perch and it is essential that the flight feathers of one hawk are not able to be reached by the feet of its neighbour should both bate towards each other. Goshawks are especially dangerous to other hawks in this respect and will seize a wing tip in their talons and pluck out the feathers if they get the chance.

If short-wings are kept it is useful to line the wall behind the screen perch with some removable waterproof material, such as roofing felt, painted canvas or polythene sheeting so that the wall is not fouled by the mutes of the hawks. The floor, of course, is strewn with a thick layer of sand or sawdust which is removed as soon as it is soiled. An attempt must be made to keep the mews as dust free as possible because in dust there often occur the spores of a mould called *Aspergillus fumigatus* which is responsible for a fatal pneumonia of hawks. This disease can be best avoided by ensuring that the air breathed by the hawks is as dust free as possible.

The perch for short-winged hawks should be rounder in cross section than that provided for the long-wings. Goshawks and Sparrowhawks are arboreal birds and are used to perching on the limbs of trees. The perch need not be carpet-covered and should have the natural bark left on. The screen should be tacked to the lower side of the perch to hang double as described before. The diameter of the pole should not exceed 2½ inches for Goshawks or 1¾ inches for Sparrowhawks.

When hawks are tied on the screen perch they are limited in their movements by the length of the jesses. To tie a hawk on the screen the falconer pulls the leash through the lower ring of the swivel until it hangs in a loop half-way along its length. Both the free and the button-end of the leash are then put over the pole and the free end is brought through the slit in the screen. The free end is now pushed through the lower ring of the swivel and brought back towards the falconer. The button end is then brought through the slit and the two ends are tied together in a bow with a single loop. Both ends are then put through the loop and the dependent parts of the leash are pushed through the first slit so that they hang inside the screen. The swivel is now held tightly in an upright position on top of the pole where it is free to revolve. This is the best and safest way to tie a hawk on the screen perch.

WEATHERING SHED AND WEATHERING GROUND

Tame trained hawks can be kept out in an open lean-to shed all the year round provided the site is well chosen. It should be well drained, sheltered from high winds and, if possible, face south-east so as to catch the morning sun. (The floor should be sand on a layer of gravel.) Hawks on blocks have the full length of their leashes so they take up a considerable amount of room. A shed to house three falcons would have to be 24 feet long and 12 feet wide. The roof should slope gently from back to front and guttering should be provided to carry away the rainwater. Only tame, quiet hawks can be kept under such conditions. Passage hawks and those incompletely. manned would be too restive to be left for long unhooded in an open shed and so must be kept in the mews.

The weathering ground should be a level, well-drained area of short grass protected from the prevailing winds by a windbreak which may be natural as a hedge or artificial as a wooden fence. The area must be considerable if several hawks are to be kept as the blocks must be moved frequently to avoid killing the grass with mutes and to allow the hawks to be placed in the sun or shade as the weather conditions dictate. If the garden is not well fenced or walled it may be necessary to exclude dogs and cats with a six-foot high wire fence with an outwardly projecting overhang.

BATHS

While on the weathering ground, the hawks will be offered a bath. Some falconers advocate a static concrete bath with a deep and shallow end so that the hawk can wade in. Such a permanency must be equipped with an efficient drain-plug. A nervous hawk will certainly enter a bath of this type more quickly than the portable sort, but it has the disadvantage that the turf round the bath tends to get worn and soiled unless the falconer is in constant attendance to move the hawk as soon as she has bathed. Also, the water in this type of bath is more liable to external contamination unless frequently changed. The portable baths are usually made of a sawn-off barrel 3 feet to 3 feet 6 inches in diameter and 6 inches deep. If a hawk is at first shy of entering this type of bath a brick or two may be placed in the water to act as stepping-stones. Cream pans painted with black bitumastic paint make good baths for the smaller hawks but, having no thick edge, they cannot perch on them. These pans are improved if sunk level in the ground. But then, of course, they suffer from some of the disadvantages of the static concrete bath.

Hawks should be offered a bath three times a week when the weather is fine and less often in bad weather. They should have the opportunity of bathing early in the day so that they can get thoroughly dry before nightfall. If a hawk is flown before she has bathed, she may rake away to look for water in which to bathe. Hawks which have undergone a journey in a hamper are especially appreciative of a bath and will be seen to drink quite a lot of their bath water. Normally a few sips only are taken. Excessive drinking may be a sign of illness. Needless to say, the bath water must be fresh daily.

BLOCKS AND PERCHES

The portable perch upon which the long-winged hawks sit on the lawn is called the block. Much has been written about the optimum design and construction of the block. Ideally the block should be of such dimensions that the hawk is perched a reasonable height above the damp ground and yet not exposed to the high winds. The construction and design should be such that the sides of the block are not fouled by mutes and there is no danger of the leash getting tangled up or the jesses straddling the top of the block.

The block is made of hard wood and is tapered from top to bottom so that the mutes do not stripe the sides and the leash does not tend to wind round. The height is generally somewhere between 12 inches and 16 inches. The top of the block may be just flat wood, or a piece of cork may be glued to the top. This has the advantage that it dries more quickly than wood but the cork is less durable. Recently

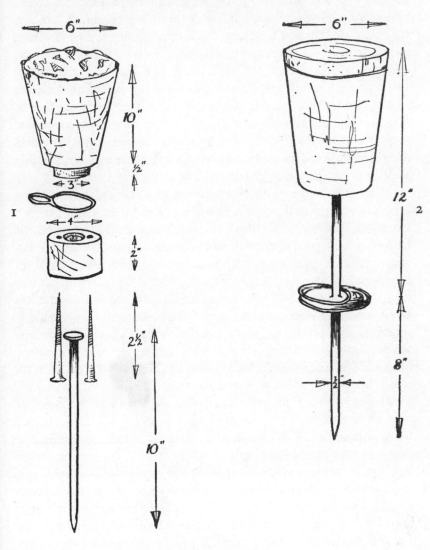

FIG. 1. THE BLOCK

1. Expanded view of concrete-topped block. The spike shown here is removable for transport.

2. Cork-topped block.

Peregrines: 12 inches high. 6 inches across top, tapering to 4 inches. 8 inches × ½ inch spike.

Merlins: 3 inches across top, 8 inches high, 6 inches spike.

falconers have been trying to overcome the corns and swollen feet which plague some falcons. In the search for the cause it has been suggested that the too regular surface of the blocks and perches may be contributory. To remedy this, blocks have been made with irregular stone or concrete tops. If concrete is used, it is attached by first stapling a rough mat of wire netting on to the top of the block and then moulding an irregular mass of wet concrete on to this. Grooves are made in the surface of the concrete while it is soft to carry away the rain water which might otherwise collect on the irregular surface. This type of block top is an attempt to simulate the rocky roosting ledge of the wild falcon.

In the simplest block the leash is tied to a staple driven into the centre of the top of the block. Other methods of attaching the leash are to cut a groove in the block about 3 inches from the ground and fit into this an iron ring with a small ring attached to its circumference. This iron ring must be so fitted that it easily rotates in the groove cut to receive it but is not so loose that the leash can get into the groove beside it and jam, nor so tight that when the wood of the block swells in wet weather it will be trapped and thus unable to rotate. If the small ring which is attached to the circumference is welded on this must be very carefully done as welds are always potential weak points which can easily rust through and result in the loss of a hawk. A method sometimes used is to have a circular plate 2 inches in diameter centrally pierced by the block spike and welded securely to the spike 4 inches from the base of the block. In the gap between the base of the block and this plate is inserted a loose iron ring to which the leash is tied.

There are various means of making the ring groove in the block. It may be turned on a lathe and the iron ring put on hot so that it shrinks into the groove. But this always results in some burning of the wood; or the block may be made in two halves, the ring put on and the two halves screwed together with long brass carriage screws.

The block has a stout iron spike driven into its base which projects about 9 inches. This spike holds the block firmly upright when pushed into the lawn or weathering plot. If the block is made in two halves it is possible to have the spike removable (for transport) by counter-sinking a large bolt into the lower half (or rather third) of the block and threading the upper end of the spike. The length of the spike will vary with the type of top soil likely to be encountered. In loose gravelly soils it is essential to have a long spike as a hungry falcon can easily pull up a block with a 9 inch spike. I have seen a falcon do this with disastrous results. She killed and ate a tiercel who was weathering next to her. In rocky soils it may be impossible to push a 9 inch spike into the ground. It is useful to have an indoor block which has no spike but which has a flat plate of lead screwed to its base. Finally the block may be painted, creosoted or stained and varnished, and the iron work painted with black bitumastic paint.

The leash is always tied to the ring of the block by the "falconer's knot." See two diagrams (Blocks and Knot).

RING PERCHES AND BOW PERCHES

Short-winged hawks are put out to weather on ring perches or bow perches. These are constructed to allow the longer tails of these birds to clear the ground.

The ring perch is more portable than the bow perch and is now in more general use. It can be made up for about £1 by any village blacksmith. It consists of a large ring 1 foot in diameter, made of $\frac{1}{2}$ inch square iron. This ring has two 10-inch spikes attached to it by a short 2-inch "neck." Round this neck is a welded iron ring 2 inches in diameter. It is to this small ring that the leash is tied. A padded leather grip is sewn on the upper quarter of the circumference of the large ring. This grip should be $2\frac{1}{2}$ inches in diameter for a Goshawk. Finally, two strips of leather are sewn on to each side of the ring so that they cross in the centre of the circle. This prevents the hawk from jumping through the ring.

A ring perch for a Sparrowhawk may be constructed using lighter iron and halving all the measurements—see diagram.

Bow perches are made of a sapling of ash or hazel. Steep in hot water and bend into a bow. Fix in position with a stout wire across the chord of the bow. The ends of the wood may be shod with iron spikes for fixing it into the ground. An iron ring large enough to run freely over the bow is put on before the wire is finally attached. The leash is tied to this ring with the falconer's knot. The diameter of the wood should be $2\frac{1}{2}$ inches for a Goshawk and $1\frac{1}{4}$ inches for a Sparrowhawk. In emergency a temporary block can always be made for a hawk using a large flowerpot. A metal pin 6 inches long with a ring on the end is pushed into the ground up to the ring. The leash is

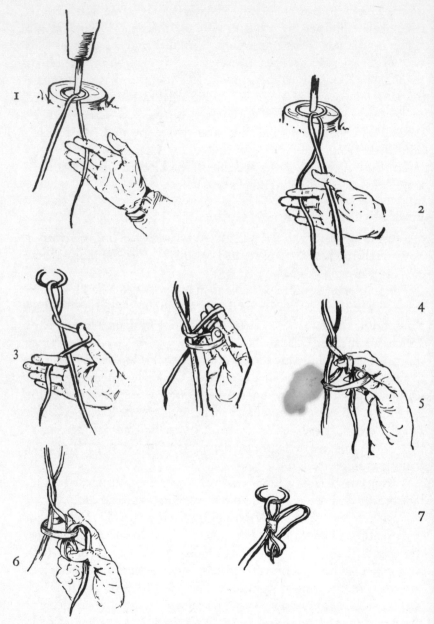

FIG. 2. THE FALCONER'S KNOT

[See Notes on page 15

put through the hole in the centre of the inverted flowerpot and the end tied securely to the iron pin. The pot is then inverted over the pin.

LEASHES

Good leashes for the larger hawks are difficult to acquire. Rawhide strips 5 feet long, $\frac{1}{2}$ inch wide and tapering to one end, can sometimes be obtained. Failing this some saddlers sell a leather strip called Helvetia which is used in the making of horse collars and to join agricultural belting. So-called "whalehide" can also sometimes be purchased from leather merchants in long 5-foot lengths but it seems difficult to get it $\frac{1}{2}$ inch wide. A button is fashioned at one end of the leash by cutting a $\frac{1}{2}$-inch square of stout leather, wrapping the end of the leash round this, punching a hole through the centre with a leather punch, passing the pointed end of the leash through this hole and pulling it up as tight as it will go. The leash is passed through the lower ring of the swivel and the button acts as a stop.

A suitable leash for a Merlin or Sparrowhawk is made from a long leather boot lace. If there is not enough leather at the end of the lace to make a button, a secure knot can be tied in the end.

Leashes must be regularly greased and inspected for soundness. The weakest spot is where the leash joins the button, and many hawks have been lost through the button breaking off. The falconer should

---

Fig. 2 Notes

1. Pass the free end of the leash down through the ring on the "block" or bow perch. Hold the free end about 6 inches from the ring with the right hand, palm upwards, under the index finger and over the second, third and fourth fingers.
2. Move hand under standing part of leash grasping the standing part in the fork of the thumb and index finger.
3. Turn hand downwards and hook the thumb under the part of the leash between index finger and ring. Bring thumb back to original side.
4. Bring whole hand back to original side of leash so forming a loop over index finger.
5. Tuck loop so formed through the loop over the thumb.
6. Draw the knot so formed tight with second finger and thumb.
7. Slide knot down to ring by pulling on standing part. Tuck free end through loop of knot and pull tight.

   If there is enough spare leash, tie a second falconer's knot for safety. Hold the hawk firmly by her jesses until the knot is secure.

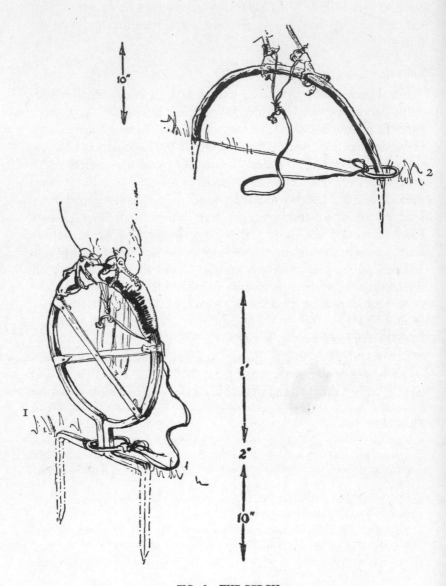

FIG. 3. THE PERCH

1. Ring perch for Goshawk.
2. Bow perch.

make a habit of inspecting this danger point every time he puts his hawk out to weather. Peregrines will attempt to bite through a leash and sometimes succeed. Goshawks rarely do this. It is unwise ever to use any other material than sound leather for a leash. Even a Merlin will nibble through thick woven ferret line in a few minutes. In hot climates where leather leashes become dry and crack and in humid conditions where leather becomes mouldy, leashes can sometimes be made of light nylon rope. The ends are whipped and the button consists of a knot behind which is a disc of leather.

JESSES

These are the strips of leather which are attached to the hawk's legs and by which she is restrained on the glove. They are joined at their free ends by the swivel. They are never taken off except for renewal. Jesses are made of pigskin or calfskin, well stretched and greased, for the small hawks (Merlins, Kestrels or Sparrowhawks) and of kip or other stout pliable leather for the large hawks (Peregrines, Goshawks or Buzzards). Their length and strength is of some importance. It is sometimes necessary to use heavier, stronger jesses during the training stages as many hawks bite persistently at their jesses until they get used to them. Later on, when the hawk can be trusted, her jesses can be made shorter, lighter and narrower. It is helpful, too, during training to have the jesses fairly long as it is much easier to pick up a shy, incompletely manned hawk which has long jesses than one which has short ones. But the jesses must not be so long that they can fall on either side of the block and so pin the hawk down. This is a serious accident as it results in great strain on the hawk's legs and often in broken tail feathers. Nor must the jesses be so short that they are difficult to hold between the fingers. Short jesses are dangerous, too, on the screen perch as they do not allow the hawk enough play to bate off and climb back again. It will thus be seen that any measurements which I give are only approximate and will depend a lot on circumstances.

Jesses for Merlin, Kestrel, Sparrowhawk. Length 6 inches—A–B $1\frac{1}{2}$ inches (outside to outside). Jesses for Peregrine, Buzzard. Length 8 inches—A–B $2\frac{1}{2}$ inches. Jesses for Goshawk. Length 10 inches—A–B $2\frac{1}{2}$ inches. (See diagram.)

Traditionally the leather was cut wider in the part which encircles the hawk's leg, but this is not really necessary in long-winged hawks.

C

Short-winged hawks tend to bate more and perhaps the wider leather gives more support.

In the Middle East the trailing jesses on a trained hawk's legs would attract other birds of prey, thinking that the trained hawk was carrying a kill. The wild hawk's attempts to rob the trained bird would spoil the flight so a method has been evolved to circumvent this. A short strip of supple but strong leather, rounded at each end, is taken round the hawk's leg and is riveted on to ensure a snug fit. In one rounded end is fitted a large brass eyelet and in the other a metal name disc. Both legs are so treated. Then another strip of similar leather with a button fashioned on one end (like a leash button) is inserted through the eyelet. The two free ends of these strips are then fixed to the swivel in the same way as are conventional jesses. When a hawk so equipped is flown the leash, swivel and button jesses are removed and she flies with just the very short eyeletted anklets. These are called "Aylmeri."

In this country Aylmeri are sometimes used on Sparrowhawks as these little hawks frequently crash into bushes after their quarry and the longer conventional jesses sometimes get caught up in the twigs and branches.

A small metal name plate bearing the name, address and telephone number of the owner may, with advantage, be fixed to one of the jesses so that should the hawk be lost its finder may know with whom to get in contact.

SWIVELS

The traditional swivel was made of brass, the two halves being joined by a steel rivet. This was the weak point as rust could attack the rivet unnoticed and one day the swivel parted with the loss of the hawk. Dog-lead swivels are rarely well enough made to be safe and are subject to rust and corrosion. The safest swivels are those made for big game fishing by Hardy Bros., Alnwick, Northumberland. Two sizes may be used in falconry. No. 1 Alma swivels for the large hawks and Hardy Small Big Game Sea Swivels for the small hawks. The shape of these swivels is not ideal but they never break.

BELLS

Bells are an essential item of furniture. Ideally the hawk carries two—one on each leg above the jesses. One of the bells should be a semitone in note above the other. This produces a discord which can be heard a great distance. The best bells come from Pakistan where they are made by some ancient process in the Lahore region. These bells are extremely light, of good tone and, because they have an irregular shaped clapper, produce a sound at the slightest movement of the hawk. European bells are invariably heavier and are not of such good tone.

An attempt was made to copy the alloy of which the Indian, or rather, Pakistani, bells are made. But spectroscopic examination of the metal showed that they contained every sort of impurity and dross imaginable. This made imitation virtually impossible. Pakistani bells are difficult to obtain. They come in three sizes. The largest are for Peregrine falcons and Goshawks, the medium sized ones for Peregrine tiercels and similar sized hawks, and the smallest are for Kestrels, Merlins and Sparrowhawks.

The bell is attached to the leg by a short strip of leather called a *bewit*. This may be put on by passing the strip through the ring of the bell and then through again on itself so that the brass ring does not touch the hawk's leg. The strip is then taken round the leg and passed through a hole punched in the other end. It is then pulled tight and a hole is punched in the first piece. The second piece is passed through this hole and two snicks are made in the strip to prevent it being pulled back. The ends are then cut short. Another method of attaching the bell which, although not quite so safe, I prefer, because by its use I am enabled to remove and replace the bells at will, is the button bewit. Prepare a narrow strip of calfskin or thin pigskin so that it has a small leash type button at one end, is pointed at the other end and has a small hole punched in the middle. Pass the free end through the ring of the bell and back through the punched hole. Then try the bewit on the hawk's leg, making a note of the place to cut the button-hole. Cut the button-hole at the point you have decided and button the bell on to the hawk's leg.

When one first puts bells on a young hawk she may bite at the bewits and as they are of light leather she may easily bite them through. It is, therefore, customary to use a pair of old, almost worn-out bells during the early stages of training until the hawk has abandoned these habits. In any case, she will not be flown loose during these early days so that the quality of the bells is of no account.

A good pair of Indian bells will last about six months on a hawk's

FIG. 4. BEWITS

1. Indian Bewit.

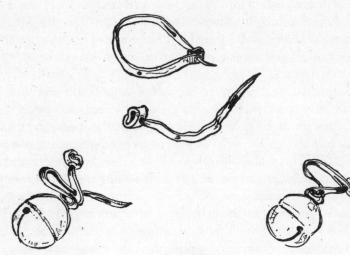

2. Button Bewit.

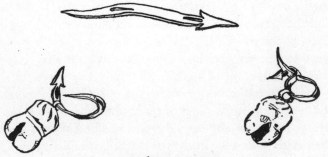

3. Traditional Bewit.

legs. In order to preserve bells I unbutton mine when I put the hawk down to moult in the spring. This has a slight disadvantage because the experienced falconer can deduce quite a lot from the sound of the bells on his weathering lawn. He knows the sound of a casual bate; he can tell when several hawks are bating at once, a sound which may mean that a prowling cat has gained access to the enclosure. He can appreciate the difference between the persistent bate of a Goshawk and the rapid ringing of the bell on the leg of a hawk which is scratching its head with its toe. If he removes the bells during the moult he is unable to receive auditory warning of danger from his weathering lawn when he is out of sight of his hawks.

Goshawks and Sparrowhawks may usefully be belled on the tail as well as on the legs. When they kill in cover the leg bells are often muffled by grass and leaves and when they take stand in a tree the tail is frequently shaken while the legs are kept very still. To bell a hawk on the tail she must first be cast by an assistant. To do this he must approach her from behind and grasp her by the body at a point level with her shoulders. Thus the wings are bound to her sides. She is then placed upon a cushion so that her feet may grip it. The bell is attached to one of her deck feathers. The fluff at the base of the feather is trimmed away with scissors, a length of adhesive plaster is cut and passed through the ring of the bell. The plaster is then wrapped firmly round the base of the shaft of the feather.

Some persons are unfortunate in being unable to hear clearly sounds of the pitch emitted by hawk bells. This is a serious disadvantage for a falconer because if a flight ends in deep cover the bells are often the only indication of the whereabouts of the hawk. This form of deafness is often hereditary and so little can be done about it. It is possible, however, to have an audiograph prepared which will show the range of cycles to which the patient is deaf. He should then obtain bells which ring within the cycle range which he can clearly hear. I myself have greatly reduced auditory efficiency between 1,500 and 8,000 cycles, so I must find bells whose note is above 8,000 cycles.

LURE

The lure is the dummy to which the hawk is trained to return after an unsuccessful flight. It may be made up in many forms and provided the hawk learns to associate the form used with food it matters little what shape the lure has or what decoration the falconer appends to it. Nevertheless, some lures are better than others. One should bear in mind that the lure may be struck by the falcon in the air while it is being swung. To have incorporated heavy wood or metal in the construction of the lure is asking for the falcon to injure herself. Gilbert Blaine always used a dead pigeon or grouse as a lure and claimed that his hawks came more promptly to this than to the artificial lure. He tied the dead bird's legs to the line swivel with "false" jesses of leather or ferret line. Many falconers now use a lump of tough beef to which is attached a pair of rook's wings tied back to back. This makes a good lure but has the disadvantage that the rook's wings get smelly. A good lure can be made by making a small chamois leather bag and filling it with sand—the size and amount of sand will vary according to the species of hawk for which it is to be used and to some extent to the stage of training. A heavy lure is often used during the early stages to counteract the vice of "carrying," that is, attempting to fly away with the lure or quarry when approached by the falconer. This vice is inherent in most Merlins. Rook's wings can then be securely sewn to the sand bag (6 oz. for Peregrine; 2 oz. and sparrow's wings for Merlins and Kestrels). A swivel, and here an old brass swivel or a well-made dog lead swivel will do, is sewn securely into the top of the bag. Two pieces of string should be passed on a sacking needle through the centre of the lure and tied. Pieces of tough meat can then be tied to these strings to "garnish" the lure.

The lure line is best made of blind cord which is strong and does not readily kink. Yellow or orange are good colours which can readily be seen if the lure is dropped in long grass. The lure line, which is 3–4 yards long, is tied firmly to the swivel on the lure. The other end of the line is attached to a lure stick made of a piece of wood the size of a broom handle and about 6 inches long. The line is wound up on this stick when not in use. I find it an advantage to have one end of this stick sharpened to a rough point so that it can be pushed into the ground. This is useful during training to anchor the lure when a shy hawk is feeding on it. She cannot then bolt with the lure. A suitable lure for a Goshawk is made of a small rabbit skin dried and stuffed with hay.

THE CREANCE OR LINE

The creance is usually a 50-yard length of woven ferret line or better, woven nylon cord wound and tied on to a short stick similar to the lure stick. Do not use fishing line as it often breaks. This line is tied to the swivel when calling the hawk to the fist or lure during training before she can be trusted to fly loose. It also has many uses in the field and should always be carried in the falconer's bag.

FALCONER'S GLOVE

European falconers carry their hawk on their left fist unless they are left-handed, in which case they adopt the Oriental practice and carry the hawk on the right. The glove for large powerful hawks is made of soft buckskin. The leather is double over the thumb and first two fingers. This double portion extends over the upper part of the wrist. The gauntlet should reach half-way up the forearm and the skirt of the glove should be full. It is convenient to have two eyelets inserted in the lower portion of the gauntlet skirt through which a small, short thong of leather can be passed—this thong is joined with a tassel and is used for hanging the glove up when not in use. Be careful not to have the thong too long or it will be for ever catching in sticks and branches when one is hawking in woods. The edges of the gauntlet may be bound with coloured leather, but it is best to avoid red as a hungry hawk on the fist is inclined to continually pull at red leather binding or thonging. The glove must be supple enough for the falconer to be able to feel the jesses through the buckskin. If it is too stiff and thick the jesses easily slip through the fingers. A comparatively light glove is all that is required for Peregrines, but the glove for Goshawks must be stout, for the Goshawk in "yarak" has a vice-like grip and its talons will penetrate any but the best buckskin. A light gardening glove is quite satisfactory for the small hawks. If it is decided to make one's own glove, get a good pattern or get a glove-maker to cut the leather out and remember to make the glove with the outside of the buckskin (chrome tanned for preference) on the inside of the glove. The talons of a hawk disengage more readily from the leather when a glove is made up in this way. After much use the glove will become soiled with blood. When in this state it is very attractive to mice which will gnaw it and ruin it, so always hang it up out of their reach.

HOODS

Hoods are stiff leather caps which are used to blindfold a hawk during transport and during training. Their use has superseded the

mediaeval practice of "seeling," that is sewing up the eyelids so that
the hawk is temporarily blindfolded while it gets over the initial
shock of capture and training. Actually, the practice of seeling, which
is still carried out in the East, was probably quite a humane act
because the hawks taken for training were almost always passagers
or haggards and for them the shock of suddenly finding themselves
in close proximity to their arch enemy, man, must have been considerable. Hoods are really only necessary for the larger long-winged
hawks. The small long-winged hawks are difficult to hood and do
not tolerate the stiff leather very well—they tame so quickly and
transport so easily, even by car, that hooding is quite unnecessary.
Some austringers like to break their Sparrowhawks or Goshawks to
the hood but this, too, is now considered unnecessary. Both Goshawks and Sparrowhawks hate the hood and it is certainly true that
the more they see the tamer they are likely to be. In the early stages of
training a Peregrine it is customary to carry her hooded. A Peregrine
is unique in that she will become manned (to some extent) while
being carried hooded. This is not so with short-winged hawks which
only become properly manned with constant bareheaded carriage.

Broadly speaking, the hoods used for falconry are of two types—
the Dutch or European and the Indian.

The Indian pattern is simpler and was probably the precursor of
the Dutch. It is believed that returning Crusaders brought the
original Oriental patterns back from the Middle East and from them
developed the present European design which has remained basically
unchanged for five hundred years.

The Dutch Hood is made up of three pieces of leather which are
sewn together to form the body and the two eyepieces. Billiard cloth
or cloth from a huntsman's pink coat are stretched over the eye
pieces and sewn into the seams to provide a light-tight junction.
Recently, coloured suede type leather has been used for this purpose.
This has the advantage that it is moth proof and is less likely to be
damaged by a falcon which persistently scratches at her hood with
her inside claw. The bright colours, apart from being gay, are useful
when the hood is dropped in long grass. A plume of cock's hackle
feathers garnished with coloured wool and bound tightly together
with fine brass wire is fixed to the crown of the hood. Again this
plume is functional as well as beautiful. It is used to hold and steady
the hood when it is being put on. The hood is furnished at the back

with two pairs of leather braces. When pulled from opposite sides the inner pair opens the hood and the outer pair closes it. Of course, when the hawk is on the left fist the falconer has to open and close the hood braces by pulling them with his right hand and his teeth. The Dutch hood tends to be somewhat heavy but some falconers will use no other, claiming that a well-fitting Dutch hood is comfortable for the hawk and that such a hood holds its shape longer than one of the Indian design. However, no hood will hold its shape for long if it is crammed in a pocket when removed from the hawk's head before a flight. To avoid this abuse of the hood, one may make a wooden block roughly the size and shape of a hawk's head. This is screwed with two short screws on to the falconer's waist belt. When the hood is struck it is placed upon this wooden block and the braces drawn tight.

The Indian hood is made of a single piece of light calf skin (or other suitable leather). It does not open and close at the back but is to some extent adjustable by being bound round the base by a thick strap of leather of contrasting colour, which is threaded through slits cut in the body of the hood. Usually there is no plume and the hood is crowned by a small turk's-head knot of leather. The beak opening of the Indian hood is much larger than that of the Dutch pattern. It extends to the commissures of the hawk's beak and so the bird is able to feed easily through the hood and may even cast through it. But this hood has the disadvantage that, having no braces, a hawk can easily pull it off. She cannot therefore be left alone hooded in an Indian hood.

A modification of the Indian hood has now been developed which is meeting the approval of an increasing number of European falconers. This entails the slitting up the back of the traditional Indian type hood and the insertion of braces similar to those used on the Dutch hood. A Dutch type plume, perhaps a little less flamboyant, is also sometimes put on.

This Anglo-Indian hood has the advantages of both designs. It is very light, and is well tolerated by the hawks. It is much more easily made and I think it is easier to make a good hood of this design than it is to make a well-fitting Dutch hood. Dutch hoods are made and "blocked out" on wooden blocks shaped like a falcon's head. Indian hoods and Anglo-Indian hoods are not so "blocked." Owing to the wide divergence in the size of the head of hawks of the same sex and

FIG. 5. HOODS

1 and 2. Dutch hood proper, front and back.
3. Dutch rufter hood.
4 and 5. Indian and Anglo-Indian hoods.

species, it is a matter of some difficulty to obtain a hood which is a perfect fit. It is often necessary to try on many hoods and to modify them by widening the beak opening with a scalpel. When not in use all hoods should be kept with the braces in the open position.

Rufter hoods are shallow, backless leather caps which used to be used to accustom the hawk to the feel of a hood on its head—they are very easily slipped on and off. Most falconers now dispense with these and break their hawks to the hood proper from the start.

THE BOX CADGE

A useful perch for hawks when they are being transported by rail or car. It consists of a square or rectangular box, the edges of which have padded battens of wood nailed to them inside the box so that a grip for the hawk's feet at least 2 inches wide is provided all round the upper edge of the box. A hole is cut with an auger in the upper third of each of the four sides of the box, through which the leash is passed to secure the hawk. A box of 2 feet square will accommodate four hooded Peregrines. All that remains is to put a 4 lb. weight on the floor of the box so that it cannot overturn. Needless to say, hooded hawks must never be left unaccompanied on a box cadge for they are much too close together for safety.

WEIGHING MACHINE

This is one of the most important items of equipment. It consists of either a dial type machine graduated in quarter ounces for small hawks or in half ounces for large ones. The pan is removed and a short piece of wood bolted in its place as a perch. Or, better, the machine may be of the counterbalance type—these are more accurate. Here again the pan is removed and a perch is substituted. It is important when using the counterbalance type to ensure that the weights are "Government stamped" as the cheaper weights are far from accurate. Always weigh the hawk at the same time of day and wearing the same furniture, i.e. hooded or unhooded. Be sure to retain a firm hold on the leash while weighing; in fact the operation is best carried out in a room or shed with the door closed. Scales vary considerably even with Government-stamped weights so that it is always advisable to take one's own set when hawking away from home.

FALCONER'S BAG

The falconer must carry a light bag which hangs on his right side and is either slung from a shoulder strap or attached to his belt. The dimensions of the bag will vary greatly as they are a matter of individual preference, but as the practice of hawking often involves running cross country it follows that the smaller and lighter the bag the better. The bag is made of canvas or leather and consists of two main compartments; one for the lure and the other, with a detachable plastic lining, for the meat upon which the hawk is to be fed. Any quarry that is captured should be carried in bags by other members of the field. The falconer's bag is generally so constructed that it hangs on a swivel so that it can be turned at will. In it may also be carried a spare leash, a short iron peg and 25 yards of creance wound on a short stick. Do not carry spare bells in the hawking field as the tinkling of these in the bag can be most misleading when one is searching for a lost hawk.

IMPING NEEDLES

These are small triangular needles filed out of bicycle spokes. They are used for repairing broken feathers in a hawk's wing or train.

Apart from the foregoing somewhat formidable list of furniture, some of which is not essential to the beginner, the falconer should provide himself with a few odd tools. These should include a leather punch, a pair of pointed pliers, a surgeon's scalpel, a nail-file (for coping), a pair of nail-nippers and a supply of leather. He may also like to make up his own dressing for jesses, leashes, etc. An excellent recipe given me by Major W. E. Poles is as follows:

> 1 oz. beeswax
> 2½ oz. white wax (good quality candles)
> 5 oz. liquid paraffin.

Shred and melt the beeswax and white wax in a tin over a slow fire. Add the liquid paraffin and stir well. When well mixed pour into a wide-mouthed jar or tin.

CHAPTER III

GENERAL CONSIDERATIONS

THERE are many things which the aspiring falconer should consider before embarking upon the task of training his first hawk. Too many beginners fail to realize that a hawk is unlike an inanimate piece of sporting equipment such as a gun or fishing rod. A hawk must have a certain amount of *daily* handling and attention. Long-winged hawks must be flown almost daily if they are to be kept at that peak of physical condition which enables them to capture their quarry. Trained hawks are not zoo animals which are kept captive to satisfy the acquisitive ego of their owner. The bird fancier and the falconer are poles apart. The beginner must remember that if he keeps a hawk it will be difficult for him to get anyone else to help him with it or to feed it should he be ill or away from home. Holidays will be almost impossible for him unless he can arrange for a fellow falconer to look after his hawk, or he can take the hawk with him and have a hawk-ing holiday. The man who in winter leaves home for work before it is light and returns after it is dark, will be unable to keep long-wings because he will not be able to exercise them sufficiently. He will just be able to keep a short-wing and fly it at the week-ends, but even then he will have considerable difficulty in keeping the bird suffi-ciently manned. The falconer who has a job of work to do and who cannot employ an assistant would be well advised to stick to eyas short-wings and to train them in the long summer evenings. It is virtually impossible to man a passage short-wing during the winter evenings in artificial light. Some carrying in daylight each day is essential. Possibly the only occupation which lends itself to daylight hawk training in winter is that of the farmer. Then there is the prob-lem of quarry. In winter when the days are short and the weather often inclement, it is often extremely difficult to find sufficient quarry to justify the keeping of a trained hawk. If quarry is not readily available near at hand and if there are too many blank days, the hawk will soon become discouraged and her performance will suffer. She will become "fist-bound" or "lure bound" and will be more inclined to look for her food upon the fist or lure than to pursue wild quarry. The man who keeps a captive hawk and does not regularly fly it at quarry is no falconer.

From this it will be readily seen that although modern falconry is not by any means the privilege of any particular class of society, there are those whose circumstances permit it and there are those whose circumstances do not. It is a wise man who will admit to himself that although he is fascinated by this ancient sport he has neither the time nor the opportunity to practise it.

It is as well before considering the training of the hawks to examine the falconer himself. To do this I cannot do better than to quote what James Campbell wrote in his *Treatise of Modern Falconry* in 1773— ".... He ought then to be of great strength to bear the fatigue of ascending hills, wading over rivers, pressing thro' thickets, and of surmounting other difficulties that may lie in his way. Agility is also requisite, that he may be able to attend his hawks in their flight, and serve them with game, while they are hanging over his head in the air in keen expectation of it. As they will often outfly his utmost speed, his voice should be full, clear and loud, in order to be heard at a distance and to bring them back to the destined scene of diversion. They demand great regularity in their food and exercises, and, that he may be seldom tempted to neglect it, he must be methodical and temperate in his way of living. His love of the sport must be very intense, to animate him to undergo, undaunted, the numberless inconveniences of attendance, weather, and soil, wherewith it is generally accompanied. This will make it his main pleasure to be always with his hawks, training them to obedience, correcting their faults and consulting their health and beauty. To do these things effectually, he must understand their temper and constitution, and ought to possess much patience and mildness in the application of his knowledge. Hawks under the management of a man thus qualified, will be always in good order for flying, exhibit the greatest boldness and address in chasing their prey, give the highest pleasure to the beholders of their motions and do just honour to the skill and attention of their keeper."

What Campbell wrote in 1773 is still true today. The most successful falconers are those who are dedicated to the sport and for whom no detail is too much trouble. There is no room for slackness and short cuts in training hawks. Some people seem to have a natural ability and confidence with hawks as with other animals and yet others seem to make heavy weather of the simplest task. Hawks, too, will quickly trust some men while remaining apprehensive and uneasy in the company of others.

The greatest mistake that the beginner can make is that of taking too many eyasses from the nest to train. He always feels that if he has more than one, he will have a spare if something untoward should happen to the first. This is true, but in practice the tyro who attempts to train two hawks at the same time invariably trains neither. He will find that, in his inexperience, the training of a single eyas is quite difficult enough. Far better to have one properly trained hawk that will show sport than two or three half-trained birds which are a discredit to their owner and whose performance is a travesty of falconry.

The training process is divided into three stages which merge with one another. The first is the stage of taming, the second is the stage of calling to the fist or lure on a creance and the third is the stage of calling to the fist or lure, loose.

Hawks vary enormously in temperament, as do other animals. The time occupied by each successive stage will depend upon the skill of the falconer, the amount of time he devotes to the task, and the temperament of the hawk. Thus a docile Peregrine tiercel may spend seven days in each stage and be fully trained, although as yet unfit to be entered at quarry, in three weeks, while a wild, suspicious female Sparrowhawk may take twice as long.

The falconer must be careful to wear the same type and colour clothing when training his hawk. Hawks can see colours and recognize their trainer mainly by sight. They also learn to know his voice, but they will not know him if he trains them in his shirt-sleeves and comes one day to them in a raincoat. Inattention to details of this sort can easily result in the loss of a hawk. Short-winged hawks are especially sensitive to any change in the trainer's appearance. Some will not tolerate certain colours and others will not be at ease in the presence of women in skirts or indeed women at all. It should be the falconer's task to accustom his hawk gradually to as many strange sights and sounds as possible. In mediaeval times it was relatively easy to man a Goshawk so that it ignored the drably clad peasant and the slow moving horse-drawn traffic. Nowadays, the Goshawk must learn to tolerate low flying jet aircraft and brightly painted, clanking agricultural machinery. Long-wings are far less sensitive to the presence of strangers and unusual sights than are short-wings.

If dogs are to be used in the hawking field, it is as well to introduce them to the hawk early in the training process so that the one will become accustomed to the presence of the other. The dog should be on hand at all times during training as he too must learn his part.

Peregrine Tiercel (Eyas) and Peregrine Falcon (Haggard).

Eyas Merlin and Eyas Kestrel showing correct age for taking.

CHAPTER IV

THE LONG-WINGED HAWKS OR TRUE FALCONS

THESE birds have dark brown irides to their eyes. The flight feathers or primaries are long, the second primary being generally the longest and the third and fourth of equal length. The wings are sharply pointed and when folded at rest, cross over one another, reaching almost to the end of the rather short tail. The beak is short and powerful. It has a characteristic notch or "tooth" on the upper mandible just behind the curved point. The toes, especially the middle one, are long and slender. The true falcons tend to be broad across the shoulders and squat in appearance. Their method of hunting is to fly down their quarry by sheer speed and endurance. They inhabit the wide open spaces. They fly at great heights and their stoop, which is the most dramatic sight in all field sport, is delivered from a position well above their quarry. If successful this stoop results in the quarry being struck a violent glancing blow with the hind talons. In many cases this blow is fatal.

As with all birds of prey the female is larger than the male. He is roughly one-third smaller and it is for this reason that he is termed a "tiercel."

THE KESTREL (*Falco tinnunculus*)

This little falcon is considered to be one of the most suitable birds with which a beginner may initiate himself into the art and practice of falconry. It is common and easily obtained. It is hardy, easily tamed and if lost is unlikely to be shot. It is, of course, a protected bird under the Protection of Birds Act, 1954, and a licence is required from the Home Office or the Scottish Home Department.

It is unfortunate that wild quarry can only rarely be taken with a trained Kestrel but the bird can be trained up to the point which, were it a Peregrine or Merlin, it would be entered at quarry.

Valuable experience in the day to day management of a hawk can be obtained by the beginner who succeeds in taming and training a Kestrel to fly to the lure.

D 33

Haggard or passage Kestrels are rarely obtainable and in any case the beginner is advised to confine his attentions to an eyas in the first instance.

Kestrels nest in holes in trees, on ledges on cliffs and buildings, and in the abandoned nests of crows, magpies, etc. Their eggs, four to six in number, are laid in May and their eyasses are ready to fly about the first week in July. The eyas should not be taken from the nest until it is almost ready to fly. Almost all the white down will now have come off and only a little will be left on the bird's head. It is possible to rear young Kestrels taken sooner, when they are but balls of greyish white fluff, but this is not advised as not only do such eyasses often suffer from faulty bone development, but they almost always become fixed in the adolescent habit of screaming. This is the infantile sound made by the young hawk when it sees the approach of its parent with food. An eyas of any species taken too young tends to become imprinted with the sight of its human foster parent and to scream on his approach. This habit, once acquired, is not often lost.

The art of falconry includes the taking of eyas hawks from the nest and it would not be out of place to discuss here some methods of doing this. If the Kestrel's nest is in a tall conifer the presence of young hawks in the nest is usually given away by the "whitewash" on the vegetation below and the bits of down which blow on to the upper branches of the trees round the nest. Should the eyrie be on a ledge on a cliff or building, it may not be so easily located. If the ledge is broad, or if the nest is in a hole, there may be no telltale whitening of the rock with mutes. The wind may also not blow the down about so freely. In these cases often the only way to pin-point the eyrie is to sit down in a sheltered spot and watch until the parent birds come in with food.

Climbing irons may be necessary in order to climb a branchless larch. Eyries on buildings or cliffs are best reached by ropes from above. (See Chapter V.) A sack or haversack is tied round the falconer's waist to receive the young hawk. When the eyas is taken from a nest in a tree it is often safer to lower the sack or haversack on a line to an assistant on the ground, as there is some danger of crushing the young bird against branches on the climb down. An assistant should always be present on the ground below whenever eyasses are taken because if the young hawks are ready to fly, some, or all of them, may jump out of the nest and plane down to the ground when the falconer reaches up to take them. The assistant must be prepared to mark down any birds that do this.

Let us assume, then, that the aspiring falconer has climbed up to the nest and successfully taken one fully fledged eyas Kestrel. In passing it would be well to note that the licence should be carried on the person when taking the hawks because it must be produced on demand to the police or other authorized person. The possession of a licence, however, does not give the licensee any right to trespass on private property in search of hawks. Permission must be obtained beforehand from the owner or his agent.

The eyas Kestrel is best taken in the evening as it will then usually have a full crop. This is important if it is to travel any great distance before it can be fed. A small hamper lined with sacking is the best receptacle for the transport of young hawks, but should this not be available, a cardboard box with sacking stretched taut across the bottom and tied with wire firmly into the corners, is a suitable sub-stitute. The sacking enables the young hawks to grip with their claws when bumped about in transit, and also helps to prevent damage to the growing feathers. Do not use hay as bedding as hawks have been known to eat wisps of it with fatal results. Air holes should be punched low down in the walls of the box.

When the young hawk arrives at its owner's home, it should be gently removed from the box inside the shed or room which is to be its home for the next fortnight or so while it grows its tail and flight feathers. If the eyas is at all advanced it is folly to open the hamper or box anywhere else than in the hack shed. While the eyas, wrapped in a silk handkerchief, is gently held by an assistant from behind, so that its wings are pinioned, the falconer will attach a pair of jesses. These leather straps are fixed, one on each leg, as follows: The jess is placed against the hawk's leg so that the leg lies mid-way between the two slits (A and B in diagram). The point C is then passed through slit B until slit A is through slit B—from the other side point D is pushed through slit A, and the remainder of the jess drawn through (see diagram). Both legs are similarly treated. It sometimes helps to open the slits with a small marline spike and pull the points through with a pair of pointed forceps. When the jesses have been put on, the young hawk should be released in the shed or loft which has been prepared with perches, vertical barred window, and double door, for its reception. The outer door is best locked and the single

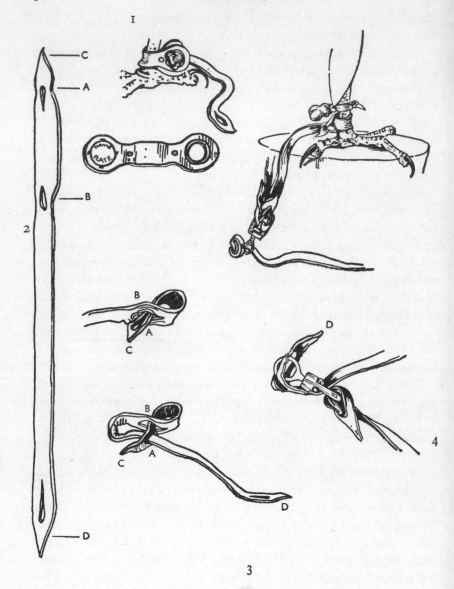

FIG. 6. JESSES

1. Aylmeri.
2. Jess.
3. Putting on jesses.
4. Putting jesses on to swivel.

key retained by the falconer. If the eyas is very young and cannot stand, an artificial nest in a box may be necessary—this should be half filled with coarse wood shavings or peat moss. Several young Kestrels may occupy the same loft. There is little difference in the size and plumage of the two sexes.

Young hawks grow very quickly and before long the eyas Kestrel will be trying to scramble up the branches which have been placed in the loft for him. When he is seen to be perching on these it will not be long before he will fly to the higher horizontal perches fixed across the corners of the room. If the window has a wide sill the young hawk will spend much time lying on it in the sun. Long-winged hawks also appreciate a shelf about 6 inches wide placed high on a wall out of draughts to roost on.

If the eyas is not very advanced it may be necessary to feed it by hand for a day or two. To do this pluck a sparrow and cut off the legs and breast meat. Small pieces of this meat are offered to the hawk on a short pointed stick or in forceps, as it stands with its back to the wall in its artificial nest box. At first it will gasp in fear and may shoot out a foot to defend itself. The falconer must be patient and when the hawk opens its beak he must adroitly present a piece of meat. If hungry the hawk will eventually take and swallow a piece of meat. It may take some pieces only to throw them out of its beak with a quick flick of its head. All the time the falconer must speak soothingly to his charge and his movements must be slow and deliberate. The young hawk will learn quickly to take its food from the stick and should be fed three times daily as much meat as it will freely take. The meat should consist of freshly killed sparrows or mice. Road casualty small birds may also be used provided they are fresh and day-old cockerel chicks are useful. Birds should be plucked and mice skinned for the first two meals of the day. The evening meal may consist of a partly plucked sparrow or a mouse in its skin. Do not remove the intestines of mice or sparrows as these contain vitamins, etc., essential for the young hawk's growth. It is fatal to stint the food during the early days when the feathers are growing, for should the young hawk be hungry for more than a few hours, a mark as if a razor had been drawn across the growing feathers will result. These marks, sometimes known as "hunger traces" or "fret marks" are often seen on the feathers of wild hawks and if they are bad they can so weaken the feather that it will break at the "fret mark" when subjected to stress. Hunger can cause these marks but it is thought that there may also be other causes, such as fright or any stress which may interfere with the metabolism of a timid, growing bird.

As soon as the young hawk snatches at its meat with a foot and bends down to pull at it with its beak, it may be fed on a board. This is a hardwood board with several small staples securely driven into it. Meat is tied to these staples so that the hawk cannot drag it about. The board is placed in full view of the young hawk. In emergency, strips of lean beef can be fed to young Kestrels, but it is best to keep to sparrows and mice. The provision of water is not necessary but once the eyas is reasonably nimble and can fly a little, a hawk bath can be placed in the loft.

Three good meals a day are given for about a fortnight. The board must be kept clean and all stale food removed after meals. An alternative to the board method of feeding is feeding on the glove. This makes for a tamer hawk but is more tedious. Once the eyas is feeding well from the stick it will quickly lose its initial fear of man and will be willing to advance a few steps towards him at feeding time. If at this stage a piece of meat held between the finger and thumb of the gloved hand is offered to it, it will probably bend down and pull at the meat with its beak. On finding that it cannot get the food in this manner it will then step on to the glove in order to get a better purchase on the meat. When this has been done for a meal or two the falconer will find that he can raise his fist a foot or so from the floor or nest and the eyas standing on it will scarcely look up from its meal. It is not advisable at this stage to stand up with the hawk on the fist as it may take fright and hurt itself in jumping down to the floor. Later when it is regularly sitting on the perches it may be allowed to feed on the fist of the falconer in the standing position. No attempt must yet be made to hold the jesses, as an unexpected bate might well break the young hawk's legs, so fragile are its growing bones.

After about a fortnight, an examination must be made of the bases of the tail feathers to see if they are hard or whether they are still soft and blue ("in the blood"). This is best done at night with a torch. If the falconer is quiet and gentle he will find it easy to approach the hawk as it roosts on its favourite perch and to spread its tail feathers and wing feathers to ascertain whether or not it is ready to take up. When all the feathers are hard at the base the hawk is said to be "hard penned" and is ready to be taken up for training. The day after it is observed that the Kestrel is ready for training the food should be a little less than usual and free from casting—lean beef is probably best for this. Next day give no food at all and in the evening enter the loft to take the hawk up. If the Kestrel has been fed on the fist this will be a simple matter for, being hungry, it will willingly jump on to its owner's fist to obtain the meat which he proffers. When it does this the trainer should, while the hawk is feeding, attach a swivel to the free ends of the jesses and finally pass a leash through the lower ring of the swivel. The jesses are now grasped in the gloved hand and the swivel drawn between the bases of the first and second finger. The leash is pulled through the ring of the swivel up to the button. It is then looped about three times and grasped by the little finger of the left hand. I must say here that there are several ways of holding the jesses and leash. I have described the way I like to do it. I distrust any method in which the leash is only half pulled through the swivel ring. I have seen hawks lost by the falconer being momentarily unaware which end of the leash is which and choosing to hold on to the wrong end!

The gloved hand is held in a lightly clenched position, knuckles outwards with the forearm waist level and parallel to the ground. The meat, cut in convenient strips, should be held between the thumb and forefinger or between the finger and the base of the thumb.

If the hawk has been fed on a board and not on the fist, it must be taken up after dark with the aid of a torch. To do this, approach it as it sits on its perch and gently pick up the hanging jesses. Now press the base of the thumb of the gloved left hand against the back of the hawk's legs. With luck the eyas will step backwards on to the fist. This is the correct way to take up a perching hawk. Attach the swivel and leash.

Once the eyas is sitting quietly on the fist in the loft, the falconer must call for an assistant who will come and bind the tail feathers about half-way down their length with gummed paper. On no account use sticking plaster or "sellotape"! The object of this is to protect the rather fragile tail feathers during the early stages of training. It should be possible for the assistant to bind the tail without much difficulty by the light of a torch. Should a bate occur the eyas must be assisted back on to the glove and the operation discontinued until it has settled down. When this has been completed the assistant should withdraw and leave the falconer to the somewhat tedious task of getting the eyas to feed on the glove. The meat, previously cut into narrow strips, is taken from the bag with the right hand and a strip slowly and gently inserted between the thumb and forefinger of the left hand. The light in the loft should be subdued during this procedure. To make the hawk look down at the food, a strip of meat is drawn slowly across its feet. Slight movements of the forefinger and thumb inside the glove may make the hawk grip the fist with its claws and look down at the meat. The falconer should stop all movements and "freeze" as soon as the hawk looks down and offers to bend its head down to the meat. Some eyasses will soon start to feed and, provided there are no visual or audible distractions, will continue to do so, but others are more difficult. These seem terrified of being caught at a disadvantage with their heads down in the feeding position. To help them to overcome this fear a piece of meat may be offered on the tip of the forefinger of the right hand. This piece of meat is offered at breast level. The hawk may seize the meat only to flick it away but sooner or later, if the falconer has patience and is slow and deliberate in his movements, the hawk will start to feed. Once this has occurred the falconer must keep absolutely still, scarcely breathing, for a fright now will undo the progress so hardly made. It may be necessary to try all the dodges described above including gently squeezing one of the hawk's toes between the thumb and forefinger to make it look down at the fist before it will finally give in and feed.

When the hawk has eaten as much as it will willingly take—this is usually about two-thirds of a crop—it should be slowly carried to the screen perch upon which it is to spend the night. The falconer now faces the centre of the screen perch and with his right hand frees the leash from his left little finger. He now places the swivel between the thumb and forefinger of the left hand and grasps it firmly. The leash is then pulled through the swivel until the half-way mark is reached. The hawk is held above the screen perch and the hanging leash is manoeuvred so that the button end falls on the far side and the free end on the near side. With the swivel still firmly held the hawk is lowered gently so that its tail clears the top of the perch and comes down on the far side and its feet, still sitting on the fist, are just below the top of the perch on the near side. The button end of the leash is now passed through the slit in the screen and the two ends held tight.

If the knuckles are now turned slowly upwards and the back of the hawk's legs are pressed gently against the perch, it will step back-wards on to it. When it does this the falconer releases his hold on the

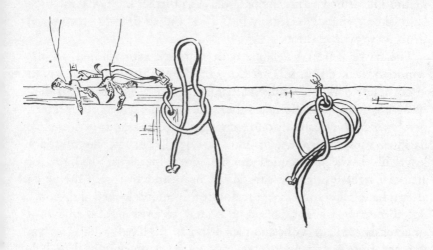

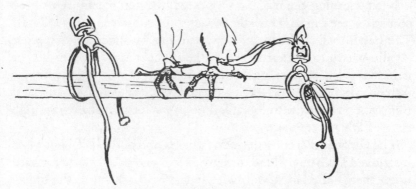

FIG. 7. TYING HAWKS TO SCREEN PERCH

swivel and pulls firmly downwards on the two ends of the leash. Thus the swivel is securely anchored on top of the perch. The correct knot is now tied. This consists of an ordinary single loop bow tied tightly beneath the bar of the perch. The free ends of the leash are passed through the loop of the bow and are finally pushed through the slit in the screen to lie between the two layers of material. The swivel should be left in an upright position on top of the perch. This method of tying up a hawk on the screen perch differs slightly from a method described earlier in this book. The former method is safer for large short-wings which may bate a lot and so dislodge the swivel from its proper position.

The hawk is now left alone with all lights extinguished and the window blacked out. It is necessary to leave as yet untrained hawks in complete darkness while unattended, for they will find that they will have some difficulty in climbing back up the screen of the screen perch when they bate off on receiving a sudden fright. In complete darkness most hawks remain absolutely quiet. The falconer must not leave his hawk unattended on the screen perch in daylight (or artificial light) until he is sure that it has learnt to regain the perch after a bate. He should keep the door of his mews locked and should not allow any stranger, person or animal, to enter until the hawk is sufficiently tame to withstand such a shock. All hawks, during training, are more docile indoors than out and in artificial light than daylight. I think this is because when outdoors they can see places to which they would like to fly, whereas indoors in artificial light all around is strange.

Next morning the training proper will begin. The objects of the course of training to which the eyas is to be subjected are as follows: The hawk shall (1) fly at and take wild quarry suited to its species; (2) allow itself to be approached by the falconer as it sits on its kill, or if it has failed to take its quarry, to return without delay to the trainer's fist or lure. (3) Develop enough physical condition so that it can come to terms with its natural quarry which is usually in a high state of athletic training.

The falconer will enter the mews quietly and in the half-light place his gloved left hand behind the hawk's legs and press gently forward upon them—the hawk will, with luck, step back on to the glove. Having taken the jesses between his thumb and forefinger, the falconer now unties the leash and pulls it through the swivel until the button engages the ring. The leash is then looped round the little finger of the left hand as described before. Light may now be let into the room. The greatest care must be exercised when taking up or setting down hawks on the block or screen perch. This is a time of grave danger and a time when many hawks have been lost due to the inattention of their trainer. A sudden unexpected bate and a loosely held leash whips through the fingers and the hitherto tame and gentle hawk is flying away into the top of a tall tree trailing a leash behind it. This is a disaster of the first magnitude and any falconer to whom it has happened should hang his head in shame. For the leash will soon become entangled in the branches of the tree and the wretched hawk will hang upside down to die a miserable death. Rescue, of course, may be possible by climbing the tree but prevention in this case is far better than cure.

All training of hawks, whatever species, takes place at feeding time and progress depends upon the bird being hungry and keen for its food, but not starved. The meals, two a day for the small hawks and one a day for the larger species, are graduated in size so as to allow sufficient keenness to develop by the next mealtime. This, of course, requires some skill on the part of the falconer, but he will quickly learn by trial and error. When the eyas Kestrel is first taken up from the loft, it will be in fat condition. It is evident that some of this so-called "internal fat" will have to be removed by dieting before real keenness for food will develop. To assist in judging when this fat has been used up, the young hawk should be weighed on the weighing machine on the first morning of its training. Fat young Kestrels will be found to weigh 8–9 oz. and a reduction of $\frac{1}{2}$–$\frac{3}{4}$ oz., or about 10 per cent of their total weight, will be found to be necessary before much progress will be made. As I have said before, hawks of all species vary enormously in temperament and some require more cutting down in the early stages than others. Usually, those that have been reduced more drastically can be allowed to regain their normal weight once they have become tame. It should be remembered that the whole art of falconry is that of flying one's hawk in the highest possible condition consistent with obedience. Slapdash cutting down of the hawk's condition as a substitute for manning and training is to be deplored as it results in a hawk that is not really tame and is physically incapable of catching quarry in any style at all.

When the eyas Kestrel has been taken up for the first time on the fist she will probably look around her for a second or two then, after bobbing her head once or twice, will bate off the fist. After a few flaps of her wings she will hang motionless from her trainer's fist. When she does this, place the palm of the right hand on the bird's breast under the wings and lift her gently back on to the glove. She may now grip with her feet and stand upright, or she may pretend to have lost the use of her legs and lie as paralysed across the fist. If she does this, gentle rocking of the fist to and fro usually results, in time, in the hawk losing her balance and gripping the glove again with her feet. She should then resume the normal upright stance. These perverse actions may be repeated many times but sooner or later if the falconer's patience prevails, the hawk will give in. Care should be taken when the hawk is indulging in these uncontrolled bates, to ensure that the wing-tips do not strike chairs, tables, door-frames, or other hard objects. It is very easy to break primaries and difficult to repair them satisfactorily.

When the first few panic bates are over and the hawk is sitting on the fist, beak open and "button eyed" with fear, an attempt must be made to feed her. This is done in the same way as described for the night before. All food is given on the fist at this stage and between feeds the hawk must rest on the screen perch in the darkened mews. At first she is fed twice daily indoors alone, then, gradually, as her confidence increases, she may be fed out of doors. Gradually she is introduced to strange people and sights, always while feeding. It is in order to try her as highly as possible as long as she does not bate. But the skilful falconer will anticipate when he has gone too far and will retreat before his pupil bates. He will notice that she is more fearful of approaching vehicles or persons than of stationary objects which he approaches with her on his fist. Likewise, she will fear the passage of persons behind her more than those who pass in front. If a friend accompanies the falconer when he is feeding the hawk, this friend should stand on the right hand of the falconer so that the hawk can see him and not on the left hand side where he will be the cause of constant apprehension.

This twice daily carrying of the hawk on the fist at feeding time is the process, called manning, by which she is tamed. It stands to reason that the more prolonged the feeding times can be made the more rapid will be the manning process. To do this, part of the meal may consist of a tough bought pigeon's wing or chicken's neck. This is called "tiring" and will keep the hawk occupied for a long time. While the manning is in progress, the falconer may stroke her breast, back and thighs with his right hand. At first she may resent this and bite viciously at his hand, so he may substitute a feather or pencil for his hand until she gets over her resentment. Beware of too much stroking with the hand, however, because it tends to remove the bloom from the feathers of the back, and feathers that have lost their bloom are less impervious to rain than those which have not.

When the meal is nearly finished, the falconer should contrive to arrive back in the mews so that the hawk may be placed safely upon the screen perch before the absence of food causes her to take fright and bate. It is always a good plan when picking a hawk up from the perch or block to have a small piece of meat—a bechin—on the glove so that in time the hawk will look forward to the approach of the gloved fist of her trainer.

Carriage on the fist and manning are concurrent but the falconer must beware of overdoing it. If the hawk is perverse and bates a lot in spite of the presence of tiring on the fist, it is advisable to replace her on the screen and retire for an hour or two until she is a little keener or she is in a better frame of mind.

The amount of food given at each feed will depend on several factors. Firstly, her weight at the last weighing and whether it was going up or coming down. It helps to use a piece of graph paper and to plot the hawk's daily weight against the date line. Secondly, her behaviour. A very little more or less food can make all the difference between a tractable and obedient pupil and a suspicious, ill-tempered bird. Thirdly, the quality of the meat given. This can only be learned by experience, but, briefly, sparrows, mice and all small birds seem to be more nourishing than an equal quantity of lean beef. The sheep's heart, often recommended for small hawks, seems to become sour and stale very quickly and in my opinion is a poor substitute for the more natural sparrow/mouse diet. Rabbit is a light meat and not very nourishing. In the early stages of training, casting need only be given once a week. The hawk should not be fed at the next feed after casting has been given until the pellet has been found underneath the screen perch. A newspaper spread on the floor will often facilitate the recovery of the casting. Small feathers and mouse skins make the best casting for small hawks. The bones of mice and small birds are almost completely digested. I think it is always advisable to break the wing and leg bones and to remove the rather sharp beaks of small birds before feeding them to the hawk because there is some danger of perforation of the crop when casting is not fed. Half-trained hawks are more irregular in the time at which they cast but as training progresses casting can be given more frequently at the evening meal and it will be found more regularly beneath the screen when the mews are opened in the morning.

As the young hawk becomes tamer she will come to regard the approach of her trainer with pleasure and will be anxious to take her stance upon his glove in the expectation of a tit-bit. When she shows signs of this willingness to step on to the glove, she may be taught to jump a leash length to the fist. To do this the hawk is taken up from the screen at feeding time in the usual way. When the leash has been pulled through the swivel up to the button it is held by its free end with the right hand and the hawk is set down again on the screen. The fist is now garnished with a small piece of meat and held in front of her, level with her feet, just out of her reach. At first she will bend forward and try to take the meat with her beak. When this fails she may try to reach it with her foot. After a bit she may very cautiously hop on to the glove and take the morsel. If she won't come, do not delay too long but advance the glove to her feet and allow her to bend down and take the meat. Or, she may just step on to the glove. In any case reward her and try again. Once her initial lack of confidence has been overcome, she will soon jump a leash length, but do not try her for too long because her appetite will wane with each reward.

As soon as she will come a leash length indoors, she may be tried off a fence or gate post out of doors. It is quite likely that although she was coming to the fist promptly indoors, she will now refuse to come at all. She will stand looking fearfully round her and ignoring the garnished fist thrust in front of her. So the falconer must go back to the beginning and coax her to step from the fence to his glove in the same way as he did indoors. When she will come a leash length promptly out of doors, the leash can be removed and a creance attached to the swivel. She can then be called increasing distances up to ten yards. This distance should be reached gradually, for any attempt to force the pace and call her too far will result in her losing heart and sheering off to fly away on her own. The creance will pull her down but ground will have been lost. Creances are necessary evils and the sooner they can be dispensed with the better. Take care to see that the creance does not get caught up on snags on the ground while the hawk is coming to the fist. With luck the hawk will not attempt to fly away and will never be aware that it is on a line at all. During these calling-off exercises, the falconer may either whistle or call to the hawk or, if he can't whistle satisfactorily, he may blow a referee's whistle with a warbling note. The object of this is to associate the sound of the falconer's voice, or the whistle, in the hawk's mind with the presentation of food and so establish a simple Pavlovian reflex.

Once the hawk will come ten yards to the fist as soon as it is presented—and it is promptness of response rather than distance that counts—the lure may be introduced. There are two ways of doing this. One can either put the hawk on a block or a smooth lawn with the creance attached to the swivel and place the lure, garnished with small strips of meat, a foot or two from the block on the ground. If she doesn't jump on to it at once a few twitches on the lure-line will call her attention to it. Or the hawk can be held on the fist and the lure also held on the glove so that she can take small pieces of meat from it. After a few moments her claws are gently detached from the lure and it is thrown to the ground. Then, bending down, the falconer encourages the hawk to leave his fist and jump down to the lure. Once she has gone to the lure, whatever the method of introduction, she must be allowed to feed a little on it while the falconer kneels beside her and offers her tiny scraps of meat from his fingers. After a few moments she must be encouraged to step on to the fist again by offering her a piece of meat on the glove and covering the lure with the gloved hand. She may try to drag the lure on to the glove by holding on to it with one foot, but if she does this her claws can be gently detached from it and placed on the glove. The lure is then placed in the falconer's bag, out of sight.

After a few days the distance is gradually increased and the hawk will soon be coming several yards as soon as the lure is swung and dropped upon the ground. If only small strips of meat are attached to the lure, several calls can be made before the edge of the hawk's appetite is dulled. It is always necessary to put a piece of meat on both sides of the lure so that it doesn't matter which side it falls on. Some hawks, however, soon learn to turn the lure over and so get both bits!

When approaching a young hawk on the lure the greatest care must be taken not to frighten her. Never stand over a hawk while she feeds on the lure—rather kneel or crawl towards her, stopping every time she looks up and stops feeding. Do not stare at her for she has an innate fear of a fixed gaze which, to wild animals and birds, is usually a prelude to an aggressive action. If the falconer is clumsy or rough when he "makes in" to his hawk while she is on the lure, she may reward him by either leaving the lure and trying to fly away or, worse still, she may try to bolt with the lure in her talons. Thus the seeds of the vice called "carrying" are sown. It pays to take every possible precaution to avoid the thought of carrying entering the hawk's mind, for a hawk that tries to carry the lure away will eventually try to carry away the quarry that it has captured and this will lead to no end of frustration for the falconer. So always be careful to offer scraps of meat from your fingers while the hawk is feeding on the lure. After a few calls to the lure it is a good plan to attach the rest of the food to the lure and allow the hawk to finish her meal on the ground. This is more important with small hawks as if always fed on the fist they may refuse to eat if offered food at the block or the ground. In the early stages of feeding on the lure it is useful to gently pin the lure to the ground with a metal pin so that any attempt to carry it away can be foiled from the start. The lure used at this time may be a good deal heavier, too, than that used later on in training.

When calling to the lure choose a place where the grass is mown very short, for it takes very little to foul the creance and pull the hawk down. Once the hawk will come 25 yards as soon as the lure is swung and before it is thrown to the ground the creance can be removed and she may be flown loose. The swivel is, of course, removed too, but the jesses are left on. Before flying loose for the first time, be sure that the hawk is really keen and have at least one trial run with the creance on. The gummed paper which has up till now protected the tail, must be removed before the hawk is called loose for she will now need to spread her tail to steer herself. The best way to remove the gummed paper is to dip the whole tail in a jug of hot, but not boiling, water. Immersion for a few seconds is enough. This dipping of the tail is also the method employed to straighten bent tail feathers, but it must not be done too often for it makes the feathers brittle.

When the hawk will come any distance that she can see the falconer as soon as he swings the lure and calls or whistles, she may be taught to stoop to the lure. This exercise is designed to build up her muscles and increase her flying powers. The lighter lure (1½ oz.) is now used. The hawk is called from a block or from an assistant's fist into the wind and instead of allowing her to alight on the lure it is twitched away from her at the last moment. She will either then

The Kestrel is an ideal beginner's hawk.

Merlin on scales.

pitch on the ground looking bewildered or will swing round in a circle in the air looking for the expected lure. In either case the lure must be quickly thrown out and the hawk allowed to take her reward from it. Soon the hawk will attempt to follow and seize the lure when it is twitched away and will fly backwards and forwards while the falconer swings it to and fro and just keeps it in front of her. This manipulation requires a great deal of skill on the part of the falconer and the best way to learn it is to go and see an experienced performer swing his lure. Care must be taken to avoid hitting the hawk with the lure-line. If the hawk manages to make contact with her claws on the swung lure, it must at once be allowed to fall to the ground and the hawk be permitted to take her reward on it. All meat must be tied very securely on the lure, for should the hawk manage to detach a piece when she stoops she may be tempted to fly away with it. To begin with, one or two stoops will be sufficient to make the hawk pant and breathe with her beak open. When the falconer sees this he must take her down to the lure, for her condition must be built up gradually and if he overdoes the stooping she may get tired and either pitch on the ground or go and sit in a tree while she regains her wind. After a few days the number of stoops can be progressively increased until the hawk is on the wing, flying hard, for a quarter of an hour at a time.

Kestrels, like Peregrines which are to be flown at game, can be trained to "wait on." This is done by hiding the lure as soon as the hawk has been called off and is on her way to the falconer. If the falconer stands in long grass on the first occasion there is less likelihood of the hawk settling on the ground. When the lure is not forthcoming the hawk will circle the falconer and follow him as he walks into the wind. At first she must only be kept waiting for a quarter of a minute before the lure is thrown out for her. The falconer must get clear of the long grass before he throws out the lure because some hawks are reluctant to come down to a lure in long grass or stubble. Each day the hawk is kept waiting for the lure for a longer period until she is on the wing for twenty minutes at a time. Kestrels will sometimes hover over the falconer's head if they are trained to wait on in the updraught on a hillside.

Now the assistant from whose fist the hawk has been called can be dispensed with and she can be cast off the falconer's fist into the wind. But if after a few days without exercise due perhaps to bad weather,

E

there is any reason to doubt the hawk's keenness, it is advisable to call her first from the assistant's fist or from a fence post rather than to cast her off. For, if cast off when not keen she might fly right away before the lure could be produced. Whereas, if called from a post she might show her lack of keenness by refusing to come and so be taken up and not flown. Thus a possible loss is avoided. It is useful to occasionally call the hawk to the fist to keep her in practice, for there are occasions when it is more convenient to call a hawk to the fist rather than to the lure. This can be done when the falconer is in a field of some high crop in which the lure would be invisible. The lure is swung and pulled up on to the glove and the fist is held high in the air. A properly manned hawk will then alight like a butterfly on the upheld fist.

Beware of flying a hawk too late in the evening, for some hawks will not come in to a lure when the light fails. I once got a Peregrine down to the lure at dusk by tying a white handkerchief on to the lure so that she could see it in the grass. Always make sure that any meat or birds' wings which may be tied on the lure are really securely attached so that they cannot be snatched off and carried away. Do not fly half-trained hawks if there is a high wind for they may be swept away down wind and lost.

In all stages of training it pays to make haste slowly and if the keenness of the hawk is in question put off flying her that day. After the first week or so of training the Kestrel may be put out on the lawn to weather on the block. In order to save her a lot of unnecessary fright and bating, I usually put a young half-trained hawk on the block for the first time in the evening just before it gets dusk. Hawks are quietest at this time and she will be unlikely to take fright. Next day she can be put out a little earlier and on the third day she can be put out during the morning and provided she sits quietly on the block, she can be left out all day. See that she is moved into the shade if the sun is hot. A bath may be offered at midday—always allow plenty of time for a hawk to dry after bathing. There is no better way of reclaiming a hawk than to offer her small titbits from the finger-tips as she sits on the block on the weathering ground. Offer a bechin, then withdraw and come to her again from a different angle and offer another. In this way she will be taught not to bate away when her trainer approaches, but rather to bate towards him in expectation of a tit-bit.

If the trainer has only time to train his hawks in the evening, it is possible to train Kestrels, Merlins and Sparrowhawks while only feeding once a day. If this procedure is adopted care must be taken to see that the hawk is fed a sufficiency at this one feed. In most cases it will be found that after the initial reduction the hawk may be allowed to eat all it can each evening. The weight must be carefully watched and should it fall in spite of one full crop a day, an extra feed must be given for a few days in the morning.

Kestrels are rarely rapacious enough to take quarry for their trainer, but recently a falconer has caught a number of starlings with his eyas Kestrel. He entered it to some starlings which were bathing in a puddle. Being wet they were slow to rise and one was caught. After this success the Kestrel caught others some of which were dry. Mice and voles have been taken too, by trained Kestrels, but these birds are exceptional.

HACKING BACK

The occasion will sometimes arise when the falconer will wish to return an unwanted hawk to the wild. In the case of eyasses that have never killed for themselves, it must be arranged to put out food for them until they no longer require it.

As when hawks are hacked in a district, so when they are hacked back must all neighbouring gamekeepers and shooters be warned of the falconer's intention. If the regular exercise field is in a good place then this is the place to release the hawk. After the daily exercise the hawk is fed up, her jesses and bells cut off, and she is "let down the wind to prey at fortune." Next day at feeding time the falconer must return to the exercise field and swing his lure. If he has been in the habit of blowing a whistle or calling vocally while luring he must do this now. Should the hawk be in the vicinity and not have killed that day, it will come down to the lure. After it has fed it is left out again. This procedure is repeated daily until, after becoming irregular in its appearances, the hawk fails to turn up altogether. Do not attempt to start a hack back when the weather is unsettled, excessively cold, or windy. High winds will blow a young hawk miles downwind and it will be lost. Merlins and Kestrels are best hacked back in early autumn before the bad weather sets in and while the north–south migration streams are in full flood. There are few places where it would be safe to release a Goshawk and it is probably

unwise to attempt to hack back foreign birds of prey in this
country.

THE MERLIN (*Falco columbarius*)

In olden times the Merlin was reserved for ladies. This little falcon
is the daintiest and most docile of all the hawks used in falconry. The
traditional quarry at which Merlins were flown was the skylark. It
was not by accident that the lark was chosen as the most desirable
quarry for these game little hawks. The two birds are very evenly
matched in flying powers and few trained eyas Merlins could catch
full-winged larks that had completed their moult in September. Now
the skylark is protected by law and falconers who train Merlins must
seek other quarry which is not on the protected list. This is not at all
easy for the Merlin, being a long-wing, requires a large open space in
which to manœuvre and few suitable birds are to be found on the
open downs. It has been suggested that starlings might make a substitute quarry for the trained Merlin, but I think the falconer would
have to walk a very long way to find sufficient slips for his hawk
that were far enough from cover. One thing is certain and that
is that a Merlin that is to be flown at starlings must be entered
in the first instance at starlings and kept on them. If the first
flights at starlings are successful the hawk will become wedded to
this quarry and will always fly it. But should the falconer be so
unwise as to allow his Merlin to fly and catch a smaller bird, say
a sparrow, he will find that she may in future refuse to fly the
larger quarry.

The training of the Merlin differs little from that of the Kestrel.
Eyas Merlins are obtained on licence from the Home Office from
their nests on the moors of Northern England. They are usually
ready to take during the first week in July. I have found that eyas
Merlins are much more intelligent and quick to respond to training
than are the more phlegmatic Kestrels. Female eyas Merlins weigh
about 7½ oz. when taken up from the hack shed and hard penned.
Male or Jack Merlins weigh about 6 oz. in the same state. It will be
found that a reduction of ¾ oz. will be necessary before progress is
made in training. I have found that once this reduction in weight has
been made it is possible to feed some Merlins *ad lib.* once a day and to
maintain their weight at about 6¾ oz. At this weight most Merlins
will be found to be strong and keen. Later on in the season the flying

weight may rise to 8 oz. Scales for weighing small hawks must be accurate to the nearest ¼ oz.

During training the greatest care must be taken to discourage the vice of "carrying" to which many Merlins are addicted. Take the same precautions as described for the eyas Kestrel but be doubly on guard when "making in" to the Merlin on the lure. Time spent in carefully "making in" is never wasted.

Merlins are delicate feeders and to be kept in good health must be fed on sparrows, mice and road casualty small birds. Lean, tender beef may be used in emergency but I have noticed that Merlins fed exclusively on beef for any length of time become noticeably sluggish and less fit than those fed on the sparrow/mouse diet. Some Merlins are very slow feeders so if they are to be fed on the ground by the block, allow at least an hour for them to take their fill. Two sparrows a day are just too much for a female Merlin, so if two are given one day, one and a half will be enough the next.

It is not customary to handicap trained Merlins by belling them. Snipe have been caught by trained Merlins but they are difficult quarry. Merlins are delicate and it is not wise to attempt to keep them through the winter when it is difficult to procure suitable food. They should be released at the end of September in a place where they would be unlikely to be shot. If they have taken quarry for their trainer, they should be well able to fend for themselves in the wild.

Those interested in Merlins cannot do better than read *The Art and Practice of Hawking*, by E. B. Michell, published by Methuen in 1900. E. B. Michell was a Merlin specialist. His book is now rare and may cost £8 to £10 but a reprint has been published in 1960 by the Holland Press at 30s.

CHAPTER V

LONG-WINGED HAWKS OR TRUE FALCONS (*continued*)

THE PEREGRINE (*Falco peregrinus*)

THE Peregrine or falcon gentle has long been greatly prized as a bird of the chase. She is, when trained, an even-tempered and courageous bird who can give a good account of herself in an aerial encounter with a variety of quarry. It is undoubtedly the speed and style of her flight which has thrilled falconers through the ages.

The rocky coasts of Britain and the inland cliffs of the mountains of Scotland and Wales provide many nesting sites for the Peregrine. Unfortunately, decades of persecution by trigger-happy game-keepers and their ill-informed employers have rendered this fine bird much rarer than it should be. The eyrie is usually located on a ledge about two-thirds of the way up the cliff. Naturally there are many exceptions to this statement but generally the nest is nearer the top of the cliff than the bottom. The ledge may be only a foot or so wide or it may be wide enough to drive a car along. Very often the eyrie site is beneath a formidable overhang of rock which besides giving shelter from the elements makes the ledge virtually inaccessible from above. Peregrines also nest in holes in the rock and often in the old nests of eagles or ravens. Many of the eyrie sites have been known for hundreds of years, and in spite of being frequently shot out fresh Peregrines keep returning to the same cliff, often to the same ledge. It seems that some cliff faces are eminently suitable for the birds for they return there year after year.

Most pairs have an alternative site a mile or so away upon which they will occasionally nest. A pair of Peregrines will rarely nest within three miles of another pair.

If the eyrie is on a narrow ledge, its position will be evident, when the young have hatched, by the white streaking of the rock below with mutes and by the white down which will blow along the cliff face. It is, however, often extremely difficult to pin-point an eyrie on some cliffs especially if the rock is light in colour.

As the young grow up so the falcon broods them less. While she is not hunting, and when the young are small the tiercel does most of the hunting, she sits on some rocky vantage-point from which she can survey the surrounding countryside.

If a human intruder should approach within a hundred yards or so of the eyrie site the falcon will leave her sentry post and fly round in large circles, screaming angrily. Occasionally the tiercel will be attracted by his mate's discomfiture and will add his voice in protest, but usually if he appears at all he keeps higher and swings round in large circles. If the man now searches the cliff face from below with binoculars he should be able to locate the eyrie. Some indication as to its position can often be gained by the intensity of the falcon's distress. The nearer the intruder gets to the nest the bolder she becomes in her stoops. I have never known a falcon attack a human being but some will stoop very close especially if the interloper is alone. Nothing in nature is invariable and some Peregrines will slip silently away upon the approach of danger, giving no indication whatsoever that an eyrie exists.

Sometimes the eyasses can be seen standing on the ledge and often they can be heard. Their screams are of a higher pitch, calling to their mother as she wheels round in the sky above them. If they can be seen their stage of development can easily be judged, but if the ledge is wide or they are in a hole, it may be necessary to descend to the eyrie from above on a rope to inspect them. Most falconers have their own ideas about climbing techniques to reach the eyrie. The basic equipment is two sound ropes both 125 feet long. One, the safety line, is of $\frac{3}{4}$ inch diameter Alpine manila, the other, the hand line, is 1 inch diameter manila. A short, stout crowbar is essential. This can be any sound steel spike about 4 feet long and 1 inch diameter. Farm crowbars are much too heavy to be carried to the inaccessible places where the Peregrines nest. A referee's whistle and a cap with some padding in the crown to ward off falling stones complete the equipment.

The climbing party should consist of not less than three persons, all of whom must be certain that they do not fear heights.

When the eyrie is located from below, it is often useful to try to get a bearing on the spot and relate this to a bush, tree, crag or other natural feature that can easily be recognized when the climb to the top of the cliff has been made. If there are enough persons in the team, one may be left below to guide the main party when they reach the top. The look-out below can also spot and mark any eyasses that may attempt to fly from the ledge should they be so far advanced. Often the summit of inland cliffs can only be reached after a considerable detour. The deer or sheep paths are sometimes the best route up. The best footwear to use on these expeditions is rubber- or rope-soled canvas shoes.

Once the top of the cliff has been reached and the marker tree or bush recognized, the crowbar is thrust into the ground and made secure. This may be difficult as the soil is often thin and peaty and the rocks hard and unyielding. It may take some time before a safe hold is found for the bar and it may be that this hold is some yards back from the edge of the cliff. The end of the hand line is now tied with a round turn and two half hitches to the bar, and the whole rope thrown down over the cliff so that it hangs from the bar. Two of the party sit down one behind the other and dig their heels into the ground. The leading man holds on to the top of the bar. The climber hangs the whistle about his neck, ties the safety line round his waist with a bowline, dons his padded cap and prepares to descend. The safety line is wound once round the bar near to the ground and the rope is paid out by the second rope man as the climber goes down. At all times this safety line must be kept taut. The hand line is used by the climber to steady himself as he climbs down and to help himself to climb over rough rocks as he ascends. The whistle is used for signalling and the code, one blast for UP, two blasts for DOWN and three blasts for HOLD, must be clearly understood by the whole team. There is often a considerable wind blowing up in the hills and this makes these signals difficult to hear. The climber, of course, has a basket or bag slung round his waist into which he will put the eyasses if they are old enough to be taken.

If the young hawks are still covered with down, they are too young and should be left for a further ten to fourteen days. The correct age to take eyasses is when most of the body down has been replaced by feathers and when the tail feathers are at least three inches long. In an average year it will be found that most Peregrine eyasses are ready to take about the 7th to 10th June. But there is considerable variation here and one may find an eyrie that is ready to fly by June 5th and another in the same county that still has eggs on that date.

If one has any choice in the matter, the best time of day to take the eyasses is in the evening for then their crops will be full and they will be less likely to jump off the ledge at the climber's approach. Sometimes an eyrie will contain two eyasses, a falcon and a tiercel, and the tiercel is often considerably more advanced than the falcon. In these cases the tiercel will take fright and leave the ledge to plane down to the ground or on to a lower ledge. The spotter left below must now mark and as the young hawk will as yet be unable to gain height, he must be dislodged from his refuge and induced to plane down to the ground. This can sometimes be accomplished by dropping the hand line over the cliff near him. The number of eyasses in an eyrie varies between one and four. In recent years the numbers have been low and many nests have only contained one eyas.

When as many eyasses as the falconer has licences for have been taken they must be transferred from his basket or bag into a large laundry type hamper which has been lined with canvas or hessian.

If their crops are empty when taken they may be fed on chopped lean beef or pigeon by placing the pieces in their open beaks with the fingers or with blunt forceps.

Food must not now be stinted for the young hawks will be growing apace, and it is upon the regular supply of suitable nourishing food that their physical development and the perfection of their feathers depends. It is thought that shortage of food at this stage may be responsible for the flaws—called "hunger traces"—which are often seen on the feathers of young hawks. These defects are to be seen on the feathers of wild hawks too. There may be other causes for the apparent temporary arresting of the growth of these feathers.

When the falconer reaches home with his precious hamper of eyasses, he must at once fit them with jesses (no swivel slit) and if they are to be "hacked," with bells.*

Whether to hack the young Peregrines or not is a vexed question. Modern falconers are divided on this issue and I shall try to put forward the salient points of the arguments used by both sides.

The advocates of hack say that the weeks of freedom spent on the wing develop the muscles and flying powers of the eyas to a much greater extent than is possible in those confined in a loft. They say, too, that the eyas at hack has an opportunity, towards the end of the hack period, of killing quarry for itself and so of learning valuable

---

* If it is decided not to hack the young peregrines they must be confined in a loft or shed, as described for the eyas Kestrel, until they are hard penned.

tactical lessons. Hacked hawks rarely scream and because, when taken up, they are in fine athletic condition, they do not need to be stooped to the lure to develop their muscles. This is important for eyasses that are destined to be game hawks because stooping to the lure, although fine exercise, tends to lower their pitch. It is essential that hawks which are to be flown at partridges or rooks in fairly enclosed country should be hacked, for only thus can they learn the futility of chasing wood-pigeons in such country. Hawks flown in the area in which they were hacked are less liable to stray if left out when trained. It is also difficult for unhacked eyasses, which are owned by falconers who have only the time to fly hawks during their two to three weeks' holiday in August or September, to achieve their full flying powers in such a short time.

Now the antagonists of hack claim that nowadays few people live in an area that is really suitable for hacking hawks and that on balance the risk of losing a valuable eyas at hack is too great. It is no longer possible to take a large number of eyas Peregrines and hack them together. At most, a falconer will be granted a licence for two, and he may decide that these two were so much trouble and expense to get that he dare not risk them at hack. Of course, two or more persons can combine and hack their hawks together. Some falconers say, too, that the unhacked hawk is less independent and less likely to rake away while "waiting on" than the hacked hawk, especially early in the season. Unhacked hawks are certainly trained quicker and are sooner flying loose than those that have had a month's freedom. This is important if the hawks are to be entered at grouse on or about August 12th, as it is essential to enter the young inexperienced falcon as soon as possible at young inexperienced grouse. In the case of tiercels designed for partridges the reverse is true, because it can be an embarrassment to have the eyasses at the stage of training when they should be entered at quarry, in the middle of August. Single eyasses are better not hacked because they often get lost.

It is, of course, possible to take eyas Peregrines from the eyrie when they are still covered with down, to rear them by hand and then hack them. This is a difficult task because the rearing of the young eyasses demands a degree of skill. They must be kept warm and clean and must have access to direct sunlight. They must be fed every three hours during daylight on birds. And they will scream due to them substituting their human attendant for their parents. This "imprinting" is almost inevitable but some say that the risk of screaming is reduced if the eyasses are never allowed to get hungry. Another authority claims that the worst screamer will lose the habit if flown seven days a week throughout the autumn and winter. But few modern, part-time falconers could manage this.

There are many systems of hack. Blaine favoured a "hack house" made of sheep hurdles with a corrugated iron roof camouflaged with turves and heather. He gave the dimensions as 8 feet by 6 feet by 6 feet high. A similar structure could be made by bales of straw. At one end he arranged a turf-covered ramp so that the eyasses could gain access to the roof. In front of the hut, about 12 feet away, he arranged a series of rough wooden blocks, 12 inches in diameter, one for each hawk being hacked. If the hack house is built in a field to which stock have access, the area round must be fenced off with a few strands of barbed wire. Do not surround the hack area with wire netting as the young hawks may fly into it. Opinions vary as to the optimum site for the hack hut. Blaine favoured the hut against a small copse facing east or south on a high down or open moor. There should always be a tree or two near by, preferably conifers to provide roosting sites, and there must be a stream or pond not too far distant for bathing. Hawks can be hacked almost anywhere but enclosed country is more dangerous than open moorland. One modern authority hacks his hawks from an old cart parked beside a copse. Another likes his hack house in the middle of a large field with trees all round so that the eyasses can fly to the trees and yet keep the hut in sight. My co-author, Major Stanley Allen, used to hack his Peregrines from the tower of his house at Denne Hill, Canterbury. He was able to feed them through a trap door in the roof.

The eyasses are put into the hut on a bed of long straw and a board a foot wide and 3 feet long is placed before them. On the board is tied a heap of food for each eyas. The cord securing the meat is either passed through holes drilled in the hack board or attached to staples. The door of the hut is then closed—a hurdle makes a satisfactory door—and the eyasses are left for the night.

Next morning, the eyasses will have fed from the board, enough light having filtered in through the hurdles, and if the door is quietly opened they will soon come out and scramble on to the roof of the hut. At this stage the flightless eyasses could be in danger from prowling foxes and it may offer them a measure of protection to encircle the hack area with a strand of bale string 8 inches from the ground, soaked in Renardine or other proprietary fox repellent.

Food is now carried to the eyasses three times a day, tied on a board and placed on top of the hack hut. After a few days the eyasses will get more active and the board can be discarded. Meat is then tied on the tops of the blocks in front of the hut. The food should consist of rabbits, pigeons, chicken heads and, as a stand by, beef. Rabbits should be paunched but freshly killed birds should have their intestines left in, for these are a valuable source of vitamins. The feathers should be left on but a few cuts may be made into the breast to expose the meat. All unconsumed food must be collected before putting out fresh food and the blocks kept absolutely clean. When the young hawks are seen to be fully summed and are able to fly, the meals can be reduced to two a day. Ideally 6 a.m. and 6 p.m. are recommended, but provided the meals are regular it does not matter if the times are varied to suit the falconer.

While the eyasses are growing their feathers, the attendants will be amazed at the amount of food they consume. They are regular in their habits and waste little time after the falconer has left the food before coming down to eat it. It is a good plan to blow a whistle loudly each time food is brought for this will help the hawks to associate this sound with food—a reflex which will be taken advantage of later in training.

At first the eyasses will perch on the fence posts and in nearby trees, but soon they will be flying all over the surrounding country and will wander as far as twenty miles away. This, of course, exposes them to some danger of being shot, especially in agricultural areas where some of the land may be keepered. To minimize this danger it always pays to inform any local landowners and their keepers that hawks are being hacked and that they will be belled. One can assure the keepers that the young Peregrines will not interfere with their precious pheasant poults in the rearing field.

Some idea of the quality of the eyasses can be gained by watching them fly at hack. To this end, it is an advantage to be able to identify them either by coloured jesses or by the different notes of their bells.

When, after three or four weeks, usually less in enclosed country, a hawk is observed to have failed to turn up at feeding time more often than once—especially if the two absences are consecutive, it is time to catch it up. The falconer must use his discretion as to whether to chance leaving the most forward eyas out for a further day or two's hack. Undoubtedly these last few days when the eyas is just beginning to kill for himself (the most forward eyas is often a tiercel) are the most valuable of the whole hack. If all the eyasses are the same age and development it may be politic to catch them all up together.

The day before they are to be caught up, very little food is put out. This is to ensure that they are hungry and will come into the blocks without delay. No casting should be given either for they will be hooded after capture and will be unable to cast through the hood.

There are two well-tried methods of catching hack hawks. The first is a bow-net and the second a snare set on the top of one of the feeding blocks. The bow-net is a hazel rod or light metal rod bent into a semicircle on a diameter of about 3 feet and hinged to the ground by two staples at either end. A circular net, dyed a drab colour, is secured to the hazel or metal hoop and the other half of the circumference is spread out and pegged to the ground. The bow is folded back on its hinges so that it lies on top of the outer edge of the pegged half of the net. A semicircular groove is cut into the ground to correspond with the periphery of the net and the loose-folded portion of the net is secreted in this groove. The whole trap is now sprinkled with grass to camouflage it and a long line is attached to the bow a little to one side of centre. If this line is pulled, the bow will come flying over and trap in the net anything that is within its circumference. In the centre of the net peg down a tough piece of beef and remove any twigs or snags which may impede the free working of the trap. Now retire inside the hut taking the line in through a hole in the wall. A peep hole must be made to give a good view of the net and the adjacent blocks. It is essential that none of the hawks shall have seen the falconer enter the hut or that he can be seen through the holes in the wall. It may be necessary to resort to the dodge used by bird photographers of having a friend accompany you to the hut who can ostentatiously walk away when all is ready.

When a hawk comes in and settles on the meat wait until she has her head down and is feeding busily, then, if she is well placed in the centre of the net, pull firmly on the line. Secure the line by winding it round a nail or peg inside the hut and get to the net as quickly as possible. Slip your hand under the net and grab the hawk's legs. Free her feathers from the meshes and instantly slip an old, well-fitting hood on her head. Secure the braces with a piece of string to prevent her getting it off and set her down on a block inside the hut. Quickly reset the net and await the next arrival. Great care must be taken that no other hawk witnesses the capture of one of its fellows. Should two hawks come in together wait until one has fed and gone away. Do not emerge suddenly from the hut while any hawk is still around the hack area. A sudden fright thus given may result in a shy hawk forsaking the hack area for good. Blaine recollects scaring a tiercel in this way and having to wait a week before he got over the shock and came in to feed. The snare method is rather more uncertain and being likely to miscarry and scare the hawk is not recommended. However, each method has its adherents.

In 1936 when Gilbert Blaine wrote his book, eyasses taken at the right age from the eyrie were said to be worth thirty shillings to two pounds, falcons being the more valuable. Well-hacked falcons were worth five pounds. Today, 1960, two eyasses may well have cost a falconer thirty pounds in travelling expenses, tips to keepers and helpers, etc., and a well-hacked eyas is beyond price.

Now to return to the freshly caught eyas. After allowing her to settle down for a couple of hours, hooded, on her block, pick her up on the fist and carry her about. Speak to her occasionally to accustom her to your voice and stroke her gently on the breast and back with a feather. At first she will behave like the Kestrel eyas described in a previous chapter except that she will be a lot wilder. She will draw sharp breaths, hiss and puff at her feathers and try to bite at the feather. Being hooded, she will be spared the shock of visual contact with her enemy but will show her resentment of the stroking and talking. Carry her about for an hour or so, occasionally sitting down and doing simple one-handed tasks so that she is aware of her trainer's proximity. If she panics and offers to bate a lot, set her down again and let her regain her composure. It is interesting to weigh the falcon at this stage. To do this, set her on the scales hooded and hold firmly on to the leash. A newly caught falcon will weigh about 2 lb. 5 oz. and a tiercel about 1 lb. 8 oz.—but as Peregrines vary considerably in size there will be some variation. When in flying condition the falcon will weigh 1 lb. 15 oz. to 2 lb. 2 oz. depending on her size and the quarry at which she is to be flown. Quarry such as partridges or grouse are well liked by the falcon and so she can be flown at a higher weight. Rooks are less attractive to her and she may have to be reduced a little before she will take them on. The tiercel will probably not be flown at rooks, and if flown at partridges, which are the most suitable quarry for him, he will weigh 1 lb. 4 oz.–1 lb. 6 oz.

The training processes are exactly the same for the unhacked eyas except that she will be a little less wild. If several hawks are being trained simultaneously, try to give each an equal time on the fist. When approaching a hooded hawk on the block remember that she is blindfolded and cannot see you—speak to her before picking her up so that she can prepare herself for the shock of being touched. During the evening of the first day of training the falcon must be taken into the mews or into some room where absolute quiet is assured and induced to feed. Some falconers remove the hood for this procedure averring that if a hawk is allowed to feed through the hood she will for ever afterwards pull at the glove as soon as the hood is put on, in the expectation of being given food. This is an annoying habit. It is important, however, to get food into the newly caught hawk as soon as possible as the shock of capture and the subsequent trauma to her nervous system during taming will cause enough loss of condition without starvation to add to it. For this reason I think it advisable to allow her to feed through the hood on the first night. A strip of lean beef is probably the easiest meat to use for the rather tedious job of getting her to feed. All the tricks described for the Kestrel eyas may have to be tried. She will, at first, not know where to find the meat on your fist so it must be held against the ball of the thumb by the last three fingers and must project up on to the glove so that her claws can be hooked into it in the feeding position. Slight movements of the fingers and hand inside the glove will often make her look down, and if her feet and legs are touched with the right hand she may bend down and try to bite. If meat is now interposed she may bite a piece out. Beware that she does not catch your finger for a Peregrine has an extremely powerful beak—it can bite chunks out of the breastbone of a pigeon—and she will take a chunk out of your finger if she can. When she starts to feed, and she will in time if patience is exercised, keep absolutely still. Place the meat beneath her beak as she blindly gropes for it. When she has eaten all she will— usually half to two-thirds of a crop—clean her beak and make sure that no meat has gone up beside her beak into the hood. If it has, shade the light until you can only just see her outline and remove the fouled hood, replacing it immediately with another clean one. It is of some advantage to have a supply of old hoods for these early days of training because feeding through the hood is bound to make the beak openings dirty and the hawk being unused to wearing the hood will often scratch at the side pieces and will fray the coloured panels. She should now be set down on a block for the night. A hawk should never be disturbed after feeding. I find a block with a lead base extremely useful at this stage for it can be put in the middle of the floor of an empty room on a sheet of newspaper and the falcon tied to it by her leash. She may jump blindly down on to the floor but she will come to no harm if she does. She must not be put on the screen perch yet for were she to jump off the odds are that she would be unable to regain the perch.

Next day the eyas must be carried on the fist, still hooded, for several short periods. She will soon stop the hissing and other signs of fear and the feather can be discarded. She can be stroked with the bare hand with impunity but do not overdo this for fear of removing the waterproof bloom of her feathers. On the second or third night, depending on progress, the hood may be removed while she is feeding in subdued light indoors. With luck she will merely stop feeding for a moment—look around her and then continue feeding. Do not stare at her, and remain absolutely still while she continues her meal. Hawks always hate being stared at; it frightens them, for a fixed stare among animals usually precedes an attack. Replace the hood before the meal is finished and draw the braces up gradually. Allow her to complete her meal through the hood so that she does not associate hooding with the withdrawal of food.

On the third or fourth day she will feed freely bareheaded indoors by artificial light or outdoors at dusk.

Unlike short-winged hawks, the Peregrine becomes manned and so tame while hooded. During these first three or four days the braces of the hood should have been occasionally loosened and drawn up again so as to accustom her to the feel. On the third evening go into a dully lighted room and loosen the braces. Now remove the hood by lifting it forwards over her beak by the plume. Do not lower the hood from her head but slip it back on again almost at once before she has the chance to bate. Continue doing this occasionally, keeping the hood off a little longer each time until she will sit bareheaded for a few seconds. If she bates off the fist help her back on

Peregrine Falcon (Haggard).

again, hood her up and allow her a little time to settle down before attempting to unhood her again. If she proves very difficult, darken the room further until you can only just see what you are doing.

It is essential that she be broken to the hood early in her training while she is still more afraid of you than she is of the hood. If this exercise is delayed for any reason she will have lost her fear of you and will be able to concentrate on dodging the hood. As it is, she will be easy to hood for the first few days then will come a period when she will try a few tricks like dodging, shaking her head about and drawing her head down between her shoulders so that it is difficult to get the hood on properly. She will shake her head and may try bating off the fist blindly as soon as the hood is put on. This can all be most disconcerting for the beginner who begins to wonder where he has gone wrong. He need not fear; if he keeps his temper and persists with the hooding and unhooding as if nothing was amiss the falcon will pass through this stage and in a day or two completely submit to being hooded. This submission is complete when the only reaction to the approaching hood is the momentary flicking across the eyes of the third eyelid or *membrana nictitans*. When you see this you know that you have won the battle.

After the first three or four days you can start carrying the hawk bareheaded indoors. Be careful of door posts and projecting furniture and be ready to slip the hood on at the first sign of a bate. Avoid windows as she may attempt to bate out through them. In the evening when it is dark she may be carried out into the garden. A day or two later she will sit bareheaded on the fist in full daylight but even now great care should be taken that she is not frightened by the sudden appearance of a strange object or person from behind or from round a corner. If a hawk is suddenly terrified by a dog or a car she may for ever afterwards fear dogs and cars, which will be a nuisance. Introduce her to dogs, which must not jump up at her and other strange sights when she is feeding. Always have the hood ready to protect her from shocks and carry a piece of tiring on the glove so that her attention can be diverted if she shows signs of fear.

In the evening she may be put out of doors unhooded on a block for the first time. Do not leave her long, especially if she bates a lot. The time can be increased and she can be put out earlier as she becomes tamer.

When she is first put out in full sunlight she can be offered a bath.

F

Put her on the block hooded. Prepare the bath, fill it with water and put it beside the block. Strike the hood and retire ten or fifteen yards away. With luck she will hop down into the bath and bathe. When she has finished she will jump back on to the block and hang her wings to dry in the sun. When she is wet she will be unwilling to bate off and she may be approached to within three or four yards. Walk slowly round her, moving farther away if she shows signs of taking fright. When she is dry she may get restless and start bating. So approach her very carefully with a little piece of meat on the glove. Pick her up and hood her. As soon as the young falcon will sit bare-headed in full daylight on the block practise approaching her from different angles and offering her a tit-bit with the bare hand. After a bit she will always turn to face you when you approach in expectation of a morsel. Do not always offer one but do not deceive her. Offer the meat level with her breast. If you put your hand lower she may strike at it with her feet.

At the end of the first week, try her on the screen perch and watch her until she bates off to see if she is able to climb back again. When she has been seen to do this two or three times, she can safely be left unhooded at night in the darkened mews on the screen. Until now she will have spent her nights hooded on the indoor block. Now she is unhooded at night casting may be given with her food and the pellet should be looked for each morning beneath the screen. She must not be hooded up until she has cast, for a hawk cannot cast through a Dutch hood. If she is late casting she must be left unhooded in the dark until she does.

The training now proceeds exactly as that of the Kestrel and at the end of the third week from when she was taken up, the eyas should be flying loose to the lure. However, the falconer should never be afraid to lengthen the training period a little for an individual hawk whose response has perhaps been slower than that considered usual. There is a tendency among some falconers to cut short the training period and to boast that they have had a hawk "going loose" ten days after taking up. There is no merit in such a boast, for although an experienced falconer may get away with such practices, it only requires some minor unexpected happening like the sudden appearance of a strange dog to destroy the tenuous link between falconer and pupil. A hawk whose veneer of training is so thin will easily take fright and cause her owner endless trouble to recapture her (if he can) and once so scared may take a long time before she gets over the effect.

The beginner will find that he will take longer to reach a given point in the training programme than the experienced falconer. This is because he lacks the judgement required to tell him when it is safe to pass from one stage to the next. Provided he does not take an inordinately long time to train his hawk there is no reason why the end result should not be as good as that of the experienced falconer. In fact, in the case of short-winged hawks, the speed of progress is closely linked to the amount of manning that the falconer can give his hawk and the longer the hawk is upon the fist the tamer and so the more obedient she will become. Falconers will quote Sir John Sebright who killed a partridge with a passage Sparrowhawk ten days after taking her up. While this was a creditable feat one would hesitate to describe that Sparrowhawk as fully trained and safe to fly in any company at any suitable quarry. Sir John omits to say whether he lost this spar on its next flight!

It would be politic at this stage to say a few words about hooding. The art of hooding a hawk is not easily learned and while some persons seem to be able to do it naturally, others experience the greatest difficulty. The reason for hooding a falcon is to blindfold her and so render her impervious to external visual stimuli. These visual stimuli are of overwhelming importance to a hawk, for it is through them that all her actions and reactions are governed. Once hooded she immediately becomes immobile; she can be carried from place to place in the confined space of a car or 'bus without the danger of a bate which in such a situation might result in the breakage of flight feathers. She is conserving her energy, and if keen cannot waste her strength by useless bates at possible quarry. All her fears are allayed and shocks to her delicate nervous system are reduced to a minimum. It used to be the custom in Europe to follow the Eastern practice of "seeling"—that is to sew up the eyelids of a newly caught hawk with thread so as to render her more tractable.

This is probably not as barbarous as it might appear, but the use of the hood in training has long since superseded "seeling" in Europe. Once the hawk is trained, the hood serves as a blindfold when hawks are in transit from one place to another, and its use prevents those hawks which are waiting their turn to fly from bating at the lure which is being swung to attract those already on the wing.

The best way to hood a hawk, in my opinion, is to hold the hood by the base of the plume with the thumb and forefinger of the right hand. Bring the hood slowly up the hawk's breast and with a twist of the wrist when it reaches her head slide it over and down into position. This is easier said than done and it must be accomplished with one single smooth movement. It helps considerably to have the hawk standing in exactly the right position on the glove. She must be standing squarely with her feet in the correct position and with her head looking forwards. If her feet are wrong or if she is not balanced properly, rotate the gloved fist until she regains her proper stance. As the hood is put on, the gloved fist should be lowered downwards and backwards so that the hawk's body is tilted slightly forwards. She is then off balance and her head should come forward into the hood. There must be no "pushing on" of the hood and the hawk's head must not be thrust into the hood from behind with the fingers of the right hand as it holds the hood. The hawk should not be hooded with such a heavy hand that she loses balance and falls over backwards, nor should she twist her head about like a snake or sink her head into her shoulders. Once the hood has been lightly placed in position, and the lighter the falconer's hand is, the less likelihood there is of an attempt to dodge or dislodge the hood, shift the hand from the plume and grasp the outer closing brace with the thumb and forefinger of the free hand and slowly pull the braces tight. The beginner will soon appreciate that there are moments when it is difficult to hood a hawk and yet others when it is easy. Never try to hood her when she is wrongly placed on the glove or about to bate. Immediately after a bate when she has regained the glove is a good time, but should she beat you to it and bate again—have patience and before long she will give in and submit. Never use force and do not attempt to "dash" the hood on suddenly. Such practices will only make the falcon suspicious of her trainer and "hood shy." Once she has come to regard you with suspicion she will prove extremely difficult to train and manage. It is unlikely that one beginner's slip will undermine her confidence in you, but should you display any repeated signs of ill temper you will make your task impossible, for the falcon will win in the end. The trainer's manner must be one of conciliation and he must be gentle but firm so that both parties are able to retain their dignity.

The hood is removed by raising the gloved fist with the hawk

upon it until her head is level with your chin. Then taking the opening braces on the inside in your teeth and the opening braces on the
outside with your thumb and forefinger of the free hand, pull
sharply. This is termed "striking" the hood. Now take the base of the
plume in the fingers of the free hand and remove the hood with an
action which should be the exact opposite of putting it on. It is
important to have the hawk's head in the right position before striking the hood and minor adjustments can be achieved by touching
her on the right or left shoulder according to which direction she is
required to look.

In the early stages of breaking to the hood it will be found that it
is easier to hood a hawk indoors than outdoors and in dull light
rather than full light. If a hawk proves difficult and some that are easy
to start with become difficult for a few days as a "try on"—the best
time to break down her resistance is in a quiet room by the light of a
dull blue bulb.

Blaine finished his chapter on hooding with a well-known quota-
tion from Bert on the hooding of Goshawks and I make no apology
for doing the same, for Bert's treatise is one of the rarest of the
hawking classics and few people have the opportunity to read it.

"I will show you my manner therein: I shew her the hoode, put
it to and over her head many times. I find her so truly manned as
that she will no more dislike the stroaking there with, than the bare
hand; I put it on gently and very leisurely, and I could never meet
with any dislike thereof in my Hawke; I would either put it on
with my full hand, or else holding it by the tassel whereby you
may know that it was leisurely and gently done, which wil be
means that she shal never hereafter be coy of it: But if my fine
Austringer will shew his dexterity and nimblenesse of the hand,
and with his finger in her necke thrust her head into the hood, if
he misse the right doing it, the next time he commeth in such a
manner, he may peradventure find her dislike, this is the next way
to make her thinke her head shall be pulled off; for the putting it
on in such a quicke manner, or thrusting her head into the hoode
with the finger behinde, will make the Hawke understand that it
is no kindnesse, but violence and churlish usage, which must never
be offered a Hawke, and then you shall perhaps finde her dislike
your hand and hoode comming to her and so being a little coy or

angry, never be content to carry her beake right, but turne it in the hoode; and so any fine quicke hand bobbeth his hawk, and make her utterly dislike the hood.

"There is no way but gentlenesse to redeeme a Hawke so bobbed, and therefore I advise thee not to trust to the quicknesse of the hand, but rather to hold the hood by the tassell to her head and then to put it on leisurely, with a light carriage. You may say she will not suffer this; so think I also, after she has once taken a dislike thereof: use her as I have used mine and you shal find yours as I find mine. Admit your Hawke shal turn her heade, away from the hoode, I know she will not bate from it, perhaps she will likewise turne her body, by the removing one or both of her feete; upon the putting of her head aside, I would still hold my hoode within an inch of her head, until she should turne her head and then to put it on leisurely; but if she stirre her body and remove her feete, then pull back your hand, and by turning your body and your fist whereon she sitteth, set her right and fit, and then hold the hoode gently to her nose, which she will be willing to put her head into, rather than stirre any more, for she knoweth there is no hurt ensueth."

This was written by Edmund Bert in 1619 and as a description of hooding a hawk it has never been bettered.

CHAPTER VI

GAME HAWKING
Written from Notes
Supplied by
MAJOR S. E. ALLEN

WHEN I was asked to write this chapter I felt a little diffident, for although I have more years behind me as a falconer than most, I considered that few, if any, would have the opportunity to fly hawks at game as Gilbert Blaine and I did between the two World Wars. We had large areas to hawk over, he for grouse and I for partridges, with falconers, dogs and plenty of time. To attain a high standard of game hawking one must have access to suitable land upon which there is available a good stock of game. This is because only by almost daily flying throughout the season do most Peregrines become steady and climb to their pitch which may be anything up to 1,000 feet. This is the most spectacular sight in all field sport and can only be achieved when conditions are absolutely right. There is no sport better than good falconry and nothing worse than the bad version.

I started falconry 61 years ago and in my time I have hunted hounds, shot and fished a lot, but it is my considered opinion that falconry is the most difficult of all field sports. Am I a pessimist when I feel that only those born with a great love of hawks and who are content with limited success can help to keep this, the finest of sports, alive?

With the exception of game hawking most flights with falcons and hawks are from the fist "out of the hood." In the case of the Peregrine the quarry is then the rook or crow which are not often its natural food. The falcon's condition, then, must be a fine balance between a sharp appetite and strong flying powers. To achieve this she is regularly flown at the swung lure during training. When game, grouse or partridge is the quarry, the flight is from a height and the Peregrine is allowed to climb high in the air before the game is flushed. To obtain the full beauty of this flight, which is acknowledged to be the most difficult branch of the falconer's art, the higher the pitch the better. A game hawk, therefore, is not stooped to the lure but is called off from a distance, preferably from higher ground and up wind. On the approach of the falcon the lure is hidden for a short time and this will cause her to mount in the air while she circles the falconer in her efforts to ascertain the whereabouts of the expected lure. This process continues each day while the lure is hidden for increasingly long periods and the falcon should begin to wait on higher and higher. When some progress has been made a covey should be located and accurately marked. Now the falcon is called off and when she rises to find the lure the game should be sprung, downwind, as quickly as possible. A kill is now important to encourage the young hawk. If you are successful at the first attempt you may consider yourself very lucky. Often the hawk will not be sufficiently high and the game may get up when she is too far away on the downwind side. Do not keep her on the wing too long in these early days as she may get bored and rake away or worse still, develop the awful habit of settling on a rick or tree.

Setters or pointers (English or German) are used to locate the quarry. To this end it is important to have a dog handler in the field who is responsible for running the dogs and who has adequate control of them. The hawk and dog soon get to know the part each has to play and develop a high degree of co-operation. The dogs must be well trained, steady and staunch on the point. Nothing ruins a young falcon quicker than a series of false points. Larks are said to have a game scent and many otherwise good dogs will point them. I remember this happening one day when my tiercel was waiting on for partridge. The dog pointed a lark and to show his disgust the tiercel stooped at the dog and caught it an awful clout! A spaniel is a very useful ally for the pointers and setters for he will be on hand to rout the game out should they take refuge in thick cover, or run ahead of the point. German pointers have an advantage over the setters and English pointers in that they are genuinely dual purpose and the best of them will enter brambles and dense cover as well as ranging the moors and stubbles and pointing. Dogs are not absolutely essential when hawking partridges on stubble which has been cut with the binder, for in this case the game can often be spotted if the fields are examined closely with binoculars. But if the corn has been cut with a combine and the stubble is long, or if the partridges are to be found in roots, the services of either pointers or setters are a *sine qua non*.

It is well to examine at this stage the technique of using the dogs and serving the hawk with game.

Pointers or setters are run on the ground into the wind so that they may pick up the scent of the hiding birds. When a dog comes steadily on to a point, and it is usually easy to judge from the dog's demeanour whether the point is solid or not, the hood is struck and the hawk is released. Some falconers cast the falcon off while others prefer to let her rouse and take a look round from her perch on the upheld fist before she takes wing in her own time. Once on the wing she will circle the falconer several times in great circles of a diameter of up to half a mile. It may take several minutes for the falcon to complete her circuits and gain height. While she is circling and rising in the air the "field," including the dog handler, must circumvent the pointer and giving the dog a wide berth to avoid accidentally flushing the quarry at the wrong moment, must reform in a straight line facing the dog about 50 yards in front of him so that they have the wind behind them and the expected quarry before them. Now, at the precise moment that the hawk comes in over their heads flying towards the dog down the wind, the spaniel should be sent in to flush the game. As the game rises all the field may shout and wave their arms in the hope that the game will avoid this human "fence" and decide to seek safety downwind rather than upwind. All this is very difficult to engineer and obviously depends a lot on the quality of the dog employed and not a little upon luck. But should things go well a kill may be expected. It is vitally important that the opportunity to stoop downwind be offered to the inexperienced Peregrine. Should the game break away upwind a futile stern chase will result. One thing is certain. The falconer and his assistants must not themselves attempt to flush the quarry. In most cases if they do attempt it, the game will not be found to be lying just where they thought it was and there results a frantic rushing about in the heather while valuable seconds are lost and the falcon drifts away. The only occasion when the falconer may flush the game himself is when he can actually see it squatting in the cover.

After about twenty successful flights, the danger of raking away or settling on a rick passes because the Peregrine loves game and knows that if it waits on it will eventually be served. Wild Peregrines kill most of their quarry by a stoop from a considerable height and have been known to wait on over shooting parties and driven sheep expecting game to be flushed. The act of waiting on is thus merely an extension of a natural instinct which is being developed for the falconer's benefit. The young hawk, after she has been successfully entered, will quickly learn that the higher she waits on the greater are her chances of success and the more she kills the higher she will go and the steadier she will be. The first few flights are all-important for it is during these that the hawk, be she a falcon flown at grouse or a tiercel at partridges, learns that if she tries hard enough she can catch and kill her quarry. Once she has made a few kills she will become thoroughly wedded to that quarry and will fly it with increasing determination whenever she has the opportunity. Nothing succeeds like success and the vital importance of the early attempts at quarry must be understood by the falconer if he is to develop the necessary confidence in his hawk. Therefore great care must be taken that conditions for the first few flights are as good as they can possibly be. If there is any doubt, do not fly the hawk, for a disappointment now may make your task a lot more difficult. It is important to get the young eyas falcons ready to be entered at grouse as soon as possible after August 12th and to arrange, if at all possible, that the first few flights are at young inexperienced grouse and not at old birds. The same applies to tiercels which are to be flown at partridges after September 1st.

Unhacked eyasses can be successful at flights from the hood, but for game I much prefer either a well-hacked eyas or a red passage hawk because both of these have learned so much about stooping and the value of height while flying at liberty.

The young game tiercel, in the early part of the season, often starts its stoop at one partridge and then, at the last moment, changes for another. The result of this is always a miss. In the next stage the tiercel sticks to the partridge he has chosen and strikes it down. If the stricken partridge falls in roots or similar cover, it is not always easy to find it again and serve the tiercel who will have ringed up over the spot to get into position for another stoop. In the final stage the tiercel will wait on steadily at anything up to 1,000 feet and at the end of the vertical stoop will always bind. When this happens the bag will rapidly grow. But it is well to remember that in game hawking, as in other branches of falconry, the bag is of secondary importance and that style, not kills, is the criterion. There can be no finer sight in the world of sport than a dog on point, a Peregrine waiting on at a vast height, then the grand stoop when the game is flushed. While quality of the flight and not quantity of kills gives the most pleasure, I knew of one falcon, called Sibella and owned by the then Major Portal (now Marshal of the Royal Air Force The Viscount Portal of Hungerford), who in one day took three and a half brace of partridges and waited on as high for her last stoop as she did for her first. In the 'thirties I rented 3,000 acres around Shrewton and Tilshead at 1/- an acre. There were lots of partridges and in 1931 I took 334 head of partridges with my three tiercels.

Most falconers prefer to fly the tiercel at partridges and the falcon at grouse; the latter is heavy and is better able to manage the stronger quarry. There is some temptation for falcons to carry if flown at partridges.

Grouse will lie to a dog up till the end of August and partridges up till the end of September. By that time the game hawk should know the job and can be unhooded and allowed to mount before the dog starts to range. If this is done game will be afraid to move under the falcon and can be induced to lie to a point until almost the end of the season. After August a falconer would probably bag more grouse than one man with a gun and he would leave nothing wounded.

All Peregrines become very wedded to game and a dog on point is their lure. They should be flown in the highest condition consistent with obedience. A little independence makes them wait on higher, which is what is desired.

As the season progresses, partridges will often throw themselves to the ground just before the end of the stoop. Then, as the tiercel throws up, they fly low up wind and usually beat him for he has now to overtake them and make an upwind stoop. Grouse, too, will often adopt this successful stratagem.

Before 1914 most falconers set great value on Peregrines from Lundy Island for game hawking, and it is a fact that most of them were exceptional performers when given a long hack. Why this should be is difficult to understand, for the one or two eyrie sites on Lundy must have been occupied by falcons and tiercels from the mainland of England or Wales. But other eyries elsewhere in Britain have been famous for centuries, too, for the quality of the falcons produced by them. Perhaps some of these eyries are so situated that the food supply during the fledgling period is more plentiful than in other less favoured sites.

Before and after the First World War many red passage Peregrines were obtained from Valkensward in Holland, and these hawks were often absolutely first class at rooks and game. They were netted on migration in the autumn by the Mollen family who lived at Eindhoven. Adrian Mollen, an early member of the family, was falconer to the famous Dutch Loo Hawking Club. In my opinion it takes a well-hacked eyas more than one season before it can compare with a passage Peregrine either in style of flight or footing ability.

The Old Hawking Club used to order fresh passage hawks every year because they found that if flown at rooks these red hawks did not always fly honest in their second season. The contrary was found to be true for passage hawks flown at game. These tend to improve as one season succeeds another. I had one passage falcon for nine seasons.

It must be remembered that not all Peregrines make good game hawks. I have had many duds. I think an eyas that has flown for a season at game will often subsequently make a good rook hawk for she realizes the value of pitch and stoop which is so difficult to teach to most eyasses that are flown at rooks first. I have had many hawks that waited on fairly well for game but which loved to chase after a Kestrel or other birds. These I noticed often turned out to be good rook hawks when later entered to the sable quarry.

I think that the modern, post World War II falconer who wishes to try his hand at hawking partridges with Peregrine tiercels must realize that his venture will be doomed to inevitable failure unless he can provide certain essential ingredients for success. If these ingredients are not to be had I most strongly advise him not to abuse the noble Peregrine but to turn his attentions to the humbler forms of falconry.

I consider that the minimum requirements are two well-hacked eyas tiercels, a steady pointer or setter, and an assistant to handle the dog. Well over 1,000 acres of reasonably flat land consisting of large arable fields, well stocked with game and a minimum of tall crops like kale or sugar beet. The falconer must be able to devote six weeks of September and early October to his sport. Only in this way will his tiercels become experienced enough to show real style. Access to a reasonably large area is important because although hawking certainly does not drive game away, constant disturbance by man and hawk, or man and gun does, and in either case they may be tempted to seek safer homes on adjacent land. When I had the 3,000 acres on Salisbury Plain, I divided it into four beats and never visited the same beat on two successive days.*

The same principles apply to grouse hawking except that the area needed will be even larger. Grouse hawking is considered by some to be easier than flying tiercels at partridges because large areas of open moor are more easily obtained and grouse tend not to run in front of a point like partridges, so can be flushed more easily at the right moment. There are, too, fewer distractions in the shape of wood pigeons and other birds on the grouse moor. The moor must be reasonably flat and not intersected by too many deep braes into which grouse can put. There must, too, be a minimum of deep heather and bracken, for many grouse will escape in this type of cover even after they have been struck down by the falcon.

Whether to feed up after a successful flight will depend on several factors of which the falconer will be aware. He will take into consideration the length of time the falcon has already been on the wing, for he may decide that although the day is still young a falcon who has been waiting on for some considerable time would be better rewarded after a successful stoop than just given the head and neck of the quarry and flown again. It is always best whenever possible to feed up after a successful flight whether this flight be the second or the seventh of the day. A lot, of course, will depend on the abundance or otherwise of the game and the falconer must gauge whether it is wise to risk a further flight being unsuccessful. It must be a bit of an anticlimax for a hawk who has been patiently waiting on for some little time expecting game to be flushed beneath her to be tamely taken down to the lure. Game hawks love to eat game, but a word of warning must be sounded about the feeding of grouse to game hawks. Grouse meat is very rich and if a falcon is given a crop of grouse she will be out of sorts for some days afterwards.

When out game hawking, and equally when out after more humble quarry, one must endeavour to keep the spectators, both invited and uninvited, under some sort of control. They must prefer-

* A further factor, essential for success, but of course outside the falconer's control, is good weather during the early days of the short Game Season.

ably be briefed before the start of the expedition, that is, if they have no previous experience. After the briefing, lure and spare hoods may be issued to those who are to act as "markers" so that they may be able to "take down" and hood up a temporarily lost hawk. The "field" must be instructed to keep together in a small knot well behind the falconer. They must never crowd round him. I have seen Peregrines show signs of confusion by being unable to distinguish the falconer among a crowd. The spectators must not talk loudly or shout to one another for this will cause game to take wing long before the dog has found it. In no case must anyone other than the falconer "make in" to the falcon on the kill. Even the falconer himself must exercise great care when he does this, especially if the hawk is a young one and apt to be shy. "Fields" should be kept small until the hawk is well made. In fact, apart from essential helpers, I think it is best not to invite spectators at all until one can be fairly certain of putting on a creditable show. It is always wise when flying trained hawks at quarry to warn one's immediate neighbours and their keepers of this fact and to enlist their interest. To a falconer a well-trained hawk is a pearl beyond price but to an ignorant man with a gun merely vermin. It helps, too, to exhibit notices in local public-houses to the effect that hawks wearing jesses and bells are being flown, for thus many countrymen will be aware of what is taking place. Their help will be of great assistance in the event of a lost hawk.

It is not often that a passage Peregrine becomes available for the modern falconer to try his hand upon. Most of the old trapping methods relied upon the use of a tethered pigeon as bait and are now illegal. But very occasionally a passage or haggard falcon finds its way to the United Kingdom from Pakistan, the Middle East or from Belgium where it has been caught in the nets set by the finch trappers.

The passage falcon is generally a superior performer to the eyas but is rather more unreliable to fly. She is inclined to rake away at distant quarry and if flown in spring and autumn when the migrations are on, there is a very real danger that she will be tempted to join the northward or southward procession.

It is important that the wild-caught hawk, whatever the species and whether passage or haggard, should be taken up for training as soon as is possible after capture. This applies to eyasses, too, once they are hard penned. For to delay in making a start is to make the task of training much more difficult, if not impossible.

The training programme for the wild-caught hawk is similar to that of the eyas except that the various stages tend to be more drawn out and the falconer must proceed from one stage to the next much more carefully. The passage hawk once manned is much better mannered than the eyas. She is more aloof and does not become so "close" to her owner. She never screams or mantles.

To start with she must be kept hooded day and night on a screen perch. The wild-caught hawk, being much stronger than an eyas, is better able to regain the screen perch should she bate off. She must always receive her food on the fist, indoors, in the evening in dull artificial light. Encourage her to feed, at first, through the hood, then, when feeding is well under way, remove the hood and carefully help her to continue her meal unhooded. Before she has finished feeding and while she is still eating hungrily, replace the hood and allow her to complete her meal through the hood. She will not then come to associate hooding with the termination of a meal.

During the day the passager may be carried hooded on the fist at intervals and stroked on the back and breast first with a feather and later with the bare hand. But do not overdo this for fear of removing too much of the bloom from the feathers.

As soon as she will feed freely bareheaded by artificial light without bating, she may be left unhooded at night on the screen perch in a blacked-out mews. Carry her to the mews hooded and unhood her after she has been set down on the screen. In the morning she may be approached carefully in the darkened mews and taken up on the fist with a small quantity of meat on the fist. Hood her up before she has finished eating this.

Her main meal will still be given in the evening unhooded, indoors. As her confidence grows she may be carried out of doors at dusk and induced to feed unhooded outside. If the falconer lives in a town or village he may find that his passager will be disposed to feed by the light of the street lamps. In Germany the German falconers always carry their newly caught passage Goshawks in the towns at night. Later she will be asked to feed indoors by daylight and then outdoors in full daylight. Choose a quiet corner for this exercise at first and allow no interruptions. Soon the evening meal may be offered with other people in sight and after a day or two with people standing nearby. If the hawk shows her apprehension by bating or refusing to feed, the careful falconer will retreat a stage in the training. She must always be hooded up before the end of these meals and allowed to finish her food through the hood. As she is now left unhooded on the screen at night she may receive casting with her food. As with the eyas it is essential to get the passager to take a crop of food as early as possible in her training before she has lost too much condition. It is important, too, to break her to the hood on the third or fourth night after starting her training. Generally speaking, passage and haggard falcons are a lot easier to break to the hood than are eyasses.

It will be a considerable time before the passager will be tame enough to be weathered on the block bareheaded. She may, of course, be put on the block hooded. Probably it is best to make sure that she is thoroughly manned by carriage on the fist before she is tried unhooded on the block. The first time she is put out bareheaded should be in the evening at dusk. Hawks are always quieter then. She must not be left alone on the block unhooded and these periods of bareheaded weathering must not be prolonged for wild-caught hawks quickly get restless at this stage. The exercise described in the training of the eyas where the falconer offers the falcon on the block tit-bits from his finger-tips as he walks round her, should be practised as this is a very good way of reclaiming her.

It is sometimes difficult to enter the passage hawk or haggard to her quarry. In spite of the fact that she will have killed many times for herself while she was at liberty she seems to lose all interest in quarry once trained. This is not invariable but it can be very disconcerting. It is more likely to occur if the passager is entered to a quarry which is not her natural food, such as rook. In these cases it may be some time and take a great deal of patience before the passage falcon will fly at a rook. Only by repeatedly throwing her off at rooks at a disadvantage, such as sick ones, will she eventually be induced to fly them. However, once she has started to fly rooks she will usually continue to do so and will become wedded to them. It was not the custom of the Old Hawking Club to fly their passage hawks at rooks for more than one season as they considered that the falcons could not be trusted at this distasteful quarry for longer than this. In the case of passagers trained to wait on for game, there is usually no difficulty encountered in entering them and they become so wedded to this their favourite quarry that they can be flown at them for many seasons. Passage or haggard Goshawks will not often fly hares when trained. This may be because they have tried to catch them in the wild

Lanner Falcon (Passage).

and received such a buffeting that they will not attempt to take so large and strong a quarry again.

The members of the Old Hawking Club never ordered haggards from Mollen as they considered them far too unreliable for rooks or game.

Eyas Peregrines, whether hacked or not, should not be made too tame but only sufficiently so to be picked up on the lure or kill. George Oxer, head falconer of the Old Hawking Club, always said: "When I slip my Peregrine I want her to leave me and not hang around me for the lure."

BARBARY FALCONS AND LANNERS AT GAME

by J. G. Mavrogordato

BARBARY FALCONS (*Falco pelegrinoides*) (red or haggard—I have no experience of eyasses) make first-class game hawks for partridges. They are not heavy enough for grouse. On the only occasion on which I put up a Barbary falcon over a point at grouse, she knocked down two out of the covey into the heather by successive stoops, but did not pack a big enough punch to do them any damage.

The falcons are, however, just the right size for partridges, and although I have never had one to wait on at stupendous heights, four or five hundred feet is quite high enough for success at this quarry. The stooping and footing of a good Barbary, even from such a comparatively modest height, are incomparable.

The tiercels are too small for serious work at partridges; they are best kept for smaller quarry such as starlings, which I will come to in due course.

Barbary falcons average about 1 lb. 6 oz. in weight, and tiercels about 15 oz. They must be flown in very high condition, for they are birds of the arid desert and the English climate does not suit them. They lose condition with alarming rapidity, on the least excuse, even in fine weather, and are not likely to tolerate the damp cold of our English winter. They are as a rule much tamer than European Peregrines; but I do not subscribe to the view that they are more heavily armed, or faster. I recently watched a palaearctic Peregrine outfly, out-stoop, and generally make circles round a Barbary falcon in a successful attempt to rob it of the sparrow it had just caught. Moreover Barbaries are, even in the wild state, remarkable for their

G

lack of perseverance; so that, apart from their tameness and their looks, they really have no "edge" on the Northern races of Peregrine.

The Red Shahin (*Falco pelegrinoides babylonicus*) of the Indians (I use the word in its pre-partition sense) is for all practical purposes the same bird as the Barbary, and can doubtless be flown at the same quarry in the same way.

The Indian Black Shahin (*Falco peregrinus peregrinator*), which is comparable to the African Peregrine, is a falcon of the forests and jungles, and is much rarer. It is rather larger, and the Indians prefer it to the red. It is said to be perfect for the smaller kinds of duck. The only example which I trained, a passage African tiercel which I kept through two seasons, was a grand little bird, better than any Barbary tiercel of mine. He weighed about 17 oz. Had he been a couple of ounces heavier, he would have made an ideal partridge hawk. His waiting on and stooping were perfect, and he was extremely tame, and as obedient as one could wish.

Lanners (*Falco biarmicus*) are also potential game hawks, though their capabilities have not yet been fully tested. I have only once slipped a Lanner at grouse, and then, as so often happens, things went wrong. There was a good point, and I unhooded the falcon. At that very instant an old cock grouse on passage flew across the moor about a quarter of a mile away, and the Lanner flung herself off the fist in hot pursuit, chased the grouse out of sight down a valley, and was lost for half an hour. So what would have happened had she waited on over the point until the grouse were flushed beneath her must remain a matter for conjecture. My guess, however, is that Lanners are neither fast enough nor heavy enough to be able to cope successfully with full-grown grouse.

With partridges, it is another matter. Both the falcons and good sized lannerets can kill partridges well; and somewhat curiously lannerets often seem better at the game than the falcons, all but the best of which appear sluggish and clumsy in comparison.

As I point out elsewhere, in dealing with magpie-hawking, Lanners excel in close and steady waiting on, invaluable characteristics where great height is not essential. The best killer of partridges which I have ever had was, however, a lanneret who adopted a highly unorthodox technique. While the dog was being run, he used to cruise about down wind of it at about tree height, keeping a very close and intelligent watch on the proceedings. When a point was found and the partridges were flushed downwind towards him, he would tear into them at great speed, and often take one head on, hitting it a smack that could be heard all over the field.

Now that partridges are becoming almost annually more scarce, more expensive, and more inaccessible to the average falconer, I feel I need make no apology for promoting the starling to the rank of "poor man's game bird," and adding a few words about the sport to be had at starlings with the long-wings.

Starlings have always, of course, been regarded as suitable quarry for Sparrowhawks and Merlins; but their potentialities for falcons were neglected so long as flights of partridges were the order of the day. Now, however, the starling is beginning to come into its own, as a quarry in its own right, even for falcons, and not merely an occasional "various" in the game book. Starlings in fact provide excellent flights for Barbary tiercels, lannerets and Red-headed Merlins (*Falco chicquera*) (and what would one not give for a chance to try the miniature African Taita* falcon at this quarry.

Starlings for such flights must naturally be looked for on the open sheep-walks and downland, and not in the hedgerows or on cultivated ground, where the Sparrowhawk with its short, sharp attacks is the right weapon to use. On such open ground, a flock of starlings will provide an exhilarating flight for the smaller falcons.

A Barbary tiercel is fast enough to outfly starlings and force them down into cover, so no particular difficulty is experienced in organizing the slip. Once the starlings have put in, the tiercel, if he knows his job—and he soon will—after making his point, will wait on over the cover and so pin them down. It is now the falconer's task to drive out the starlings under the tiercel. Each time he does so, they will go out in a reluctant tight-packed bunch, and after swirling round in the open and running the gauntlet of one or two breath-taking vertical stoops, they will plunge back into cover—as often as not the bush they had just left, or perhaps, if nothing better offers, a bed of nettles, tussock of grass, or a flock of grazing sheep. The process is continued until a stoop makes contact, the starlings succeed in making themselves scarce, or the tiercel tires.

Lannerets are too slow to be able to put down starlings on the wing but good sport may be had with a high-mounting lanneret, if he be given the opportunity to gain his pitch before the starlings take

* Kilimanjaro Falcon, Falco fasciinucha, Reichenow & Neumann.

wing. This can sometimes be arranged if the starlings are engrossed in feeding, or resting in good cover in the middle of otherwise open ground. The method, then, is to go off some two to three hundred yards, put the hawk on the wing, let him gain his pitch, and it must be a good one, over you, at leisure, and then bring him back over your head, without loss of height, until you reach the quarry, which by then (if it has not already taken flight and made off) will be successfully pinned down, and ready to be flushed under the hawk at the right moment.

The so-called Red-headed Merlin (not really a Merlin at all, though bearing a superficial resemblance in size and shape to a European Merlin) is a resident of tropical Africa and India. This beautiful little falcon is much more heavily armed than a Merlin, having a thick heavy beak and large strong feet with the long toes typical of a bird-catching falcon. The females weigh up to 9 oz. and the males between 6 and 7 oz. They are very fast and dashing little fliers both in the wild and in the trained state. It is almost impossible to keep up with one in a car, even in flat desert, when actually flying quarry. They can be taught to stoop beautifully to the lure, throwing up 50 to 100 feet between stoops. They will wait on overhead for two or three minutes (which is longer than you might think until you have timed it) after putting in quarry, but are not inclined, indeed cannot be trusted, to stay overhead for long, if only because they are sure very soon to spot and dash off after some other quarry.

In the wild state they prey on any bird up to dove size. In England a good female would, I believe, not hesitate to tackle a partridge. But the best and most sporting flight to be had with them is probably that at starlings, at which they should be slipped from the fist. Males as well as females should be capable of this flight and have no difficulty in out-flying them and forcing them down, even if the starlings have a considerable start. They are not prone to carry the kill.

If the best is to be got out of them, they must be kept in extremely high condition (there is no trouble here as they are very tame by nature), and given plenty of exercise; at least twenty stoops to the lure on days when they are not flown at quarry. Unfortunately, these little birds are very delicate and are susceptible to a particularly virulent form of frounce. Their ability to stand an English winter must be considered very questionable.

CHAPTER VII

ROOK-HAWKING AND MAGPIE-HAWKING

ROOK-HAWKING

by J. G. MAVROGORDATO

ROOK-HAWKING, as a recognized branch of falconry, is, I believe, of comparatively recent date. It seems to have been introduced as a humbler substitute for Kite-hawking and heron-hawking, when the disappearance of the Kite, and the draining of marshes, put an end to these nobler forms of "flying out of the hood."

However that may be, the rook has many advantages as a quarry for the modern falconer. It is common and easily found; it is regarded with disfavour by farmer and gamekeeper alike; it does not enjoy the protection of the law; and, last, but not least, it provides a sporting and even spectacular flight which will test the skill and staying-power of both falconer and falcon. Moreover, it is not as a rule necessary to own land or sporting rights of one's own in order to fly this quarry: many landowners and shooting tenants can, with the exercise of a little tact, be induced to grant permission to fly vermin; and, provided that this permission is never abused, they will in due course come to recognize that the flying and killing of rooks and crows on their land, far from having an adverse effect on their game-birds, will actually improve the shoot. For just as the partridges will soon take no notice of falcons passing harmlessly overhead, so will the rooks and crows become increasingly conscious of the unusual menace in their midst, and more and more reluctant to go "birds' nesting" far from the shelter of their rookeries or roosts. Before long, one glimpse of the hawking van will be enough to make them abandon their nefarious activities and send them scurrying home.

Good rook-hawking requires three things—good country, good hawks, and good slips.

Rooks may be found on almost any ground, but it is only on good ground that the best flights are to be had. While I have the greatest admiration for those who can kill rooks in small fields, surrounded by hedgerow timber, and with perhaps a wood at one end, that, with all due respect, is not the highest form of rook-hawking. For the real thing, really open country is needed—downland, fens, marshes, or even moors, if rooks can be found on them. Woods, trees, hedges, farmyards and cottages must be few and far between; even fences can spoil a flight and should be eyed askance.

As for hawks, the traditional hawk for the "sable quarry" is the female Peregrine. There have indeed been good tiercels, but they are exceptional, and in any event ought not in my opinion to be slipped at the carrion crow, for which even the falcon is barely strong enough.

Female Sakers (*Falco cherrug*), if carefully trained and entered to this flight, will also make good rook-hawks, and a first-class Lanner would, I believe, occasionally prove capable of killing rooks. They are also, of course, well within the scope of a jerkin, but it seems, judging from my experience, that this quarry has little appeal for these powerful but unpredictable performers.

The following observations will, accordingly, be based on the assumption that the hawk to be flown at rooks is the female Peregrine.

It remains to consider whether she should be unhacked, hacked, passager, or haggard. With all respect to those who hold a contrary view, in my opinion an unhacked eyas should be avoided. It may take months or even years before the unhacked eyas develops into a stylish performer at rooks; in fact she may never do so. Even hacked falcons can be very disappointing, but they do have one big, perhaps commanding, advantage over passagers and haggards: they are much less likely to be lost, and, after loss, much more likely to be recovered, particularly if flown in the area in which they were hacked.

As for passagers and haggards, no one who has ever enjoyed good flights with these can ever, I fancy, be really satisfied with the performance of even the best of eyasses unless and until years of experience have taught them what the wild-caught hawk already knew. It is my personal belief that, for sheer perfection of style, haggards are even better than passagers: but the haggard is, on balance, inferior to the passager because of her wildness, obstinacy, and independence.

Rooks may be flown at any time of the year: the best time for entering a hawk to this quarry is as soon as practicable after the rooks' breeding season, before the young rooks are strong on the wing, and when the old birds are becoming very ragged with the onset of the moult. Young hawks should be entered as soon as they are ready. It can, however, be very dangerous to fly rooks in July and August in the neighbourhood of standing corn: the rook may put into the corn, or perhaps worse still, be taken by the falcon in it: to locate and extricate her from a hundred-acre field of waist-high wheat is no easy task—nor one the performance of which is likely to endear you to the owner of the crop. The best flights are obtainable in the early spring, when both rooks and falcons should be at their best: this is the traditional season for "spring rook-hawking."

We now come to the training of the rook-hawk, and I shall assume that we start at the stage where the falcon has been properly manned, and made to the hood and lure. I shall merely add that I, personally, attach considerable importance to an adequate degree of manning: there is nothing I dislike more than having to drag up, tail first, a wild and reluctant hawk who has bated away from me as I approached the block: it is small consolation to me that such a hawk may, half an hour later, behave herself well in the field, nor do I believe in the theory that "rook hawks can be too tame." Tame falcons are a delight to handle, wild falcons the reverse: and I have so far met with nothing in my own experience to suggest that falcons which behave well at home are any the worse for that at flying and killing rooks. Be that as it may, I certainly expect of any rook-hawk of mine in flying order that she shall bate from the block *towards* me, not away from me, when I approach to pick her up: nor is this expectation often disappointed, even in the case of a haggard.

As for hooding, it is obviously important that a falcon which is to be flown out of the hood at quarry should not be hood-shy, should have a well-fitting hood, which keeps her pretty well in the dark even when the braces have been "struck" (loosened) in preparation for a slip, and should submit without a struggle to the striking of the braces and the removal of the hood.

The lure for a rook-hawk should be a dead rook, or the usual leather foundation with a pair of rook wings sewn on to each side, and a pair of thongs or cords fixed to the middle of each side for the attachment of food.

It is a mistake to think that a falcon, which can have had little or no flying since her training began, can, as soon as she comes promptly a hundred yards or so to the lure, be taken out and thrown off at a rook. If the rook is poor enough, she might conceivably catch it after a stern chase, but that would be a travesty of rook-hawking. No. You must assume that the rooks you are after are *very fit* birds, constantly on the wing in all weathers, and you must try to make your falcon almost equally fit before you launch her against them. How is this to be done? By stooping her to the lure, daily if practicable, until she can put in not less than twenty hard stoops running without becoming distressed or out of breath.

To stoop a hawk well to the lure requires considerable skill on the part of the falconer as well as the falcon. The whole art lies in the timing. The lure, which has been swung round in a vertical plane during the falcon's run-in, must, just before she approaches, be swung out into her path, and then in the nick of time swung back out of her reach, and the process repeated until she has had enough, when the lure should be thrown out on to the ground for her, or, if you have the necessary skill, swung up at the critical moment so as to allow her to take it in the air, without getting hit by it or entangled in the lure line. If the falcon is skilful enough to grasp or even hit the lure before you intended, she should, by way of reward for her skill, be allowed to have the lure without further ado.

These stooping lessons should be progressive: at first one or two stoops will suffice, but each day the number of stoops should be increased, until the number has reached twenty. This may take ten days or more. The lure for these stooping exercises must be a light one, so as to minimize the risk of injury to the hawk from an error of judgement on the part of either falconer or falcon: 8 oz. is quite heavy enough. The line should be three to five yards of blindcord, with a free-working swivel between lure and cord to obviate kinking.

When the falcon can do her twenty stoops without distress, and, let us hope, with increasing speed and severity, she is ready to be entered to her quarry.

At this point I may perhaps anticipate the objection that repeated stooping to the lure makes a hawk lure-bound and likely to refuse live quarry. I have not myself found this to be so: prior to the 1959 Game Fair, I stooped both Saker and Red-headed Merlin to the lure almost daily for the best part of a month, in preparation for the exhibition they were to give there; two days after the Game Fair, both flew live quarry really well, and killed. In Pakistan I saw falcons stooped to the lure on every day on which they were not flown at quarry, and I was told that the normal ration was fifty stoops—though I must confess I myself never counted more than twenty.

I shall not say much about entering, for the answers to the problem are really obvious. You want your falcon to kill as soon as possible. The first few rooks at which she is slipped should, therefore, be easy ones. Keep your eyes open, and try to take your first rook or two at a disadvantage. Look for young rooks, sick rooks, wet rooks, or rooks deep in the moult, and get a close slip at them—not more than fifty yards. Needless to say, such flights are not sport, nor are they meant to be so. But they are a necessary prelude to sport. If your falcon starts, and the slip is a reasonably good one, she will have a fair chance of killing, and once she has made two or three kills, and gained confidence in her powers to take this quarry, she may be promoted to proper flights.

If all else fails, and you are lucky enough to have a "made" rook-hawk in flying condition, you may fly them together in a cast, in the reasonable expectation that the beginner, when it sees the "make-hawk" pursuing a rook, will be tempted to join in the flight and share in the kill. Unless the rook is a singleton, it is advisable not to slip the beginner until the make-hawk has cut out her selected rook from the flock. There is, of course, always a risk in such cases that the two falcons will crab, particularly if the beginner is an unhacked eyas and so has never previously been on the wing with another falcon; but this is a risk that will have to be accepted, and in any event not much damage is likely to be done.

One point that requires consideration at this stage is, should the falcon be allowed to feed up on a rook that she has killed? On this, opinions differ. Some experienced falconers hold the view that in no circumstances should a falcon be allowed to taste rook flesh, in case its taste should permanently disgust her with such a quarry. Others consider that, unless the falcon shows obvious signs of dislike for rook flesh, there is no harm in allowing her to eat it. I myself rather incline to the latter view. It is certain, in the first place, that wild falcons do kill and eat rooks (one has even been trapped on a rook kill), though that is probably in default of anything better: some wild Peregrines even make a habit of preying on the more strongly and unpleasantly flavoured jackdaw. In the second place, it is a great convenience to be able to allow the falcon to take her pleasure on her own kill, and to be spared the complications involved in substituting the flesh of a freshly-killed pigeon for that of the rook. In practice, my experience has been that most Peregrines killing rooks regularly soon learn to devour them eagerly; even if the taste for rook flesh is an ácquired one, it seems to be acquired fairly readily. Sakers never have any hesitation—but then their natural diet includes comparatively unpalatable food in any case, such as rats and lizards. I therefore recommend that for the first two or three flights, a pigeon be held in reserve, and at the slightest sign of distaste for rook flesh, that of the pigeon should be substituted; but that the substitution should be stopped if and as soon as it becomes practicable. I should add that, apart from considerations of flavour, rook flesh is good red meat, and will keep a falcon fed on it in high condition. But, of course, a falcon should not be fed exclusively on rook, any more than on any other diet: they appreciate variety as much as we do, and on their off days, or, if they are killing regularly, even sometimes on the kill, should have a change of diet.

We have now arrived at the crucial point in rook-hawking—the slip. The slip is the key to success. Assuming good country, and a good falcon, a good slip spells success, a bad slip failure, involving possibly the loss of the falcon herself.

The art of slipping can probably only be learnt, in the last resort, by actual experience in the field, but there are certain rules, neglect of which is likely to produce failure or disaster.

I will now proceed to set out these rules in order:

1. *Do not slip in unsuitable country*

Make as sure as you can that the rooks cannot reach safe cover—trees, woods, farm buildings, thick hedges—upwind or downwind or on either flank, before the falcon has had a real chance to dominate them and put in several stoops. It is impossible to suggest safe distances, for everything depends on the direction and strength of the wind. If the wind is strong, the upwind cover can be much closer, but the downwind cover should be correspondingly more distant than if the wind is slight. A rough-and-ready rule, propounded by my friend Robert Spens, was that the distance from rook to upwind cover should be double the distance from the falconer, at the moment of slip, to the rook.

You cannot know whether or not country is unsuitable unless, before slipping, you have adequately reconnoitred it. You must, therefore, know what is beyond the upwind sky-line, and the downwind skyline (unless they are so far distant that the answer is irrelevant) before you slip, and have clearly in mind the nature and position of every piece of cover which the rook may conceivably attempt to reach.

2. *Always slip dead into the wind*

This means that you must manœuvre yourself into a position exactly downwind of the rook or rooks to be flown. The reason for this—the most important rule of all—is difficult to explain shortly on paper, though it can be seen easily enough in practice. By slipping the falcon at the rooks from downwind, and so forcing the rooks to fly into the wind, the falcon's superior wing-power is at once brought into play: she not only gains on them more rapidly, but gains height in a way only made possible by flying into the wind. This enables her to dominate the rooks from the moment that she "fetches," or reaches them, and even if the flight thereafter takes a downwind turn (as it probably will) the falcon will remain in command, and bring the rook or rooks back towards, or over, the falconer, who will thus retain much better control of the flight than if it continued straight on in one direction.

If the slip is downwind, rooks and falcon go helter-skelter, without height, to the nearest downwind cover, the falcon is never in a dominating position, there is merely a stern chase without stoops, and the falconer himself is in danger of being left rooted to the spot, an idle spectator at the outset, and then not even that.

Slips on a cross-wind are nearly as bad, for the rook will probably manage, before it is under the falcon's control, to swing round her and dash downwind, with similar results to those already described. Time taken to get the wind dead right before slipping is never wasted.

3. *Do not take too close a slip*

The beginner is generally tempted to get as close as possible to the rook before slipping. This may be permissible when the hawk is being entered, but as soon as she knows the quarry, short slips should be avoided. A hundred yards should be regarded as the minimum. If the slip is too short, the rook will manage to whip round the falcon before she has got height or even flying speed, and the result, even if the rook was upwind to start with, will be a downwind flight of the kind already described. A good falcon, "wedded" to the quarry, will think nothing of slips of up to a quarter of a mile; but in such cases, naturally, the area free from cover in all directions must be correspondingly large.

4. *Do not slip if there are rooks, other than those to be flown, downwind of you or on either flank.*

This is another important rule. The falcon cannot be relied upon to pursue the rooks so carefully selected by you if, at the moment of being slipped, she catches sight of others which in her view (however mistaken it may be) are more desirable. Make sure, therefore, before slipping that there are no other rooks downwind (perhaps over the brow) or on either flank, and, if there are, go and drive them off. That will sometimes, perhaps often, result in the selected rooks also taking flight: but that is a risk that must be taken. Sometimes they move off into an even more suitable position!

5. *Do not slip at a very large and widely-scattered flock of rooks*

Such slips are dangerous, particularly if, as often happens, a mob of wood-pigeons, lapwings and starlings gets up with the rooks. You are faced immediately with a scene of indescribable confusion; you will probably lose sight of the falcon in the middle of the mob, rooks on the flanks will almost certainly manage to break away downwind, they may be the very ones that tempt the falcon, and it will be the easiest thing in the world to lose the falcon even if she kills. I once slipped a falcon at about a thousand migratory rooks: she killed, but I never knew where, and was lost for several days.

6. *Do not slip at rooks until they have risen*

One is sometimes tempted to try and take advantage of the rooks by slipping the falcon while they are still on the ground, so as to give her a flying start at them. This seldom works out in practice. Predators are notoriously bad at picking out anything that is motionless, and the chances are that the falcon will fail to spot the rooks, and start off in the wrong direction. In this event, it will be the rooks and not the falcon that will generally get the advantage. If, then, the rooks do not rise when you are within correct slipping distance, frighten them up by waving your hand at them and shouting, or send forward an assistant to force them to take wing, and hood off the falcon the moment they do so. Alternatively, you may wait patiently in the hope that the rooks will every now and then flutter up and down, or be joined by other rooks, so that there are at least some on the wing to catch her eye at the moment that the falcon is unhooded.

7. *Do not slip an inexperienced falcon at a rook "on passage"*

A falcon should not be slipped at a rook on passage, that is to say, a single rook making a long-distance flight from point to point, unless she has already killed several rooks; and the rook should be less than 30 feet high and travelling upwind away from the falconer. This is the rule, but it may be progressively modified as the falcon becomes more skilled in dealing with such slips. Rooks on passage are generally strong, self-reliant birds, harder to bring to book than the average member of a flock: it needs a really experienced falcon to tackle them successfully.

8. *Do not slip at jackdaws*

Jackdaws are slippery customers and may well outfly the falcon, or take her so far that she is lost. It is easy in the excitement of the moment to mistake a flock of jackdaws for a flock of rooks, so it is prudent to make quite sure that the proposed quarry consists of rooks and not jackdaws. There is no objection, however, to slipping at a mixed flock of rooks and jackdaws: the falcon will almost certainly have enough sense to choose a rook.

9. *Do not slip at crows*

This is a less absolute rule than the preceding one. Perhaps, instead of an absolute prohibition, one should say: "Be very cautious about slipping at crows." There is more than one reason for such caution. In the air, though he looks slower than the rook, the crow seems to be definitely more skilled in shifting from the stoop, and is also more stout-hearted, so that he may succeed in surviving from six to ten good stoops and reach cover that would have been beyond the reach of a rook. On the ground, he is a bigger, heavier, and stronger bird than the rook, and fights back much more strenuously, so that even a falcon finds difficulty in killing him. Nor is this all. Crows are nearly always to be found in pairs or family parties, and there is every likelihood that the mate, or the whole family, will fly in to the succour of the captured bird, and either force the falcon to relinquish her grasp, or worse still, seriously injure her by stabbing at her with their great pick-axes of beaks. Falcons have been known to lose an eye or have the crop torn out as the result of such an attack.

On the whole, therefore, the falconer will be prudent not to slip deliberately at a crow unless it is in an exceptionally good place, and is either solitary or on ground over which the falconer can ride or drive very rapidly to the succour of his falcon should this be necessary.

How does one distinguish a crow from a rook? In the case of an old rook, it is of course, easy: the bare white patch at the base of the upper mandible gives it away. To distinguish crows from young rooks is not so easy, and needs experience. As a rough-and-ready guide, however, it may be said that solitary birds, pairs, and parties of up to five or even ten birds, *none* of which have the tell-tale white patch, are probably crows, and better avoided, or tackled with caution. Flocks of rooks may, of course, include crows, but that is a natural hazard that can be accepted: and should the falcon chance to capture one, rescue operations by its relations are much less likely to be attempted in such a case.

Some falcons, probably as the result of an unpleasant previous encounter with crows, distinguish them instantly from rooks and absolutely refuse to fly them. Such falcons should, of course, on no account be slipped at crows, whatever the temptation: for they will at once swing off in search of other quarry, probably downwind, and, if you are unlucky (as I once was) may never be seen again.

10. *Do not slip in unsuitable weather*

This point is too obvious to require much more than its mere statement. Unsuitable weather includes gales, heavy rain (light rain can be ignored), fog or mist with reduced visibility, and excessive heat. Some wind, even stiff breezes up to 15 or 20 m.p.h., is a definite help: it increases the margin of superiority in speed of the falcon over the rook while both are flying into the wind, and makes it more or less certain that the flight will take an upwind-downwind direction without much lateral deviation. A flat calm is embarrassing, because of the difficulty of anticipating the course that the flight will take.

11. *Resist all temptation to accept a slip against your better judgement*

Even if your guests are "V.I.P.s" with trains to catch, remain adamant. All they stand to lose is an afternoon's sport: you stand to lose your falcon.

So much for the eleven golden rules of slipping. Something must now be said about the methods by which one gets into position for a good slip. In the old days, and ideally even now, the falcon was and should be slipped from horseback; but that method is so little likely to be practicable, or practised nowadays, that I shall devote no more attention to it, sincerely though I deplore the passing of so exhilarating a way of initiating and following a flight at the rook.

In modern days the car has replaced the horse, and this holds good for rook-hawking too. The rook-hawks will be transported on a screen-perch or box-cadge in the car, which will be the base from which the flights are carried out. The falcon may be slipped directly from the car, if this can be manœuvred into the correct position for the slip. Otherwise, the falconer will have to approach and, if necessary, stalk the quarry on foot.

As the car will probably be required to negotiate rough trackless downland, stubble, and the like, one of the jeep or land-rover type is indicated; and a very useful refinement is a hole in the roof, enabling the falconer to stand up in the car, whether for the purpose of spotting distant rooks suitably placed for a slip, or of actually slipping the hawk at them (thereby obviating the inconvenience and delay involved in getting out of the car in order to slip) or of following the subsequent flight, while the driver drives on after the line of flight, or, if circumstances warrant, makes a bee-line for the nearest cover in order to anticipate and forestall the putting-in of the quarry.

Where the stalking on foot of shy and uneasy rooks is necessary, it is a good plan to shelter during the approach behind a companion, who will serve both to screen the falcon from the rooks and to shelter the falcon from the wind, the impact of which might otherwise induce her to give herself away by a premature spreading or flapping of her wings.

When the slip is imminent, the braces should be struck, so that the hood can be whipped off the moment that the rooks rise. What next? There are two schools of thought. One believes in the instantaneous swinging forward of the arm, on the fist of which the falcon is held, so that she is at once catapulted into space: after the initial spring, the falcon will probably hang on her wings for a second while getting sighted on her quarry, and will then start off in pursuit. The second method is to unhood the falcon and hold the hand aloft, leaving her to look around, sight her quarry, size up the position, and take off in pursuit at her own discretion. On the whole, and particularly for young or inexperienced hawks, I prefer the latter method. If the falcon has no inclination to fly the rooks, then throwing her off at them is not likely to make her change her mind: while if she intends to fly them, there is no harm in letting her choose her own moment and method of departure, and little real advantage, in a flight that is sure in the nature of things to be a fairly lengthy one, in giving her a catapulted start.

Once the falconer has slipped his falcon at the rooks, his task is by no means at an end. He must keep the falcon in sight, evict the rook from light cover such as a fence, a sheep pen, or a bed of nettles, into which the falcon may have put it, call back the falcon *instantly* to the lure if she has been beaten in the air, or if the rook has put into thick cover, such as a wood, or belt of trees, or farmyard buildings, from which it cannot be promptly evicted; or make in and pick up the falcon if she has killed. Flights may extend over distances of up to half a mile or a mile, so that all the above tasks demand a high degree of mobility in the falconer and any other members of the field. In my own circumstances, I have found a combination of car-driving and running on foot not unsatisfactory: but this really requires a minimum of two persons, one to drive, and the other to run when further progress in the car is stopped by barbed wire, fences, or the like. Each,

Saker Falcon (Haggard).

of course, should have a lure, leash, swivel, and hood, so as to be able to take up the falcon at the end of a flight, whether successful or unsuccessful. A good pair of field glasses (with 8 × or 10 × magnification, and a good field of view) is indispensable, both to locate distant rooks, to differentiate crows and jackdaws from rooks, and to keep the falcon in sight if she rakes away, or checks after wood-pigeons or other quarry, or it proves impossible for any reason, such as the nature of the ground, or the distance covered, or the direction taken, to keep up with the flight.

The nature of the actual flight will vary according to the weather (strength of the wind), the ground (availability and nature of cover), and the physical condition, courage, and perseverance of both falcon and rook. Just as a bad falcon makes a good rook, so does a good falcon make a bad rook. By this I mean, in the first case, that if the pursuit is weak and the falcon never gets into a position to control and dominate the rook, the rook will ring up in airy circles over the falcon's head, and leave her looking the fool she is. He may even add insult to injury by stooping at *her*. In the second case, that self-same rook, flown by a first-rate falcon, will be dominated from the outset, he will be given no time or opportunity even to think of ringing up, his sole idea will be to plunge into the nearest cover at the first available moment, and if the slip was a good one he will probably be killed—not because he was a bad rook, but because the falcon was too good for him.

Flights at rooks, unlike those at game, are capable of almost infinite variation; this is one of the attractions of rook-hawking. You get every kind of flight, from that where the rook drops into any available cover, however inadequate, as soon as he sees the hawk driving at him, and is very likely killed after an exciting and perhaps exhausting but by no means spectacular kind of rat-hunt, in which "the field" will have an active part to play; and that where the rook or rooks strive their utmost to beat the falcon in the air, in which case the falconer and the field may well remain mere spectators until its conclusion.

The classic ringing flights, so graphically described in the Badminton Library volume, and in Captain Blaine's book, are scarcely ever met with in these degenerate days. It is difficult to say just why this should be so, but I am inclined to suspect a combination of circumstances—much more cover on the Plain, tempting the

H

rook to seek safety by the less dramatic tactic of plunging into cover, instead of attempting to beat the falcon in the air; many more rooks, tempting the falcon to check from a rook that is proving unco-operative to easier ones sighted still on the ground or only just air-borne over the neighbouring brow; and the greater mobility and less leisure of the modern falconer, tempting him to waste no time wait-ing for the solitary rook on passage who is alone likely to provide a ringing flight, when he can, by scouring the countryside in his car, be reasonably certain of finding, sooner or later, a ready-made slip at a flock.

As in other forms of hawking, it is the quality of the flights and not the size of the "bag" that counts. And the quality of the flights depends, in the last resort, on the style of the falcon. Let me illustrate this, by way of example, by comparing the style of my last eyas falcon with that of my Adenese haggard. The eyas, a good killer with over fifty rooks to her score, flies straight at the rooks as they rise: by the time she reaches them most of them are still above her, though she may be level with the middle or bottom layers of the flock: the only rooks she can control from that position are those that drop out, because they are either physically below par or lacking in courage. (I myself doubt the theory, held by some, that the rook falls out because it knows that it has already been marked down by the falcon.) Any considerable flock will contain one or more who will drop out in this way, and such a rook will come under the control of the falcon, who will put in several stoops at it, but may fail to bind to it or knock it down, owing to "poor footing," until the rook has been driven too low for manœuvrability: the falcon then comes in from behind and below and clutches it, with a marked absence of impact; alternatively, if she knocks it down, the blow is so lacking in punch, and the falcon so slow in taking advantage of her hit, that the rook will probably be given the opportunity of picking himself up and shuffling off into cover before the falcon can come back on him and secure him.

Now, by way of contrast, for the Adenese haggard. When slipped, she shoots up from the fist and climbs so rapidly that by the time she fetches the rooks she is as high above the *topmost* rook as he is above the ground. She will not dream of stooping at them until she is ver-tically above them. Even then, she holds that devastating vertical stoop up her sleeve. She starts to stoop, the rooks drop down in panic, she at once rebounds from the feint, and goes still higher: another feint, after which the rooks are lower still, and the falcon yet higher: then comes the real stoop, vertical and deadly. In the particular flight I have in mind, the haggard's perfect footing hit the rook she had marked down a blow that sent it another fifty feet earthwards: after this blow, the falcon shot up again in preparation for the *coup de grâce*: meanwhile the rook had somehow managed to right himself and resume level flight, only a second or two later to be hit with a crack that could be heard from hundreds of feet away, and to go into a spin earthwards with a shattered wing, from which he was retrieved and carried off by the falcon before he hit the ground.

When a rook is killed by a falcon, the other rooks of the flock "sky up" over the site of the kill, circling upwards in a tight spiral to a considerable height, giving vent to their anger and alarm with harsh caws of protest. Occasionally some of the bolder spirits may dive down and make ineffectual dabs at the falcon's back. These habits, and also the later habit of diving down with closed wings into the tops of trees and clustering there in uneasy silence, are very useful guides to the whereabouts of a falcon that has killed out of sight or become temporarily lost. When a falcon has been lost, the falconer should be constantly on the look-out for such signs: if he is lucky (and few falcons are recovered without an element of luck) they will lead him straight to the missing falcon.

I shall conclude this chapter by listing the faults of a rook-hawk. The first, and worst, is refusing, or turning tail, that is, ignoring the rooks at which she is slipped, either at once or after a half-hearted pursuit, and raking away aimlessly downwind, or circling round the falconer in anticipation of the lure. The reasons for such refusal may be the use of an unsuitable hawk (a tiercel or a lanneret instead of a falcon), wrong conditioning (the falcon is too high, and cannot be bothered, or too low, and has not the energy for such a flight), inadequate entering (the falcon is given difficult slips before she is ready for them) or dislike of rook-flesh (insufficient care has been taken to test her reactions, and in case of doubt to substitute pigeon). Once the reason for refusals has been diagnosed, the remedy should be sufficiently obvious.

The second fault is checking at other quarry. Very often rooks will be found feeding in the company of other birds, for instance, pigeons on stubble, or lapwings on pasture or plough, and it can be very irritating if, after great pains have been taken to obtain a perfect slip for the falcon, she ignores the rooks and goes chasing off after pigeons or lapwings. Luckily this checking seldom meets with any success, and the fault is, therefore, likely to cure itself in the course of time. The falcon will soon learn to contrast successful flights at rooks with unsuccessful flights at these other quarries, and eventually abandon these unremunerative flights.

A similar fault is to check at rooks other than those at which the falcon has been slipped. But in most cases this fault will also be that of the falconer, who should before slipping have made reasonably sure that there were no rooks, other than those upwind of the falcon, at which she *could* check. If, as sometimes happens, the falcon passes over the nearer upwind rooks in favour of others still farther upwind, little harm will normally result, and if the country is open enough, you may get an even better flight. The remedy, accordingly, lies in taking greater care with the slip.

The last fault, lack of style, in which I include such things as poor tactics and bad footing, arises from lack of experience, and lack of intelligence, and cannot be cured by the falconer. Some eyasses will gradually improve in style, as they gain in experience and intelligence, until they become almost if not quite the equal of the wild-caught hawk: others seem to have a definite ceiling beyond which they cannot rise. But such falcons will probably have other qualities which will to a greater or lesser extent compensate for this lack of style.

MAGPIE-HAWKING

by J. G. MAVROGORDATO

Magpie-hawking is an excellent form of the sport, particularly for a party of young and active falconers. In some ways it is, I think, a more difficult flight than rook-hawking, for the magpie makes up for his lack of speed by his cunning, and his refusal to lose his head, or admit defeat until he is actually within the falconer's grasp.

The country for this flight must be very open, and free from woods, spinneys, or belts of trees: but it is improved, rather than spoilt, by scattered bushes, small farmsteads, turf ricks, and the like. Indeed it is only in such places that magpies are likely to be present. The cream of such country is to be found in Ireland, but some of the English downland has possibilities which should not be overlooked.

The classic hawk for this flight is the Peregrine tiercel, or rather a cast of tiercels, for one tiercel, however good, is seldom able to bring a magpie to book single-handed, and much of the art lies in the way in which the two hawks team to co-operate with each other and with the falconers to bring a flight to a successful conclusion. I have never seriously tried Lanners at this flight, but experience with them in the Sudan in flying great grey shrikes amongst the scattered bushes of the desert (which is in all essentials a form of miniature magpie-hawking) leads me to think that they would prove even better than Peregrines. They wait on much more steadily over the bush into which the quarry has been put, lacking the tendency of the Peregrine to rake away downwind once the quarry is out of sight; and, having a much smaller turning circle, they maintain command over the quarry in a way that seems beyond the average Peregrine. A first-class cast of large lannerets might well prove to be the ideal for this flight, but on the whole Lanner falcons would be more reliable, since small or poor-spirited lannerets would tend to refuse a quarry substantially bigger than any they habitually prey on in the wild state. Barbaries have been tried at this quarry and found wanting; the tiercels are too small, and the falcons lack the necessary perseverance.

Whatever type of hawk is used, avoid the unhacked eyas, for unhacked eyasses, reared in isolation, are certain to crab when flown in a cast, and most of the early slips will be spoilt by this irritating vice. Hacked hawks, used to flying in company, will be less inclined to crab, particularly if both members of the cast were hacked together. Passagers and haggards are also unlikely to crab.

Finding a magpie in suitable country which is known to harbour magpies, would appear to the uninitiated to be a simple matter. You just drive around in a car until the tell-tale and conspicuous piebald plumage reveals itself on top of a bush or post, or the weak flight of a pair or a party of magpies across the green landscape gives an even more unmistakable proof of their presence. In fact, we learnt by experience in Ireland before the 1939–45 war that it is possible to drive through country comparatively thick with magpies without spotting a single one in a whole morning. The reason for this is that magpies spend a lot of their time walking about on the ground, and are then hard to spot and easily overlooked. Just after the car has passed the magpie may jump out of some ditch on to the top of a bush, too late to catch your eye. The way to find magpies in suitable country is to walk, listen for their chatter, and periodically sweep the ground with powerful binoculars.

When one or more magpies have been located, careful thought must be given to the slip. As in rook-hawking, the slip should be upwind, and the stronger the wind within reason the better, for a magpie can make no progress at all against a stiff breeze, and is bound to turn downwind, where the members of the "field" can be making preparations for his reception.

With young or inexperienced hawks, old magpies (whether single or in pairs) should be avoided; they can be distinguished by the extra length of the tail. What is wanted is a family party, consisting of, say, four young birds and their parents, such as is commonly found travelling about the countryside together in early autumn.

When such a family party has been located, the hawking party should get into position downwind of them, and not too close. The magpie is so slow that the hawk will always overtake it with ease, however long its start, and the farther it is driven into the wind, the more certainly will it be brought back to the falconers. I once had an old experienced tiercel that would take on a magpie on the wing so far off that I could barely see it, would force it to drop to the ground like a stone, then land within a few feet of it, and wait for me to come up and drive it out of its hiding-place for him. With the tiercel on guard, the magpie was pinned down indefinitely.

Only one tiercel should be slipped at first; otherwise they may exhaust themselves (and the "field") by chasing separate magpies. The tiercel slipped will before long succeed in cutting out one magpie—almost certainly a young one—from the bunch, and putting it into cover. The second tiercel should now be brought up, and hooded off at the magpie as soon as it is flushed. From then on, both the tiercels should fly the magpie, driving and stooping at it alternately every time it takes wing, and it is now up to the "field" to see that it does this frequently. It will become harder and harder to evict as it becomes more closely pressed, but it will never lose its head. It will make use of the slightest piece of cover, a cart-rut, or a tussock of grass, to give it temporary shelter from the stoop. Hence the need for a very active and well-disposed "field"; there is no point in everyone "following my leader." If the magpie is sheltering in a hedge or ditch it should be headed and then, by means of a "pincer movement," forced out into the open. Meanwhile, spare members should be marking down the bushes or other cover for which the magpie is likely to make next, and should forestall him by getting there first. Eventually, if hawks and humans co-operate in this way, there will be one stoop too many for the magpie, and one of the hawks will bind to it, probably on or near the ground. The other hawk will generally rush in too, and there will be something of a mêlée on the ground but no damage is likely to be done, except to the quarry. The owner of the second hawk should take his hawk off on to the lure with the least possible delay, and the first hawk can then be dealt with in the usual way. If both hawks are to be fed up, the magpie can be divided between them; but don't overlook the fact that there is surprisingly little flesh on a magpie. It's all wings and tail.

Sakers (*Falco cherrug*)—at least the passage females—make excellent rook-hawks; far better, in my opinion, than indifferent eyas Peregrines. They generally require careful entering, and, even after they have been entered, have an annoying habit of ignoring the carefully selected rook at which they have been hooded off, and checking at pigeons, lapwings or starlings; all the more annoying because these are quarries at which they have little hope of success. In due course, however, the Saker will become "wedded" to its legitimate quarry, and will thereafter be less inclined than the Peregrine to fly at check. In fact the danger from that moment is rather the opposite one, that the Saker, after being beaten by the rook at which she was slipped, will refuse to admit defeat and return to the lure so long as she thinks that there is the slightest chance of her finding another rook in the area.

Sakers when familiar with this quarry will take on slips of astonishing length—upwards of a quarter of a mile—indeed most Sakers seem actually to prefer long slips, and to dislike short ones, probably because they need plenty of time and space to attain maximum speed and manœuvrability. Owing to their large expanse of "sail" they are more buoyant than Peregrines, and can rise very steeply and easily against the wind. A good Saker, like a good Peregrine, will go right above the whole flock of rooks before putting in her first stoop. The stoop itself is not so hard as that of the Peregrine, but this is largely compensated by excellent footing, assisted by a great length of leg

There is no doubt that Sakers are perfectly capable of ringing flights at rooks. I have myself enjoyed one such flight, and a favourite flight in India for Sakers is the ringing flight at the "grass-owl," in which the alternative to a kill is the loss of the falcon, since the quarry, unless mastered, will take the falcon clean out of sight overhead in a cloudless sky.

One curious advantage which the Saker enjoys over the Peregrine, when flying a flock of rooks, is the ease with which she can be picked out from the mob owing to her larger size and wing span. A Peregrine can quickly be lost to view. A Saker's position in the flock is always obvious.

Sakers kill even crows without trouble. They also have little difficulty in carrying them, but are not usually inclined to do this. They are fond of rook flesh, and can safely be fed up on the kill.

Saker falcons weigh about $2\frac{1}{2}$ lb., sakrets about 2 lb.; flying weights are about 2 lb. 3 oz. or 4 oz. for the falcon, 1 lb. 10 oz. or 11 oz. for the sakret. A good sakret is capable of killing rooks, but is likely to need a good deal of initial encouragement. The Arabs do not consider him worth training, but then they are only interested in killing bustard (houbara) and hares. Lanner falcons which range between $1\frac{1}{2}$ lb. and 2 lb. in weight, should, if they have sufficient courage, be capable of killing rooks, but I have not yet seriously tried them at this quarry. One falcon, used for game, occasionally checked at rooks and put in a good stoop or two, but I am not sure how far she was in earnest. Lannerets, weighing from 15 to 20 oz., are too small. So also are Barbary falcons which average about 1 lb. 6 oz., and I have never tried these at anything but game.

CHAPTER VIII

SHORT-WINGED TRUE HAWKS—GOSHAWK AND SPARROWHAWK

THE short-winged hawks have yellow irides to their eyes which gradually change with age to a deeper orange and turn red. The wings are broad and round in outline. The tail is long. These two features enable the hawk to fly successfully in wooded country and to manœuvre in dense covert. The fourth primary in the wing is the longest and the feathers are softer and more elastic than those of the true falcons. The legs are long and powerful and the talons more developed than in falcons of the same size. The beak is slender and lacks the notch or tooth. Hawks hunt by stealth and taking their quarry by surprise outfly it in a short, swift sprint. Once they have caught their prey they kill by the sheer pressure of their extremely powerful feet which drive the needle-sharp talons deep into the captive's body. Sparrowhawks sometimes administer the *coup de grâce* by breaking the quarry's neck with their beak.

THE GOSHAWK (*Accipiter gentilis*)

Those who aspire to train the true hawks are called austringers. Their problems are somewhat different from those of the trainer of falcons. The temperament of the short-wing is not the same as that of the long-wing. Generally speaking, long-wings are more easily tamed and once manned remain so without a great deal of "maintenance" manning. The reverse is true of short-wings. They are difficult and tedious to tame and, even when manned, quickly revert to their former indocility if they are not given a certain amount of daily "maintenance" manning. However, they have the advantage in that they are relatively easily obtained and once trained they will bring a greater variety of quarry to the bag for the average falconer than will his long-wings.

The last eyas Goshawk to be taken from the nest in the British Isles was taken by Colonel Thornton from Rothiemurchus Forest in 1786. Since then the Goshawk has only been a rare vagrant to these islands. There is evidence that an attempt to re-establish themselves as. a breeding species may be being made, but some at least of the Goshawks in the country now are undoubtedly escaped austringers' birds. Nowadays eyas and passage Goshawks are obtainable from the Continent. Norway, Sweden, Denmark, Holland and Germany are all sources from which these birds have been recently acquired, usually through the good offices of a Continental falconer or gamekeeper.

The eyasses are taken during the last week in June and may be flown over to London Airport or shipped to Harwich. On arrival they must be collected as soon as possible and taken to the shed or loft in which they are to live until hard penned. I say "they" because although it would be folly to attempt to train more than one short-wing at a time, sometimes several Goshawks are sent over together to be distributed later to their trainers. The basic requirements of the loft shed or room are the same as those pertaining to long-wings described in a previous chapter. Several Goshawks may be put in the same loft together provided that the loft is a fair size and that the hawks are of the same age.

The box containing the eyas must only be opened in the loft and if the hawk is unwilling to come out it may be left in the box with the lid open so that it may emerge when all is quiet. Food must be tied on a board on the floor for the bird will probably not have eaten for more than twelve hours. Most eyasses coming from the Continent are "branchers" and are well taken. They arrive at an age when they can pull food for themselves and usually can fly up on to any perches that have been provided. The food is the same as that supplied to Peregrines at hack and it should be available *ad lib.* for the fortnight or so that the bird is finishing the growth of its feathers. Needless to say, all stale food must be collected and removed for at this time of the year it quickly becomes putrid and fly-blown. It is not usual to make any attempt to clean out the loft while it is occupied by the eyas because to do so would only terrify the bird. If any adjustments in the loft are necessary these are best made at night by the light of a torch. A spy hole in the wall of the loft through which the hawk's progress can be observed is useful. If several eyasses are being reared together one then has the opportunity of gauging the quite marked differences in size, colour and conformation which can occur in Goshawks of the same origin, age and sex.

The female Goshawk is prized more highly than the male or tiercel because she is able, by virtue of her larger size and greater weight, to overcome a wider range of quarry than is her smaller brother. Female Goshawks in England are worth, at the time of writing, every penny of £10 and while males are just as much trouble to procure, they may command a slightly lower price.

Goshawks from Scandinavia tend to be considerably larger than those whose origins are in Southern Europe. There is, however, no evidence that these larger types are any better performers than are the smaller. It all depends on the individual bird. There have been good big ones and good small ones, and a good small one will take the brown hare, the largest quarry likely to be flown in the British Isles, just as efficiently as a good big one.

When an examination of the primaries and train feathers by torch-light reveals that the eyas is hard penned, she may be taken up for training. The preliminaries for this are exactly the same as those de-scribed for the Kestrel. Short-wings are not normally hooded, for the more they see the tamer they become. But if it is decided to break the eyas to the hood it must be done in the first few days before the hawk loses its initial fear of its trainer. It will soon be apparent to the young austringer that the task he has set himself is a lot more tedious than that of training a Kestrel. The female eyas Goshawk when taken up from the loft will weigh anything from 2 lb. 12 oz. to 3 lb. 8 oz. and the male 1 lb. 10 oz. to 1 lb. 14 oz. She will be virtually unman-ageable until some 4 to 6 oz. of internal fat have been dispersed by judicious dieting. To achieve this she must not be starved but must rather be fed on food of a lower quality from that to which she has been accustomed in the loft. Rabbit, if it can be had, is ideal for this purpose and if the eyas is given a daily crop a little larger than a golf ball plus a rabbit's foot with the bones smashed for casting, she will gradually lose weight and become more tractable. This downward trend in her weight may be watched by daily weighing and it is some advantage to plot her weight against the date on a piece of graph paper. Most female Gosses fly at about 2 lb. 3 oz. and males at 1 lb. 6 oz. but there is considerable variation.

The periods of carrying on the fist must be much more prolonged for a Goshawk than for a long-wing. In fact the speed with which a short-wing is reclaimed is directly proportional to the number of hours which her trainer can afford to carry her on the fist. Progress will be slow unless two to three hours a day can be spared and it will be found that an intensive period of manning will produce better results than a longer, more leisured spell. In the long summer evenings it is a pleasant task to take one's eyas Goshawk on the fist and go for a walk around the fields accompanied preferably by the dog which later on will hunt with the hawk. It is best at first to go alone on these excursions but later on a friend may be taken for company. When one or more persons are out walking with the austringer, always be sure that they walk on his right hand side for the hawk will not be at ease if someone is walking on the left behind her. While carrying the hawk on the fist, keep moving from one place to another avoiding any object which is likely to upset the hawk and precipitate a bate. Avoid clanking agricultural machinery especially. Later on when the hawk is a little tamer she may be tried a little more sorely but always be ready to retreat if she shows signs of fear. A hawk is not being manned properly if her trainer is sitting in a chair in the garden reading a book. A hawk so treated will be continually looking around for some refuge and eventually her eyes will light on a branch or fence post to which she will continually try to fly. It is a poor falconer who will sit unheeding while his hawk bates thus. By being carried the hawk gets used to the rhythm of the human step and learns to balance herself on the fist upon which she is going to spend a great deal of her time. As the scene changes frequently on the walk so temptations come and go and few are before her long enough to provoke her to bate.

In these early stages the young Goshawk must spend her time in a darkened mews on a screen perch when she is not being carried on her trainer's fist.

It will be found that after about ten days the eyas will be prepared to step from the screen perch on to the fist and from then on progress will be more rapid. Once she will come to the fist a leash length out of doors she can be called from gateposts and fences during the manning walks. When she will fly from the fist to the gatepost a leash length and immediately on alighting turn round and return to the proffered fist garnished with a tit-bit she may be called longer distances on a creance. She will by now be allowed to rest by day in full light in the mews and will be spending some of her time weathering on the lawn on her ring or bow perch. She may be offered tit-bits from the fingers while she is on the bow perch so that she will learn to look upon the approach of her trainer with pleasure. But he must be careful when offering her these tit-bits to keep his hand high and only just below the level of her beak, for were he to drop his hand at all she might be tempted to slash at it with her talons. This is no laughing matter and if a Goshawk really gets a grip on a bare hand she can apply a vice-like pressure which is agonizing. The punctures inflicted by the great black talons go septic very easily and I find that soaking the injured hand in very hot water is a useful treatment provided sepsis has not supervened. If the hand swells at all and red lines are seen to be running up the arm a doctor should be consulted without delay. I mention this because a Goshawk is a very powerful bird and it is quite difficult to prise the claws off an unguarded hand should she get a grip. Every movement of the imprisoned hand will result in fresh convulsive gripping which drives the talons deeper into the flesh. In view of this danger I do not recommend that a child of, say, under 16 years of age should attempt to handle a Goshawk.

Short-winged hawks will not stoop at the swung lure as will long-wings, so they must be exercised by flying to the fist. In order to get the maximum amount of flying the hawk should be encouraged to fly to a perching-place, say a wooden fence, turn round and fly back to the trainer's fist. The distance may be increased daily until she will come 100 yards on the creance. When calling her to the fist, the austringer may call her by name or blow a whistle. Now she must be trained to come out of a tree. This is difficult in summer when the leaves are on the trees because as yet the eyas knows little of how to alight in a tree. Also, if one is to fly her still on the creance, and it is advisable to do so for a little longer, one must be careful to choose a tree with few side branches in which the creance can entangle. The best tree of all for this exercise is a single dead tree standing alone in a hedgerow. The hawk may be encouraged to leave the fist and fly up on to a branch which must be as free from projections as possible, about ten or twelve feet from the ground. She will at first stare around her for she will be able to survey the surrounding country-side from her new-found elevation. After a minute or two she will turn round and fly down to the trainer's fist. Do not try to call her too far to start with and equally do not stand immediately beneath her so that she has to descend vertically to the fist. Call her about fifteen yards at first. When calling a Goshawk to the fist from a tree or other perch, hold the left arm out parallel to the ground and stand with your back to the hawk at right angles to her line of flight. Thus she is offered the whole arm as a possible perching-place. In the early days she may land on your forearm instead of the glove but she will not grip and if the fist is raised she will quickly run up on to the correct place. Later on she will become more efficient at judging the landing and will always land on the glove. Try to arrange things so that if there is any appreciable wind the hawk is called into it otherwise she may overshoot the fist.

When she will come fifty yards out of the dead tree, and this will be some four weeks after her training started, the creance may be removed and she may be flown loose. The day before this is done she must be given a small feed and she must be flown loose for the first time in a place where a sudden unexpected distraction is unlikely. If the preliminary training has been satisfactory she will have been unaware that she was on the creance so her behaviour will be unchanged now that she is off it. Should she have been called too far from the dead tree while on the creance she may have been tempted to sheer off while coming to the fist and seek to fly to an alternative perching-place—maybe another tree. If she does this, gently pull her down with the line. Never tie the line to a post so that she is brought up with a jerk and always tie the free end of the line to a line stick about nine inches long so that if she does fly away on the line this will drag and act as a brake. The reason for this over-shooting and sheering off must be found and avoided in future. It may be due to calling downwind, or calling too far too soon. It is always better to have the hawk come a short distance promptly rather than a longer distance after a lot of hesitation and delay. Calling too many times, too, will make the hawk bored and if she has a reward of meat each time she comes to the fist the edge on her appetite will get progressively less. She should not be called more than five times at any one training session. Another cause of sheering off is the presence behind or to one side of the trainer of another tree which seems to offer a better perch than the fist. One should avoid training a hawk in such a place. Actually, when flying the hawk at quarry later on it will often be found that she may come fifty yards out of a tree towards the fist only to swing up into another tree twenty-five yards behind the austringer. She will then turn and perhaps fly to another tree ten yards from him and from thence to the fist. Of course, the sudden appearance on the training ground of a strange person or animal will be a very potent cause of refusal to come and sheering off. It is for emergencies such as this that I think it always wise to have one's Goshawk made to the lure as well as to the fist. It is a counsel of perfection to tell an aspiring austringer that he must have his Goshawk so manned and trained that it is obedient to the fist whatever the circumstances. This may have been possible in more leisured days when professional falconers were employed to carry the hawks for many hours a day, but nowadays it is an exceptional hawk that will always come to the fist. Blaine says that the Goshawk that will only come to a lure is not properly manned and is the second-rate pupil of an indifferent teacher. This is basically true, but the teacher will save himself a great deal of time if he introduces the lure during training so that his pupil is aware of what it is. The lure can then be kept in the hawking bag for emergency use.

Concurrent with the flying exercise to and from the fist and the tree the hawk must still be carried and her condition checked by daily weighing. As her weight drops you will notice that she will suddenly grip the glove when a bird flies past or when a gate creaks. These momentary convulsive squeezes are a sign of the approach of "Yarak"—a Turkish word used to describe the Goshawk that is fully manned and in flying condition. She will now cast baleful glances at domestic hens or even domestic cats and will bate precipitately from the fist should a hen or cat come near. She will bate towards her trainer whenever he appears on the weathering ground and once on the fist will puff out her feathers and raise her crest. Her weight will probably be found to be about 2 lb. 3 oz. I say "probably" because there is considerable variation here. A lot will depend on her starting weight and to some extent the amount of carrying she has had. The more carrying and manning the higher will be the weight at yarak. An average sized female Goshawk which has had about two hours carrying per day for a month to five weeks will come into yarak at about 2 lb. 3 oz. If she is slow to come into yarak a course of three or four days on "washed meat" will often do the trick. "Washed meat" is fresh, lean beef cut into long thin strips and soaked for twenty-four hours in cold water in a refrigerator. The meat is well squeezed to remove the juices and dried with a clean cloth before use. Hard washed meat is almost white in colour. A hungry hawk will eat it but will lose weight in spite of having a medium sized crop. This is better than shortening her rations of plain meat because although washed meat is very rapidly digested her digestive organs are kept in working order. Never call a hawk to the fist for washed meat as it is somewhat distasteful, having little flavour, and may cause her to resent coming to the fist. Goshawks receive all their food on the fist except for an occasional tit-bit on the lure and are thus trained to expect to find food there.

Once well and truly in yarak the hawk must soon be entered to quarry. In the case of a female Goshawk to be flown at rabbits or hares, a young rabbit must be found lying out in an open place. With any luck she will see it move before you do and in a flash will be off the fist and after it. If it got up at your feet it will not get fifteen yards before she is on it. In the days before myxomatosis it was easy to find a suitable half-grown rabbit in a suitable place but now rabbits are scarce it is not so easy. Failing a young rabbit or half-grown hare the next best thing to enter a hawk to is a moorhen. These are easily caught by both female and tiercel Goshawks and can provide quite passable sport where there is little cover on the banks of slow flowing shallow streams. Such conditions are found on the chalk streams of Wiltshire and Hampshire. If the streams are deep and the banks high and covered with dense vegetation, it will be impossible to get the moorhen to break cover. In suitable places a moorhen may be marked down in a ditch a hundred yards or more from the main stream. With the help of a dog the bird can be flushed under the hawk's nose and should be easily taken in the air.

Should the hawk persistently refuse quarry a useful trick is to procure a dead rabbit, rook, pigeon or moorhen and tie a line to its legs. Hide it in some long grass or in a corn stook and get an assistant to pull it out on twenty-five yards of line just as you walk past the hiding-place with the hawk on your fist. With luck she will dash upon it. If she does so the assistant must immediately drop the line for fear of dragging the hawk along the ground. Allow her to feed up on the pelt. Do not allow a Goshawk a full crop of coot or moorhen flesh for it is very oily and rich and will put her out of yarak for several days.

Should the hawk kill at first-attempt, allow her a medium crop of warm bloody meat and take her home. Next day she will be keener still and there should be no further trouble in getting her to fly that quarry.

Goshawks, like the other species of raptores that are trained, quickly become wedded to a specific quarry and the first few flights

Female Goshawk on ring perch with wirehaired German Pointer.

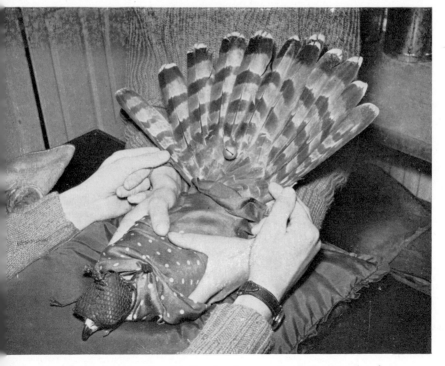

Female Goshawk with tail bell—also shows method of casting hawk.

at that quarry will make or mar the hawk for the future. If the main quarry is to be birds, as will be the case with the tiercel Goshawk, he must be entered at a moorhen and when he has caught a few he may be switched to partridges. If an easy slip can be found to start him off, so much the better. The same applies to the female Goshawk that is to be flown at pheasants. In this case there will be a delay throughout September while the austringer impatiently waits for October 1st. He may fill in the time by trying his hawk at hares, moorhens, coots, partridges and rabbits. Some female Goshawks show a predilection for feathered quarry. These will pursue anything from a blackbird upwards. Others seem uninterested in birds and will only fly rabbits with keenness. The female Goshawk that will take brown hares regularly is rare. Many eyas Goshawks will take a hare or two before getting a bad kick in the inevitable tussle. They will then refuse to fly them again. Even a good Goshawk that is wedded to hares will give them up after she has been knocked about. This may occur after her seventh or seventeenth hare. It makes no difference. She will be unwilling to fly hares ever afterwards. The hawk's size is no criterion of whether she will tackle hares or not. Some of the best hare hawks have been small ones. One successful hawk at hares in recent years weighed only 1 lb. 15 oz. when in yarak. If a hawk is to be flown at hares, she must not be allowed to catch many rabbits for if she does she will quickly learn that rabbits are easier to hold than hares and will afterwards refuse the stronger quarry.

Once the hawk has shown that she will go for a hare, do not be afraid of long slips of a hundred yards or more. She will easily overtake the hare which will be unaware of its mortal danger and will not run flat out. Beware, however, of wire fences beneath which the hare will duck and which the hawk may not see in time so intent will she be on footing the hare. At first she will tend to grab the hare by the hindquarters and will be dragged along the ground and finally kicked off. If she is to make a hare hawk she must soon learn to grab the hare by the head with one foot and by the loins with the other. Only thus will she be able to hold him. If she succeeds in binding to a hare it is important to resist the temptation to run in and help her. If this is done it almost invariably results in the hare making a desperate effort to escape which usually succeeds. So wait a bit and allow the hawk to shift her grip until she really has hold of him before making in to administer the *coup de grâce*.

I

The case of the male Goshawk at rabbits is very similar to the female at hares. The boldest, not necessarily the biggest, tiercel Gosses will take rabbits, but due to their smaller size they are never very happy with this quarry. It is at rabbits that the female Gos excels. When she is good at them she is very deadly and will follow a rabbit through cover to foot him with great dexterity deep in a bramble patch into which she has hurled herself after his retreating scut. Rabbits may be walked up when they are lying out in rough grass or they may be beaten out of bushes or hedgerows. Provided they have thirty yards or more to go before they reach cover the Gos will have a good chance of taking them.

Before myxomatosis decimated the rabbit population they were so common in some districts that a Gos would often go off self-hunting if she missed her first flight. The rabbit would get to ground in a hedge bank and the baulked Gos would throw up into a tree. From this vantage-point she would espy other rabbits feeding out in an adjacent field and would soon be after one of them. The austringer had to be very fit in those days to keep up with her, but luckily it was usually not long before he picked her up on a kill. Nowadays rabbits are scarcer and do not feed out so boldly so this rather annoying habit of self-hunting is not so likely to occur.

If the rabbits are not lying out, a ferret can be pressed into service, and provided the buries chosen are isolated and reasonably small, fine sport can be had at bolted rabbits. The austringer should stand fifteen yards upwind of the bury. The ferret used should be a white one and the Goshawk must be held back a time or two when she bates at the ferret. It is surprising how quickly the hawk comes to understand that the ferret is an ally and must not be taken. The reason for using a white ferret is that the hawk might easily mistake a polecat ferret for a stoat and be tempted to take it. Buries situated high on a hillside on the downs with a hundred yards or more to go to the hedge provide most spectacular flights akin to coursing with greyhounds. A good Goshawk will take ten or more rabbits in an afternoon before she gets tired. Rabbits may be hawked in woods and hazel coppice too, once the leaves have fallen in November. To do so before the fall is to run a grave risk of losing the hawk by becoming unsighted among the trees. Goshawks flown in or near woods should carry a bell on each leg and another on the tail.

With the virtual disappearance of the rabbit from many districts austringers have had to turn their attention to other quarries which before only provided an occasional incidental flight. Techniques have had to be developed to overcome the difficulties inherent to getting a flight at these rather special quarries. Grey squirrels can be taken by female Goshawks when they are found out on the ground well away from a tree. But this is a rare occurrence and some sport may be had by poking the squirrels out of their dreys with telescopic aluminium poles in winter. This flight is best obtained in an isolated copse on the Downs and provided there are no hollow trees or wood-peckers' holes to provide a refuge, the hunt can last twenty minutes or more as the squirrel races from tree to tree, one minute on the ground and the next high in the trees. The field below must assist the hawk by keeping the squirrel on the move and the austringer must quickly go to her assistance should she foot the quarry and bring him to the ground. If the squirrel is not quickly killed or if the hawk does not muzzle him effectively with her foot he is capable of inflicting nasty bites on her feet and legs. A male Goshawk might take grey squirrels as well but his legs are a little shorter and his feet smaller and he might get bitten rather more seriously.

One quarry which attracted the attention of the old austringers of the early seventeenth century, and one which they flew with con-siderable success, was the pheasant. Of course, many pheasants have been caught by Goshawks, both females and tiercels, since the seven-teenth century, but few people have made the pheasant their main quarry and have studied the technique required to bring the long-tail to the bag.

Pheasants can be flown by both female and tiercel Goshawks. Some austringers prefer the tiercel because they say he is more agile in cover, others prefer a female because she is able to tackle any larger quarry which may present itself. It is said with some truth that most male Goshawks are inclined to fly feathered quarry, whereas only some females will. Certainly some females have a predilection for fur and some for feather, but I think a lot depends on the success of the first few flights at any one particular quarry. The austringer who intends making pheasants his main quarry might consider rearing a few and turning them out in some convenient place so that he may be sure of having a few young pheasants on hand at which to enter his Goshawk at the beginning of the season.

The flight at the pheasant is difficult for he is rarely found far from cover and once on the wing can fly at the same speed as the pursuing Goshawk. If he can be found in open country, say on downland well away from a wood or a tall crop like kale, a stern chase will ensue with the gap between pursuer and pursued remaining the same throughout. If the pheasant is hard pressed, and he will consider himself so if the hawk is only a few feet behind him, he will "put into" the first available cover such as a bramble patch in the corner of a field or a thick hedge. When he brakes to land and run in, the hawk may find an extra spurt of speed and may be able to foot him on the ground before he disappears to lie very low in the cover. If the hawk fails to do this she will shoot up in the air over the spot where the pheasant has put in and take stand either on a fence post or in a nearby tree. The austringer will now come running up and with the help of his dog will endeavour to flush the hunted pheasant again. If he succeeds and the hawk is waiting in a tree, there is a very good chance that she will take the pheasant in the air after a short chase. If the Gos is waiting on a fence post, on a low bush, or on the ground, it is best to call her to the fist and fly her from there. In very open country it is possible to get two or three flights at the same pheasant in this way and each time the pheasant is flushed so the chances of catching it increase. Hen pheasants are far less resolute than cocks and are more easily caught; but I remember one cock pheasant that was flushed four times in a short space of time underneath my Goshawk which had taken stand in a tree. The last time he rose the cock flew a hundred yards, hotly pursued, into a large wood and I thought I had seen the last of him, but a few minutes later the dog came out of the cover carrying the pheasant. It was stone dead and hadn't a mark on it so I can only presume that it died of fright!

Another stratagem which may be employed to give the hawk a better chance to catch the pheasant is to observe from a distance a pheasant feeding under an oak tree and to walk up slowly with the hawk shielded by an assistant's body so that she does not see the pheasant and bate towards it. When you are quite a long way off the pheasant will unhurriedly run into the hedge and hide. The Goshawk is now thrown high into the oak and the dog put into the hedge. When the pheasant rises before the dog a fine flight will ensue and due to the extra height from which the Gos is able to start she may perhaps catch him. Some Gosses are very good at crashing into quite thick cover and grabbing their quarry on the ground. Those that do this will catch quite a few pheasants as they put in. I have noticed that when one is out walking with a Goshawk and a dog—I use a German pointer—and one comes suddenly upon a pheasant unexpectedly in what may seem to be a most unsuitable place for a flight, it often pays to let the hawk go even if both hunter and hunted disappear from view in the first five seconds. To my great surprise many flights of this nature end in a kill and I think this is because cover abounds and the pheasant not realizing his mortal danger does not bother to use his wings to save himself. He assumes, unwisely, that he has only to drop into the nearest bit of cover to escape. If the hawk means business she will drop in too. It may be difficult to find the hawk again after a flight such as this, especially if she has killed, for Goshawks will crouch very still with mantled wings over their kill and the bells may be muffled by the pheasant feathers and the dead leaves on the ground. The dog will be useful now in helping to locate the kill which is often deep in a ditch or beneath a bramble patch. It is rarely far from the start of the flight and I would advise the austringer who has temporarily lost his hawk in these circumstances to search thoroughly the nearest cover in the line the flight took. If the hawk has failed to kill she will have thrown up over the spot where the pheasant has put in and will be waiting in a tree. Naturally hawking pheasants in or near woods must be delayed until mid-November when all the leaves will have fallen.

In Hungary Goshawks take pheasants which are driven towards them in the maize fields. The hawk leaves the fist to intercept the oncoming pheasant and binds to it in mid-air. It was suggested to me by a German falconer friend that a useful artifice by which to circumvent the wily pheasant is to observe a small isolated copse in which pheasants may roost and from which they emerge during the day to feed in the surrounding fields. The austringer must now one afternoon make his way privily to this copse and once there, throw his hawk high into a prominent tree from which she can oversee as many lines of approach as possible. An assistant, meanwhile, must walk round the adjacent fields and hedgerows with the dog. Pheasants thus disturbed will fly back towards the spinny unaware that the hawk is there awaiting their arrival. A head-on flight may thus be obtained.

In pheasant hawking as in other branches of falconry, the falconer must not only know what lies beyond the wood and over the hill, but he must also know a great deal about the natural history and habits of his chosen quarry. In this he is like the wildfowler who, without an intimate knowledge of the terrain over which he shoots, and the habits of ducks and geese, has little hope of filling his bag.

Mallard may be taken with male and female Goshawks provided they can be stalked and the slip is short. If a tree overlooks an isolated pond frequented by duck the hawk may be encouraged to fly into the tree before the duck are flushed by the dog. Duck are more easily caught at a pond surrounded by trees, for they then have to climb vertically when they rise.

Dogs used with Goshawks may be of any type but only those to which the hawk is used should be taken out. German pointers have some advantages in that they will point the quarry and so give the austringer time to manœuvre into a good position for a flight. They will also enter water or dense cover to flush quarry when ordered to do so. The falconer's dog must be trained to walk at heel on his right-hand side otherwise the hawk will be continually looking over her shoulder at the dog. Dogs and hawks soon learn to respect one another. The hawk will follow the dog with her eyes as he works and the dog on point will look up when he hears the approaching bells of the hawk. The man is often but a spectator. It cannot be emphasized too often that the secret of success in training short-winged hawks is frequent carriage. A Goshawk that is wild and fearful when taken up in the morning will often be a changed bird after an hour or so's carriage. When possible it is always wise to carry any trained Goshawk for about half an hour before flying her loose at quarry. This is particularly important after a car journey to the hunting ground. Goshawks soon learn to travel quietly on the fist or on a screen perch rigged up in the back of a car. Try sitting in a stationary car first with the hawk on the fist and the door open. Then, when she has got over the strange surroundings, start the engine and accustom her to that. It will be found that she will sit a lot quieter when the car is moving because her attention will be occupied to some extent with keeping her balance on the fist or screen. She will be apprehensive at the approach of vehicles from behind so it may be helpful to arrange a blind over the rear window of the car and possibly the back side windows.

Passage Goshawks are sometimes available from the Continent in October. These are very fine hawks and if they can be manned at a time of the year when the hours of available daylight are decreasing rapidly, they will fly in a style which is far superior to that of an eyas. But passage female Gosses will not usually take hares. They seem to know by experience that this large quarry is really beyond their powers. An eyas is often more foolhardy. For pheasant a male or female passage Gos may prove superior to an eyas by virtue of its greater experience.

BUZZARD (*Buteo buteo*)

This predator is a member of the group of hawks classified as "broad-wings." It is a protected bird and a licence is required before it can be taken for training. Eyas Buzzards may be obtained from the nest in late June, or early July. Their treatment and training are the same as for an eyas Goshawk. It is possible to catch young rabbits and moorhens with a trained Buzzard but they tend to be sluggish and lazy. They are, however, easy to keep and a beginner may gain valuable experience by handling a Buzzard before he obtains a more valuable Goshawk. The female Buzzard will fly at about 1 lb. 12 oz. and the male at about 1 lb. 10 oz.

THE SPARROWHAWK (*Accipiter nisus*)

The female only of this species is worth training. The male or musket is very small and nervous. Sparrowhawks are ready to take from the nest about the end of the first week in July. The males will often fly out of the nest when the climber comes up as they are usually more advanced than the females. The eyasses may sometimes be seen standing on the nest platform from the ground. If the nest is in such a position the stage of development can be easily gauged by inspection with binoculars. The number of eyasses in a nest varies from one to six and if the nest is found early enough austringers have removed some of the young hawks leaving only two of the largest females. Thus the attention of the parent hawks will be concentrated on these two eyasses which will grow apace. The female eyasses, of course, are considerably larger than the males both in their bodies and in the size and length of their toes. Their heads, too, are broader and flatter. One method of rearing an eyas Sparrowhawk is to take it from the nest when it is but a few days old. It is then reared by hand and is fed frequently on tiny morsels of chopped bird meat—preferably sparrows. Such an eyas, if successfully reared, will scream on the approach of its owner especially when hungry. But the scream of the Sparrowhawk is a puny whistle compared with the ear-piercing shriek of a screaming Goshawk, and it is often an advantage to be able to locate the Sparrowhawk in a tree by its scream.

Sparrowhawks, if taken early in July, a few days before they would fly from the nest, may be hacked from an artificial nest or basket set in a tree. If this is done a ladder or pole should be leaned against the tree so that an eyas that reaches the ground too soon may find its way back up to the nest. The eyasses in the artificial nest must be force fed with forceps for a couple of days until they will take food voluntarily when it is offered to them on the forceps tip. The food must consist of chopped sparrow with the feathers on but the beak and feet removed. When food is taken freely from the forceps it may be left for them on a board placed on the edge of the nest. The secret of hacking Sparrowhawks is to always have food present on the board. They will not then stray far and will always return to the tree for their meals. The best method of catching up hacked Sparrowhawks is either to have arranged for them to feed on a table beneath the tree upon which is set a bow-net or, better, the nest in the first place may be set in the bottom of a wooden framed wire-netting box. The top of this box has a balanced lid covered with fish-netting. The lid is held open by a trigger. Then when the young Sparrowhawk is hard penned and it is decided to catch it up a string is attached to the trigger and a sharp pull at the right moment will cause the lid to fall and close the box. (See Diagram of Hawk Trap, p. 154.)

It is unfortunate that the Sparrowhawk, the last British bird of prey to be afforded legal protection under the Protection of Birds Act, 1954, is occasionally the hawk most easily obtained by the inexperienced beginner when he attempts to train his first bird. The outcome of the clash of wills that now ensues nearly always results in the death of the hawk and the despair of the would-be austringer. For the Sparrowhawk or "spar" as she is called by falconers, is an extremely difficult subject with which to start. She combines all the contrariness of the Goshawk with a constitution that is so delicate that it will tolerate no rough food or long fasts. Yet once manned the eyas female spar is an extremely sporting little hawk to own and will tackle quarry a great deal larger and heavier than herself. Like the Goshawk the secret of success is constant regular daily carriage. The food should consist of sparrows, mice, woodpigeons and road casualty small birds. Beef must only be used in emergency. When first taken up the female Sparrowhawk will weigh 9½ to 10 oz. It will be found that her flying weight will vary between 8 and 9 oz. depending on her state of manning and her size. In common with all trained hawks success will depend upon the finding of a balance between tameness brought about by carriage and condition brought about by dieting. The tamer the hawk the higher the condition in which she can be safely flown, and the higher the condition the more easily is she able to outfly her quarry. The margin between "too high" and "too low" in the case of the spar is only about a quarter of an ounce in body weight, so it will be seen that a very little food more or less will be enough to upset the balance one way or the other. Sparrowhawks, and indeed all small hawks, should be fed twice daily especially in winter. A half crop in the morning without casting and two-thirds of a crop in the evening for the trained spar will be found to be sufficient, but this may be varied slightly according to her behaviour. Especial care must be taken to feed the hawk well in cold weather. The basic training for the spar is the same as that of the Goshawk.

The traditional quarry of the Sparrowhawk was the blackbird, but this sporting little bird is now protected by law and the austringer must seek other game for his spar. If she is to be flown at large birds like moorhens or partridge it is best not to allow her to fly at small birds like sparrows or starlings. As with other hawks, the success of the first few flights is vitally important and the austringer should choose the quarry and the circumstances of these first flights with great care and by so doing assist his hawk to make a kill and gain confidence. Trained eyas Sparrowhawks will take large pheasant poults up to 1½ lb. in weight as well as young partridge, moorhens, little owls and starlings.

The passage spar or the self-hacked spar, that is, a bird that has left the nest for three weeks or so but is still being fed by its parents, is thought by some to be easier to man than an eyas. They are certainly better mannered. But I would advise any austringer, however keen, who has to earn his living during ordinary working hours, not to attempt to man a passage short-wing during the winter unless he can arrange for it to be carried for him for at least two hours in daylight. It is, in my experience, impossible to get a passage short-wing manned by carriage indoors at night.

Cooper's Hawks (*Accipiter cooperi*) are short-winged hawks resident in the United States and Canada. Very occasionally specimens have been imported into this country and have been trained. They are more like small Goshawks than large Sparrowhawks and the females particularly lack the long, slender "bird catching" middle toe of the Sparrowhawk. Proportionately their tails are very long and they have Kestrel-like "bottle shoulders" which would seem to indicate that their habitat is dense woodland. The moulting weight of a female Cooper's Hawk is about 1 lb. 2 oz. and the flying weight about 15 oz. The male weights are about $12\frac{3}{4}$ oz. and 10 oz. respectively. But these weights must not be taken as being too accurate because not only do individual hawks vary greatly in size but ornithologists recognize two distinct races of Cooper's Hawks—a western race, *Accipiter cooperi mexicanus*, which is small and has very short, round wings, and an eastern race which is somewhat larger. The weights given above would be typical of the small western race. A female of the eastern race might moult at 1 lb. 5 oz. and fly at 1 lb. 2 oz.

The quarry which female Cooper's Hawks have taken in this country includes pheasants, small rabbits, moorhens, woodpigeons and rats. They are very quick in cover, but all those falconers who have had them here report that they were difficult to enter at quarry and were all rather vicious and free with their feet. The male is undoubtedly no better than a good female Sparrowhawk, but is easier to keep. The female is not as good as a male Goshawk.

CHAPTER IX

A MISCELLANY, HEALTH, TRANSPORT, FOOD, THE MOULT, DISEASE, ACCIDENTS, LOST HAWKS

THE comfort and health of his hawk should be a prime consideration of the conscientious falconer. They are captive and cannot shift for themselves to choose a sheltered resting-place, nor can they select their food. Hawks detest wind, so the weathering lawn must be sheltered from the prevailing gales. If natural windbreaks, like hedges or shrubberies, are not available, then the falconer must improvise with canvas screens or screens made of reed matting. Rain is of less importance although it is probably wise not to expose hawks to continuous cold rain in winter. European falcons, especially if haggard or intermewed, are more impervious to rain than are the hawks and looser feathered desert falcons. And intermewed hawks and falcons are more waterproof than eyasses. Light rain in summer is of no account. If hawks have been caught on the weathering lawn in heavy rain in winter it is advisable to leave the electric light on in the mews for an hour or two after dark when they have been fed up and put away on the screen perch for the night. This allows them to rouse and preen a bit before they go to sleep. If the lights are extinguished as soon as the wet hawks are tied on the screen, they tend to sit immobile in the dark and remain damp and miserable all night. Needless to say the mews should be clean and dry and free from draughts. Cold does not matter but draughts and damp do. No scraps of food should ever be dropped and left up on the floor of the mews, for to do this would invite keen hawks to bate at it in their efforts to secure a morsel. The floor of the mews is usually covered with a two-inch layer of sand or sawdust which is changed regularly. Blocks on the weathering lawn are moved daily otherwise the grass will be killed by the accumulated mutes. Blocks in an open weathering shed are surrounded by sand which is regularly changed.

All hawks love to sit in the sun on their blocks but in high summer care must be taken that the sun is not too hot. At this time of the year it is best to allow the hawks to enjoy the early morning sun and then move them back into the shade as the day advances.

A bath should be offered two or three times a week in hot weather and less frequently in winter. Falcons are more disposed to bathe than are hawks, which seem to be more afraid of being caught at a disadvantage with their feathers wet. Do not offer a bath every day or the birds may not bathe so thoroughly; they will just hop into the water and out again without wetting themselves properly. Never give a bath on dull damp days or so late in the day that the hawk will still be wet when night falls. Some falconers remove the leather leash and substitute for it a nylon cord when the hawk is offered a bath so that the leather leash does not become hard and cracked through frequent wetting and drying.

Each morning a search must be made beneath the screen perch for the casting of each hawk, for while it is permissible to put the hawk out to weather before she has cast, she must not be hooded, fed or flown before this act has been completed. (A hawk, however, can cast through a well-fitting Indian Hood.) When the hawks have cast they may be given a tiring such as a tough pigeon's wing or rabbit bone with little meat on it to occupy their idle hours on the block. Do not leave many feathers on the wings given for tiring as these look untidy when plucked on the lawn. These tirings give the hawks valuable exercise for their neck and back muscles and help to keep their beaks in shape.

When hawks are to make a long journey by train or car as from the South of England to Scotland in August, they may either be carried, hooded, on the fist or they may sit hooded on a box cadge. If the latter method is chosen they must never be left unattended for a moment for they will be sitting within reach of one another and crabbing may easily occur. Feed the hawks up well for a day or two before the journey and on the evening before departure feed a light feed with no casting. Do not feed on the morning before the journey because hawks often suffer from motion sickness and can get themselves in a frightful mess by throwing up half digested food through the hood.

Place the box cadge as securely as possible on the seat or floor of the car or estate car, so that the vibration of the wheels on the road is minimized. Upon arrival at the destination place each hawk upon her block or ring perch and unhood. Allow an hour or so to settle down and if early enough in the day offer a bath. Hawks will often drink quite a lot after a long journey. Feed lightly with casting. It will be several days before travelled hawks are themselves again and the falconer must take care to gradually re-introduce the familiar routine. When hawks are being flown every day it is easy to predict their behaviour and performance with some accuracy, but any break in daily observation caused by a long journey or unsuitable flying weather will mean that the falconer will have to use his scales and proceed with caution before the risks involved in a flight at quarry can be accurately calculated. This is especially true of short-wings for they quickly lose their veneer of tameness if not handled and carried every day. Small hawks and those not broken to the hood may be transported in boxes, even if accompanied, by car and train. If unaccompanied this is the only way a hawk of any sort should be packed. It has been suggested in the past that round wicker baskets lined with hessian are the best containers for hawks in transit, but I do not think that these are ideal, for hessian always lets a certain amount of light through, unless very thick, and if thick enough to exclude light it will exclude air also. Hawks packed in such a container often flap about and get their feet caught in the hessian lining. After some experience I have decided that a stout cardboard box of a suitable size is the best container for adult hawks in transit. A piece of hessian can be stretched across the floor of the box and sewn securely into the four corners. The hawk then has a firm floor to grip when the box lurches about. If the box is rectangular or square the corners inside can be rounded off by glueing corrugated paper (smooth side inside) inside the box so that the cube inside is converted into a cylinder. The inside of the box is now completely smooth with no projections to damage the feathers. Holes for ventilation are cut low down so that the hawk cannot see out. Wooden laths (1 inch by 1 inch) may be tacked into the corners of the box outside the corrugated paper cylinder to give the box more strength and obviate the danger of crushing if other boxes should be stacked on top of it. The size of the box is calculated as follows. If the length of the hawk from beak to tail tip is "L" inches, then the diameter of the cylinder inside the box must be $1\frac{1}{4}$ L inches and the height $\frac{3}{4}$ L inches. If the box is a plain rectangle inside then the length must be $1\frac{1}{4}$ L inches, the breadth $\frac{2}{3}$ L inches and the height $\frac{3}{4}$ L inches. These measurements are the minimum. But remember that airlines may charge by volume as well as by weight and often place limitations upon the size of boxes that they will carry in different aircraft.

Flightless eyasses can travel together in hessian-lined hampers or in boxes as described above. All other hawks must have a box to themselves. Never put hay or straw on the floor of the box and do not put food inside. There probably won't be enough light for the hawk to feed anyway. Adult hawks should wear jesses only for the journey. The tails of short-wings are best bound up with sticky paper. They must not be hooded or belled. The sound of bells attracts inquisitive persons and encourages them to enlarge the ventilation holes so that they can see the occupant of the box. They may also be tempted to feed the hawk on unsuitable food. Hawks often arrive after a rail journey sitting in their boxes surrounded by the cheese sandwiches pushed through the ventilation holes by solicitous railwaymen! All hawks travel best in high condition and growing eyasses must always start their journey with a full crop. If the journey is not to last more than eight hours there is some advantage in not feeding well-fed adult hawks before departure because if fed they will pass a lot of mutes in the box and will foul their tails and wing tips. All airlines require that a supply of food must accompany the bird and some require water as well. To comply with this unnecessary regulation, it is best to arrange that a small container be wired to the floor of the box in one corner and that the water be absorbed by a small sponge to prevent slopping. Meat may be placed in a plastic bag and tied securely to the outside of the box with a label giving instructions to airline staff as to how many hours after despatch the food should be inserted. The label may also explain that nothing other than fresh raw lean flesh is acceptable as food, that water is unnecessary and that feeding must only be carried out via the specially arranged sleeve. In no circumstances must the box lid be opened by an unauthorized person. The consigner should inform the consignee before the hawk is sent off, of the route, flight number and times of departure and arrival. The consignee should report her arrival or failure to arrive. The box should be wired shut and should be labelled "Livestock." The label should also give the telephone number of the consignee so that he can be rung in the event of delay *en route* or to announce her arrival at the station or airport.

Remember that airlines often require freight to be handed in two hours before a scheduled flight is due to leave and that if the hawk is to travel abroad it must be accompanied by a veterinary certificate of health which may have to be legalized by the consulate of the country to which the bird is travelling.

When the consignee receives the hawk he must open the box carefully inside a shed or room. He must then show the hawk his gloved fist garnished with a piece of meat. She will probably seize the gloved fist in her talons and be easily lifted out. The swivel is then put on the jesses followed by the leash. Bent, frayed and soiled tail and primary feathers may be spectacularly refurbished by dipping them for a few moments in very hot but not boiling water. Do not overdo this however as repeated immersion in hot water makes the feathers brittle. As soon as possible the travelled hawk must be offered a bath and be fed.

A trained hawk's condition is regulated by judicious feeding and while the falcon will not fly quarry and remain obedient to her trainer unless her appetite is keen, it does not follow that she be starved into submission. Her condition and appetite must be similar to that of an athlete. There is an old saying that "A fat hawk makyth a lean horse, a weary falconer and an empty purse," but a thin hawk will not be any credit to her owner either.

Condition may be gauged to some extent by feeling the breast muscles and judging the prominence of the breast bone. Bear in mind that short-wings have more prominent breast bones and generally have to be flown in somewhat lower condition than long-wings. The weighing machine is a more accurate indication of the state of affairs and it will be found that all hawks fly best at a certain weight known as the "flying weight." This weight varies somewhat in individuals of the same species and with the quarry to be flown. Thus Peregrines flown at game will have a higher flying weight than those flown at rooks.

When dieting hawks the quality as well as the volume of the meat must be taken into account. Naturally the margin of error in small hawks is much smaller than in large ones. Woodpigeon is twice the feeding value of an equal amount of rabbit. If beef is used the daily ration for a Peregrine falcon will be about 5 oz. and for a tiercel rather under 4 oz. A female Goshawk will need about 4 oz.

There are many systems of feeding when flying. Peregrines when flown at game daily may be fed well and the flying weight of the falcon kept at around 2 lb. and that of the tiercel around 1 lb. 5 oz.

Peregrines flown at rooks will need to be an ounce or so less. Goshawks which are only flown at the week-ends may be kept on the following regime: Full crop on Sunday—preferably fed on warm quarry; nothing on Monday; half crop Tuesday, Wednesday and Thursday; small crop (walnut-sized) Friday. Fly on Saturday, feed half crop. Fly on Sunday and feed full crop. The Goshawk on this regime must be weighed daily to keep a check on her weight trend. The exact amount of food given each day will depend upon her weight. As she is not flown during the week this is the only way her condition can be judged. Naturally she must be sufficiently manned to fly at a reasonably high weight (about 2 lb. 4 oz. for a female and 1 lb. 8 oz. for a male). It is better to keep the Gos at just above her flying weight during the week and then try to cut her on to it exactly on the day she is to be flown, than to allow her to get well above the critical weight and then have to keep her very short of food in order to get her down to the flying weight on the day she is to be flown. Hawks have, perforce, to be flown in lower condition than falcons. This is because they are much more nervous creatures and the austringer finds that he is unable to keep their attention if they are too fat. But this does not mean that they must be starved. A Goshawk or Sparrowhawk is just as hungry and keen when she has been properly dieted to reach her true flying weight as is a bird which has been reduced below this weight. The difference is that the first hawk is strong and able to overcome quarry, and the second, though keen, has not the physical strength to fly properly.

All food must be absolutely fresh when fed to hawks. If hungry they will eat food which they would not dream of eating in the wild, but to force them to this in order to survive cannot do their digestions much good. Butcher's meat, if used, must be fresh and have no stale smell. Preferably it should not have been frozen as this may indicate that it was going off before the butcher decided to arrest its decomposition by freezing it. Shin of beef is the best "cut" to buy because it is relatively fat free and is easily cut into convenient strips for feeding on the fist. Remove all fat, tendon sheaths and gristle. Ox cheek is cheaper but is often a bit fatty and is sometimes stale. Ox and sheep's hearts I do not like as they go bad very quickly. Rabbit, if available, is good food for Goshawks and as a change for Peregrines, but it is too light and poor in food value for smaller hawks. I have not ever fed mutton or pork to my hawks. Rats and grey squirrels are good for Goshawks especially during the moult. The squirrels are very tough and provide a deal of exercise. Young chickens, provided they are disease free, are excellent food for all hawks. Old hens are usually very fat and if a hawk is allowed to eat a lot of this fat she will vomit and go off her food for several days. Chickens' heads, plus necks, are often available from the poulterer. These are very good food for the larger hawks during the moult and during the off season, but are very messy to feed on the fist and it is difficult to ration a hawk when feeding chickens' heads. They do not keep well but if a surplus becomes available they may be successfully deep frozen provided they are fresh.

Young house pigeons are good, nourishing food for all hawks. Old ones are tough and indigestible, so feed sparingly. This does not apply to woodpigeons, rock doves and stock doves, but hawks fed on a lot of woodpigeon tend to get a bit independent. All the pigeon family may harbour the protozoon which causes frounce, *Trichomonas gallinae*, but luckily this organism seems to be very fragile and dies out very soon after the death of its host. Whether this is due to a change in the pH of the pigeon's body fluids after death or to the post-mortem drop in body temperature, is not clear, but for practical purposes one may conclude that pigeons are a safe food for hawks if they are allowed to become cold before they are offered to the hawks. All other food should be freshly killed and fed warm when possible.

Grouse are very rich and should be fed sparingly. Falcons are usually rewarded with the head and neck after a successful flight. Pheasant and partridge are excellent foods which are well liked by all hawks.

Rooks are regularly fed to rook-hawks and may be fed to eyasses at hack. They are often full of lice.

Duck and teal are rather fat so feed with discretion.

Many modern falconers are finding that a basic diet of hare is suitable for all hawks and is superior to butcher's meat. Now that rabbits have all but vanished following upon myxomatosis, hares seem to be on the increase and may be cheaply bought almost all the year round. They must, of course, be fresh and should be paunched as soon as possible after death. Hare is much more nourishing than rabbit.

Moorhens and coots are fat and greasy. Feed sparingly. Blackbirds,

K

thrushes and other small birds which may be picked up as road casualties, are all excellent food for small hawks and may with advantage be given to a larger hawk that is off colour. If fresh, they may be fed with the entrails and crops in situ. Mice are good for Merlins, Sparrowhawks and Kestrels. Their skins make good castings. Large birds should have their intestines and crops removed only if they are not going to be fed on the same day as they are killed. Leave the liver in as it is a valuable source of Vitamin A. Where possible food should be fed warm. If it has been stored in a refrigerator it must be warmed by placing it in a plastic bag and submerging the bag in warm water. Surplus food may be deep frozen in plastic bags provided it is absolutely fresh when put in the deep freeze. It is best to disembowel and remove the crop of birds and animals to be deep frozen. Naturally deep frozen meat must be allowed to thoroughly thaw out before use. To speed the unfreezing some falconers knead the meat in warm water and dry it before feeding.

When feeding birds or animals which have been shot with a shot gun, an attempt should be made to find and remove the lead pellets, but provided plenty of casting is given these pellets are almost invariably cast up with the casting. It is perhaps safer to shoot hawk food with a rifle. I have fed cat-meat to Goshawks, and young kittens, often unwanted on farms, are a useful change of diet for moulting Gosses. Rabbit and hare feet are good for casting if they are hammered first to break up the bones.

The food question can be a bit of a nightmare for the falconer and some of us now keep a supply of white rats, guinea pigs or light breed cockerels so that we always have available food "on the hoof," for use in emergency. I think that to maintain hawks in good health they must be fed on a varied diet. It does not do to feed exclusively on any one type of meat. Young growing eyasses must be fed on an abundance of the most natural food that can be provided. Plenty of small birds with their entrails, liver and crops intact and with their bones broken into convenient lengths for swallowing. Hawks fed thus will develop sturdy skeletons. Do not feed butcher's meat to young eyasses. It is not good enough for them. There is no doubt that wild hawks will pick seeds from the crops of their quarry and will on occasion eat the entrails. It is from these sources and from the liver that they obtain certain essential vitamins and food factors. If these are denied ill health will result. Egg yolk, a valuable food, rich in

Vitamin A and minerals, is useful during the moult. It helps to impart a rich yellow colour to the cere and legs.

The moult generally starts about the end of March or in early April. The seventh primary or beam feather with its corresponding secondary are the first feathers to drop. When these feathers have been almost replaced by new ones, the eighth pair will drop and so on outwards from the centre of the wing both ways. The last feathers to be replaced are the outside or first primaries. The interval between the casting of one pair of primaries and the casting of the next is about a month. Concurrent with the replacing of the main feathers of the wings is the moulting of the train. The first to drop are the two deck feathers generally within a few hours of each other. When the two new decks are almost down the two train feathers next to them will fall and so on outwards until the last two outside train feathers are changed. It takes about five to six weeks for a train feather to be completely replaced in a Goshawk. The body feathers drop later on in the moult. The whole process may be complete in five months, but it is more likely to take six to seven months. Warmth has a beneficial effect on the moult and I have seen Goshawks moulted very quickly and completely in a small corrugated iron hen-house. The main wing and train feathers of the adult are about one-third of an inch shorter than are the feathers of the juvenile plumage of the eyas.

A hawk after her first moult in captivity is called an intermewed hawk.

It is my opinion that short-winged hawks, because of their nervous nature, are best moulted at liberty in a loft appointed as described for rearing eyasses. Before turning her loose in the loft in early March remove her bells, replace her jesses if worn or, if sound, grease them thoroughly. Cope her beak and claws, especially the hind talon. Provide a bath twice a week according to the weather and leave her to her own devices. Feed a variety of food *ad lib.* but be careful to remove any unconsumed meat and debris daily so that blow-flies are not encouraged. The yolks of eggs which are removed from the abdomens of hens when these are being dressed by the poulterer, are very good for moulting hawks. Young chicken, house pigeons and wood-pigeons are also good food for moulting hawks. Rabbit should not be fed exclusively. Hare is better than rabbit but bird fat is essential for the growth of good broad feathers. Chicken and duck heads supply plenty of bird fat. Long-winged hawks may be moulted in a

loft together provided they are of the same species and sex and are
known not to be cantankerous. But I think that long-wings generally
are as well moulted on the block and fed daily on the fist. By this
means they are kept reasonably tame.

If Peregrine falcons are to be flown at grouse in August, they must,
of course, be picked up from the moult before it has finished. To
effect this, reduce the food given for some ten days previously. If the
bird is being moulted on the block it will be much easier to get her
back into flying condition because she will have been used to being
fed on the fist and to being occasionally hooded. This is especially so
of passagers and haggards. All hawks, when taken up from the moult,
will be balls of fat. To hasten the elimination and absorption of this,
washed meat is often used. Washed meat is prepared by cutting lean
fresh beef into long thin strips and soaking them in cold water in a
refrigerator for twenty-four hours. Then squeeze out the meat in
warm water to warm it and to remove the juices, and dry it on a
clean linen cloth. Well-washed meat is almost white in colour and is
not very palatable for the hawk. It may be necessary at first to feed
her upon it hooded until she is hungry enough to eat it bareheaded.
Do not give casting with washed meat. A course of washed meat
should not last more than five days when this rather lowering diet
must be relieved by a good meal of nourishing red meat. Daily
carriage in the hood meantime will be sufficient to man the falcon
and as soon as the scales indicate that the excess fat has been absorbed
she is said to be "enseamed" and is ready to start flying to the lure.

The old falconers used to give their hawks six or eight small
smooth pebbles about the size of French bean seeds about a week
after they had been taken up from the moult. These stones, or
"rangle" as they are called, were given "over hand" every night by
opening the beak and pushing each stone in turn down the throat
with one finger. It may, however, be necessary to cast the hawk for
this operation. Rangle was given every night for a week or ten days
after the crop of food minus casting had been put over. The stones
were then retained overnight in the crop and were cast up in the
morning covered with a thick mucus. The effect of the rangle is
thought to be that it stirs up the accumulated grease and mucus in
the hawk's pannel. After a few days of this treatment the mutes will
be observed to be greasy and discoloured. Modern falconers probably
pay too little attention to the old saying "Wash'd meat and stones

maketh an hawk to flie but great casting and long fasting maketh her to die." (Latham's *Falconry*, 1615, p. 23.)

It may help a falcon to retain the stones if she is carried for a few minutes on the fist after the administration of the rangle. No casting is offered while rangle is being given.

After a further week, casting and more normal food may be given and her appetite will be improved. She will now be ready for flying to the lure, but being slack in muscle and wind the flights must be short to start with. Fly her in the cool of the evening and stop when she pants for breath. She will soon regain her athletic condition and will improve in wind daily. But care must be taken not to overdo the exercise in the early stages.

Short-winged hawks taken up from the moulting loft will need a course of re-training which does not differ in principle from the training of an eyas except that it will be considerably shorter. The end of the moult is a dangerous time for any trained hawk and many go to pieces at this time if mishandled. Short-wings, particularly, are prone to epileptiform fits which may prove fatal if they are allowed to bate a lot in hot weather before they are enseamed.

Various substances have been administered to hawks with a view to shortening the moult. These include progesterone (given to females only), Vitamin B_{12} and thyroid gland. All of these substances have their champions but so little is known of the physiology of birds of prey that I would not advise the use of such drugs which may have untoward effects on their delicate metabolism. Actually, with the possible exception of game hawks to be flown at grouse early in August, there is little justification for attempting to shorten the moult. There is little legal quarry for short-wings in summer, and even if game tiercels are not ready by September 1st, it is possible to fly them at game while they are still moulting, for they will not have to be cut down much in order to fly a quarry to which they are so wedded. Haggards, and to a lesser extent passage hawks, moult slowly and irregularly. It may be several years before a haggard completely changes her feathers. Those falconers who fly haggards and passagers tend to ignore the moult and fly right through it. Shaheens are said to moult very quickly.

Hawks are undoubtedly best kept free from disease by judicious feeding and management, but accidents and mishaps will happen in the best regulated mews and although a sick hawk is all too often a

dead hawk, there are some conditions which will yield to appropriate treatment. The falconer must learn to recognize the signs of
health in his hawk before he can hope to detect disease. He must
know the normal from the abnormal.

The healthy hawk's eyes are round and wide open. There is no
tendency for them to be oval or for the third eyelid or *membrana
nictitans* to protrude. The eyes are bright and there is no watery discharge. She will sit buoyantly on the fist, is alert and keen for her
food. Her weight remains constant unless her food is increased or
diminished, in which case it rises or falls accordingly. An early sign
of trouble is a falling or stationary body weight in spite of full
feeding.

A fit hawk "rouses" frequently and her feathers drop crisply back
into place. At night she sits on the screen perch at the full length of
her jesses away from the swivel, and sleeps on one leg with the other
drawn up into her feathers. On the block on the lawn she "mantles"
and "warbles" and after feeding she "feaks" busily. Her plumage
normally lies close and sleek but in cold weather or after she has
taken a bath, she may puff her feathers out. Food should be taken
eagerly and her crop should be put over at regular intervals. There
should be no food in her crop in the morning after an evening meal
and casting should not be long delayed. Normal castings are oval,
firm and dry. Normal mutes are white with a central clot of black.
Discoloured mutes may indicate disease, but green mutes, often
regarded as being abnormal by the old falconers, may only mean that
the hawk's pannel is empty and feeding should not be long delayed.
After casting, a healthy hawk may throw up a little oily mucus—this
is called "gleaming."

The mutes of short-winged hawks are "sliced" a considerable distance with great vigour. Long-winged hawks do not squirt their
mutes anything like so far but they manage to eject them well away
from their block or screen. It is abnormal for a hawk of either type to
frequently drop small quantities of rather pasty mutes which tend to
soil the fluffy feathers round the vent. As the hawk grows older her
feet and cere gradually assume a brilliant yellow hue which is indica-
tive of health. This colour is very largely influenced by the food, and
food which contains carotene such as bird fat, bird liver and egg
yolk, will quickly produce a good yellow colour which will last for a
month or more even if no more carotene is fed. The irides of eyas

Goshawks are at first a pale grey, later pale yellow which gradually deepens to orange and at two years plus becomes a very handsome deep red. This eye colour, too, is influenced by the amount of carotene in the food.

Any divergence from the normality described above may indicate that something is amiss. The observant falconer will be quick to detect even the most minor changes in his hawk's behaviour which herald the advent of more serious and obvious symptoms. Sunken eyes which are oval, apathetic expression, puffed feathers on a warm day, discoloured mutes, foul breath, froth round the beak, wet, misshapen castings, sitting on the block or screen on both feet, and, on the screen, sitting on top of the jesses and swivel, losing weight in spite of adequate feeding, sudden changes in behaviour such as screaming or appearing inordinately hungry when well fed, are all the signs that all is not well.

Unless the falconer is very experienced it is always wise to obtain the advice of a qualified veterinary surgeon who is *au fait* with bird disease. At the time of writing the British Veterinary Association is preparing a booklet on the diseases of exotic birds and animals. A section of this booklet, which will be circulated to all members of the British Veterinary Association, is devoted to the diseases of trained hawks, so most practising veterinary surgeons will shortly have a reliable reference book.

Much hawk disease is caused by parasites, both external and internal. A hawk in high condition usually harbours a small resident population of parasites, the size of which remains constant as long as the host is in good health. In fact, her immunity to a pathogenic infection probably depends upon a state of premunity existing. If this is so, attempts to remove low-level infestation with drugs may do more harm than good in that not only may the drugs prove toxic but the hawk may be left without the antigens to stimulate the production of antibodies which protect her against overwhelming accidental infections. *External parasites*—red mites or acari—sometimes attack the cere, nares and eyelids. They burrow into the skin and cause iritation which provokes the hawk to scratch her head and cere with her feet and to rub her head on the block. Sores which are largely self-inflicted soon develop and the feathers round the beak and eyes become disarranged. As with all parasite infestations low condition predisposes to this condition.

Treatment consists of feeding the hawk up to improve her bodily condition and painting the cere with an emulsion containing gammexane. The old remedy, which is not very effective, was to paint the cere with tobacco juice in spirit. It is seldom necessary to apply the gammexane emulsion more than three times with a four-day interval between dressings.

Feather perforating and depluming mites have been reported, but there is some doubt as to the diagnosis and the species involved. Their depredations among the feathers should be easily recognized. Dusting with anti-parasitic powder containing piperonyl butoxide and pyrethrum should be effective and non-toxic, but beware aerosols containing these drugs as in this form they appear to be much more toxic and the death of one hawk has been ascribed to them. Biting lice (*Mallophaga*) commonly infest hawks. They rarely cause trouble but a heavy infestation in a bird in poor condition could contribute to its death. Peregrine flying rooks in the spring often acquire these lice from their quarry which are always very lousy. Young rooks, too, which are fed to hawks at hack may be the source of infestation. Treatment: Paint with a child's paint brush, one drop of 40% Nicotine sulphate solution on one leg under the jesse. When the hawk draws this leg up under its feathers at night the nicotine will vaporize and rise through the feathers to kill the lice. Repeat in 10 days.

Hippoboscid flies, or so-called flying ticks, often infest eyasses when first taken from the nest. They suck blood but most hawks seem only to harbour a few. They disappear after the hawk is hard penned. They can be killed off with a dressing of anti-parasitic powder.

Internal parasites—Capillariasis is caused by a very small nematode or threadworm (*capillaria spp*). These worms, which are common in nearly all wild birds, infest the upper part of the small intestine. As with external parasites, most hawks carry a resident population of these worms which cause no harm unless the resistance of the hawk is lowered by intercurrent disease or mismanagement. In these circumstances an infestation with Capillaria can become pathogenic. In bad cases the worms can break out of the intestine and appear in the lungs, air sacs and abdominal cavity. Hawks so infested die. Infection takes place through food or drinking water contaminated with the mutes of an infected bird. The eggs of the worms are passed in the mutes. Normal hygiene in the mews should preclude many infestations occurring in this way. As all hawks seem to carry this parasite and few are affected by it, treatment, which at present is not completely satisfactory, should be reserved for those hawks which show clinical symptoms of parasitism. These symptoms, which are not diagnostic of capillariasis, are those of chronic inflammation of the intestine. The mutes are profuse, discoloured and may contain blood. The feathers round the vent become soiled and the hawk loses weight in spite of ample food. Soon she starts flicking her food about and may cast her crop of meat, undigested. This is a bad sign and generally precedes death. Before the end the hawk may lose the use of her legs. These symptoms when coupled with a high count of capillaria eggs in the mutes should justify the diagnosis of capillariasis, but even then the increase in the numbers of worms may still be due to some intercurrent disease of the bowels of which the parasites are taking advantage. The egg count on the mutes is a job for a skilled parasitologist. Only the black part of the mutes is required and about a teaspoonful should be sent to the Ministry of Agriculture Veterinary Laboratory, New Haw, Weybridge, Surrey. A letter should accompany the specimen which should be packed in a glass bottle or tube, describing briefly the symptoms and giving information about the age and species of the hawk. The name and address of the owner's private veterinary surgeon should also be given. *Treatment.* There is no known drug which is really efficient against capillaria. Probably the best is Thibendazole (Thibenzole; Merck, Sharpe and Dohme Ltd.). This drug, which is only effective against the immature stages of the parasite, is administered wrapped in a piece of meat at a dosage rate of 1 g. per 1 lb. body weight of the dispersible powder (as used to treat sheep for worms). This preparation is safe and will remove other species of round worms (including gapeworms) as well. Imported hawks, especially those from the Middle East, sometimes suffer from an infestation of round worms in the air sacs and peritoneal cavity. These may be controlled with Thibendazole. Symptoms of these aberrant infestations are loss of weight in spite of good appetite, weakness and sometimes a haemorrhage into the lungs which is followed by death. Routine treatment of all hawks is advised.

Concurrent with many infestations of capillaria, there is often coccidiosis. This is another parasite, this time a protozoon. It inhabits the caecum and/or duodenum of its host. The symptoms it causes are

similar to those caused by capillaria. Most hawks seem to carry
benign infestations of coccidia. Diagnosis is always by microscopical
examination of the black parts of the mutes. Treatment, if considered necessary, is by the administration of sulphamezathine.
Sulphamezathine is issued in .5G tablets and the dose is a quarter of a
tablet per 2 lb. body weight once daily for five days. The fraction of
the tablet is best administered wrapped in a piece of meat.

Both these diseases may result from faulty hygiene, so care must
always be taken to see that no food is ever contaminated with
mutes, that the bath is regularly cleaned out and scrubbed, and that
the bath water is changed after each hawk has bathed. Regular dis-
posal of the mutes in the mews and frequent moving of the blocks
on the weathering lawn will help to limit gross infections with these
two parasites. When a bird is known to be carrying a heavy infestation and has been treated, special disinfection of its surroundings may
be necessary. Burn any sawdust and mutes. Scrub the floor, perches
and blocks with hot water and washing soda ($\frac{1}{2}$ lb. to the bucket of
hot water), discard and burn any contaminated leather furniture and
keep a special glove, which can be washed in soda water, for the
infected bird. In the case of coccidiosis the disinfectant of choice is
10 per cent ammonia. Large round worms (*Ascaridia*) sometimes
infest hawks but rarely cause trouble. Piperazine adipate at a dosage
rate of 50 mg. per 1 lb. body weight is fully effective.

   The Gapeworm (*Syngamus trachea*) sometimes affects hawks. It is,
of course, a common parasite of domestic poultry, pheasants, rooks,
etc. When it occurs in a hawk it is probably an aberrant infection.
The life history of the parasite may be direct but earthworms, slugs
and snails can act as intermediate hosts. Larvae may retain their
infectivity for up to four years in these agents. But as hawks do not
eat earthworms, slugs or snails, they are unlikely to contract gapeworm infestations from this source.

   The barium antimonyl tartrate treatment which used to be used
for poultry is not suitable for use in hawks. The latest treatment for
gapeworm is thibendazole given in the same dosage as for capillaria
(see page 137) and continued as a daily dose for at least 14 days.
The gapeworm is about an inch long and bright red in colour. The
male is attached to the female in permanent copulation.

Tapeworms occasionally occur in hawks especially those imported from abroad. The most effective treatment is Yomesan (Baywood Chemicals Ltd.) given in food at a rate of one quarter of a .5 g. tablet per 2 lbs. body weight. Tetrachlorethylene has been used by some with success. This drug must be administered in a capsule and the dose will be .2 ml. in a capsule per 2 lb. body weight.

Metabolic disease is most likely to affect eyasses which have been taken too young from the nest and are being fed on unsuitable food.

Cramp and Paralysis are common complaints of young hawks. Sometimes the unco-ordinated muscular spasms may be so violent as to fracture a leg bone. It is possible that some of the cases of "cramp" are, in fact, a flaccid paralysis due to the virus of fowl paralysis, but this has never been proved. In any case, whatever its cause, paralysis of one or both legs in a hawk is a serious thing and is rarely curable. Fractured legs have been repaired successfully by the use of plaster of Paris bandages. The lower down the leg the fracture is situated the better are the chances of a successful union. Cramp may be treated by placing the affected bird in a small box and putting the box in a linen cupboard or similar warm place. The affected leg may be fomented with hot water and massaged with a mild liniment. Michell, in his book, recommends this treatment but says that unless relief from the paralysis is prompt, the bird should be destroyed. I have had ducks suffering from a similar paralysis recover after the injection into the breast muscles of $\frac{1}{4}$cc of concentrated Vitamin D_3. It has been also suggested that the condition is similar to polyneuritis in which case injections of Vitamin B_1 (3 mg. every forty-eight hours for fourteen days) would be indicated.

As usual, prevention is better than cure and eyasses taken at the right age, kept warm and dry and fed on small birds and mammals (including their livers and bones) are unlikely to suffer from deficiencies. Vitamins A and D can be supplied by giving a halibut liver oil capsule twice weekly, but the capsules must be fresh.

While on the subject of paralysis mention might be made of a sprain in the wing which sometimes occurs in short-wings while they are at liberty in the hawk shed. This muscular sprain must occur as a result of an inco-ordinated attempt to reach a higher perch. The result is that one wing droops lower than the other when the bird sits at rest. There is little that can be done by way of treatment as any attempt to bind up the wing in the normal position may result in injury to the shafts of the growing flight feathers. The only thing to do is to leave the hawk loose in the loft until the muscle has healed. In mild cases this may take three weeks. In bad cases a lot longer. When a hawk is flying quarry she may, by accident, fly into a wire fence or telephone wires. This can produce a sprain of the wing with similar symptoms. In this case she must be grounded until she is better. Wire can wrench a primary feather out of place, too, with the result that the affected feather does not lie snugly in place beside its fellow but sticks out at an angle. In these cases the best thing to do is to sew this feather to the one next to it by passing a needle and thread through the shafts about half an inch from where the feather is embedded in the wing. Tie off firmly. This will keep the damaged feather in the normal position and the hawk can continue flying. The stitch can remain in indefinitely but it must be cut and the two feathers separated before the moult starts. Accidentally fractured legs, provided the fracture is below the knee, may be set in plaster of Paris bandage. The plaster should be left on for three weeks. In the case of a broken wing the outlook is much more serious but wings which were not too badly smashed have been set successfully.*

"*Blain*" is a watery blister affecting the second joint of the wing. The joint gradually stiffens and becomes anchylosed. The bird is then useless. I have never seen the condition which Lascelles says is commonest in severe winters and suggests that it may be due to frostbite. Michell suggests lancing the blister and keeping the hawk quiet until the wing is healed. A counter irritant such as tincture of iodine might be tried, painted on the blister.

Swollen feet afflict hawks of all species. The swelling is a symptom of several diverse conditions which must be differentiated. Swelling occurring in a freshly caught short-wing may merely be due to contusion arising from the concussion on the heels by the jesses when the hawk bates. The remedy here is to fit soft, well-greased jesses and improve the management of the hawk so that it bates less.

There have been some reports of true gout occurring in birds of prey. In these cases the swelling is due to the deposition of urates in the joints and is accompanied by severe changes in the kidneys. This type of foot swelling is probably commonest in Sakers and Gyr falcons which tend to be phlegmatic in temperament and do not move

* Recently the fractured wings of two eagles have been successfully set by open reduction and the use of Salo Jonas self-expanding intra-medullary pins.

about much on their blocks. There is no doubt that lack of exercise and improper feeding (too much butcher's meat) are contributory causes. It is doubtful whether a bad, advanced case is curable but mild cases may respond to light feeding and increased exercise.

The commonest type of foot swelling which occurs most commonly in falcons, Golden Eagles and Hawk Eagles, and less commonly in Goshawks and Sparrowhawks, is a condition resembling bumblefoot in domestic chickens. The pathology of this foot disease is fully described in an article by Dr. K. W. Kost, reprinted in English from the *Deutscher Falkenorden Journal* of 1955 in the *Journal of the Falconry Club of America*, Vol. 2, No. 1, Sepember 1958.

The lesion starts as a black scab on the sole of the ball of the foot. Gradually the swelling increases and soon there is appreciable heat in the affected foot which the falcon will favour when she sits at rest. She may, as the pain increases, lie down a lot on the ground beside her block. Smooth, soft fluctuating swellings may develop on the sides or top of the foot. The falcon may peck at and excoriate these swellings. The interval between the development of the various stages may be protracted as the whole disease is of a chronic nature. In the final stages there is abscess formation and gross involvement of tendons and joint capsule. When the disease reaches such an advanced stage it is probably incurable.

Dr. Kost recommends a radical operation for the treatment of this type of foot swelling if it has reached the stage of causing the hawk to lie down with the pain. The hawk is cast by an assistant. A tourniquet must be applied to the leg to limit bleeding. No anaesthesia is necessary. The swelling is incised at its summit taking care to avoid any nerves or blood vessels. The inflammatory fluid which oozes out will be scanty and the main content of the cavity will be found to be a rather firm, cheesy, laminated mass—something like a small onion. This mass must be carefully removed and the cavity packed with a folded strip of penicillin tulle. The tulle is kept in place with adhesive plaster which must be well wrapped round the toes. If the falcon shows a tendency to pull at the bandage she may be discouraged from doing so by fixing a circular cardboard anklet to her leg so that she cannot see the bandaged foot. A groove can be cut in the anklet to accommodate her other leg. The wound may be dressed and the tulle removed after two days and the cavity painted with pykotannin solution. After operation the bird must be kept on a soft padded perch, be fed by hand with chopped food and not allowed to bathe. It is Dr. Kost's opinion that the probable cause of this troublesome condition is a puncture of the ball of the foot by the hind talon. This talon has a groove on its underside which is often full of decomposing meat, a perfect culture medium for bacteria. A single puncture by the hind talon when meat is perhaps clumsily pulled away from the falcon can result in a massive inoculation of the ball of the foot with bacteria of many different species.

Other factors, such as lack of exercise, stagnation of the circulation in the feet, lack of sunlight and lack of Vitamin A all contribute to this condition. The Vitamin A deficiency theory is interesting for it has been noticed that hawks suffering from swelled feet often have very pale yellow legs and ceres. Vitamin A is concerned with the ability of an animal to resist infection, especially infection of the skin. Carotene, which is pro-Vitamin A, is taken in the wild by hawks when they eat the liver and fat of their quarry. The legs and ceres of wild hawks are always bright yellow in colour and wild hawks do not suffer from swollen feet. It appears that there may be a connection between the carotene deficiency which is common in captive birds of prey, and the occurrence of swollen feet. Newly hatched chicks and the egg yolks of hens run on free range (not the pale yolked eggs of deep litter or battery birds) are a valuable source of carotene which the falconer can supply to his charges. Sunlight in the mews, by virtue of its ultra violet content, will kill off many of the bacteria. Exercise is necessary too, in order to stimulate the blood supply to the extremities. Coping of the hind talon especially at the start of the moult is a wise precaution. There does not seem to be a constant bacteriological picture or specific pathogen. In fact, the evidence is that an assortment of organisms is necessary to provoke the disease. Dr. Kost does not recommend the injection of antibiotics since severe cramps have been seen to result from this.

Kecks, Croaks and Pantas are the old names for a disease of the respiratory system characterized by wheezing, breathing and later croaking noises which are most marked on exertion. It seems that these manifestations of disease may, in fact, be but symptoms of several primary conditions. Hawks suffering from croaks lose condition rapidly. In severe cases they lose the use of their legs. It is possible that some cases are due to gross infestation with internal parasites. A mute sample examined in the laboratory will confirm or deny this.

The treatment recommended by Blaine was six or seven cardamom seeds with the casting, and as a preventive, an occasional peppercorn or a pinch of mustard seed in the food especially in damp, stormy weather. In all cases feed light, warm, nourishing food such as freshly killed sparrows or young pigeons. I have cured a case of croaks in a Merlin by giving 25 mg. Aureomycin in a capsule in food daily for five days. A larger hawk would take double this dose.*

Colds are commonly seen in hawks after a period of damp, stormy weather. The symptoms are a watery discharge from the nostrils. The hawk sneezes or "snits." The disease used to be called "*Snurt.*" Treatment consists of feeding the bird well and placing a few drops of oil of eucalyptus into the nares with a feather. A capsule of halibut liver oil might also be given in winter. Respiratory disease and conditions affecting the sinuses in front of the eyes may be successfully treated with Tylan (Elanco Ltd.) Dose: 10 mg. per 1 lb. body weight in food twice daily for 4 days.

Aspergillosis is perhaps the commonest cause of illness and death in captive birds of prey. The germ is a mould prevalent in dusty and damp conditions which causes a fatal pneumonia. The symptoms, as usual, are not diagnostic and the disease is as yet incurable largely because by the time it is diagnosed the lungs are destroyed. Very often the earliest sign of trouble is a persistent slight drop in weight in spite of full feeding. The hawk may appear to be bright and well apart from a slight shortness of breath. In a few days the weight drops sharply and the bird gets weaker. She may now refuse food and may flick pieces of meat about with her beak if she is offered them. She soon dies. I believe that this disease, caused by *aspergillus fumigatus*, is more common in passage short-wings than in other species of hawk. I have noticed that passage short-wings often die within the first two months of capture of a complaint which, on post-mortem, is revealed as aspergillosis. It may be that these hawks are already infected in the wild and that as their health runs down they become less efficient at catching their prey. This makes them more likely to risk entering the falconer's trap in search of an easy meal. After capture, the shock of handling and the subsequent loss of condition which is inevitable, both play a part in precipitating the disease which may have lain dor-

---

* Since writing the above I have completely cured a haggard lanneret (weight 1 lb. 4 oz.) of croaks by giving 50 mg. aureomycin by hand daily for 5 days. This hawk had to be force fed for a week to keep it alive.

mant for some time. Aspergillosis does not seem to be so common in eyasses. In the wild the disease may be contracted from infected prey as it is a common complaint of young pheasants especially in wet summers when weed seeds left in the cornfields by the combine harvesters tend to go mouldy. It always amazes me that the hawk affected with advanced aspergillosis often does not show any symptoms at all until her lungs are virtually destroyed by the disease. It is for this reason that treatment is unlikely to be of any avail. Antibiotics are contra-indicated for they seem to stimulate the growth of the mould by removing bacterial competitors. An attempt can be made at preventing this fatal disease by keeping the mews warm and dry and by keeping dust down to a minimum.

Frounce is a disease of the mouth and tongue caused by a protozoon called *Trichomonas gallinae*. This organism causes a similar condition in birds of the pigeon and dove family. In fact, it is considered by some to have been one of the factors contributing to the extinction of the Passenger pigeon in the U.S.A.

The symptoms are frothing at the mouth and difficulty in eating. Upon examination an evil smell will be noticed and there will be seen to be a greyish-brown or yellowish-white deposit on the tongue and mucus membrane of the mouth. In severe cases the infection spreads down the throat and may prove fatal. Dr. Stabler in America first suggested treatment with Entramin (May & Baker). Dose 40 mg. per kg. given in a capsule daily for seven days.

In some cases entramin has proved specific but in others it has been ineffective. This might lead one to suppose that there is more than one type of frounce. Entramin is so dramatic in susceptible cases that it should always be tried first. If it fails one must fall back on the older remedies of which the most successful are dressing twice daily with 1 per cent aqueous gentian violet solution and dressing the deposit twice weekly with a silver nitrate stick. This gradually burns back the diseased tissue. The hawk must be cast for this operation and treatment may have to be carried out for some weeks.

As infection with *Trichomonas gallinae* is common in both domestic and wild pigeons, it follows that they must be fed to hawks with some care. It was at first thought that provided the head and crop of the pigeon were removed the chances of infection were slight. This is undoubtedly so, but recent findings seem to indicate that *T. gallinae* is a very fragile parasite and that when its host dies it does not live long in the cooling carcase. Whether the demise of the parasite is due to simple cooling or to changes in the pH of the pigeon's tissues occurring post-mortem is not known, but it is known that *T. gallinae* is impossible to culture when attempts are made to recover it from the carcases of pigeons which have been dead more than an hour or so. In the light of these discoveries it is probably safe to feed pigeons to hawks provided they are allowed to cool after death.

While on the subject of pigeons, mention might be made of a toxic condition which has recently been diagnosed in hawks following upon their being fed on a diet of woodpigeons shot in the spring and autumn. It seems that seed corn dressed with dieldrin to prevent the ravages of wireworms is consumed by woodpigeons after the spring and autumn sowings. Some pigeons die of dieldrin poisoning but others are shot while full of the drug but as yet not showing symptoms. If pigeons so contaminated comprise the main diet of a trained hawk, it is conceivable that the hawk, too, will suffer from dieldrin poisoning. The symptoms so far seen are those of incoordination, physical weakness and depressed appetite. The hawk may lie on the ground beside her block and if placed loose in a loft will press her head against the wall in a corner. Death may ensue and post-mortem examination will reveal no definite cause of death. The danger of dieldrin poisoning occurring in pigeons is greater in dry years than in wet seasons because in dry sowing times the grain is longer germinating and so is available to the wild pigeons for a longer period. The poisoning seems to be cumulative and affected pigeons may drop dead in flight. They are thin, for they do not feed during the last few days of their illness. Many falconers store pigeons in deep-freeze cabinets and pigeons shot over the freshly sown fields in spring may not be fed to the hawks for some weeks or even months—so dieldrin poisoning can occur at a time of the year when there is no dressed grain about. Specific treatment is unknown, but if the poisoning is suspected all pigeon meat must be withdrawn and the hawk fed on other meat. If she has not received a fatal dose she will gradually eliminate the poison and will survive. It is, in any case, not a good plan to feed exclusively on any one type of meat.

Inflammation of the crop is the name given to a condition where a hawk casts up her food some little time after she has consumed it. A day or so before this symptom is evident, the castings may have been noticed to be discoloured, loose and misshapen and to contain

L

undigested food. The mutes are pasty and chocolate/red in colour. The condition is often fatal. Post-mortem examination does not reveal a specific cause of death. Treatment consists of giving a tea-spoonful of liquefied (warmed) Brand's Essence of Beef mixed with 10 grains of bismuth subnitrate. The Brand's Essence may be replaced by Protein Hydrolysate or Ovigest (Burroughs Wellcome & Co.), 10 ccs. The best way to administer the medicine is to suck up the mixture into a hypodermic syringe to the nozzle of which has been fitted 6 inches of thin rubber tubing. Now get an assistant to cast the hawk, and pass the rubber tube down her throat and into her crop. The end of the tube can be felt in the crop. Now pump in the medicine. Repeat in twenty-four hours. In between doses, give the Brand's Essence or Protein Hydrolysate every four hours throughout the day. Turn the hawk loose in an airy loft and after the second dose of bismuth offer her a little freshly killed warm flesh, say, half a rabbit's liver. Give a similar amount a few hours later. Next day feed lightly on warm flesh, not butcher's meat. Thereafter the food may gradually be increased if retained but do not fly the bird for a fortnight.

Blaine recommends that three grains of freshly ground Turkey rhubarb be given on an empty stomach, followed in two hours by a little warm food. I have tried this but the hawk vomited the rhubarb. No casting should be given for several days until the digestion is normal.

Epileptiform fits are common in short-winged hawks especially when they are fat at the end of the moult. The bird falls off the ring perch and gyrates on the ground becoming hopelessly tangled up in its jesses and leash. The tetanic spasms pass off and the hawk, when released from the tangled leash, regains the perch and seems normal. Further attacks may ensue at shortening intervals. The cause of this complaint is unknown. One case was treated with chloromycetin by mouth in capsules and did not have another fit for a year when it succumbed. Another Goshawk was given calcium borogluconate injections on the supposition that the tetanic spasms resembling eclampsia in children might be due to a shortage of ionic calcium. This hawk appeared to derive some benefit from the injections but fell into her bath while having a drink and drowned. A Saker which had several fits was confined in a dark, warm cupboard for three days and fed on the fist at night in twilight. This bird had no more fits and lived until lost flying quarry. From the above the reader will see that no one has the slightest idea of the cause of these convulsions or how to treat them. The only suggestion I can make is that the bird be put loose in a warm, dark place and be disturbed as little as possible for several days. Symptoms of inco-ordination may indicate poisoning with toxic agricultural chemicals through feeding the flesh of pigeons, etc. Change the food to lean beef and keep the hawk, loose, in a quiet, dark place. Force feeding may be necessary. Some recover.

Medicine may be administered to a hawk either over hand when the bird is cast or wrapped in food. Some hawks are past masters at casting up anything which they consider is not food. To diminish the risk of this occurring, it helps to carry the hawk on the fist with a bit of tiring for half an hour after dosing. Always avoid dosing hawks unnecessarily, for hawks cannot tolerate many drugs and if one is not careful the cure will prove worse than the disease. Purgatives particularly must be avoided. Washed meat is laxative and so is Powdered Rhubarb (*Pulv. rhei co.*), but its after effects are binding and it should be followed by a dose of butter and sugar candy. Butter and sugar candy are recommended by Blaine as being a safe laxative. His recipe is to wash a little fresh butter in water to remove the salt then mix with it icing sugar until the mass is a sort of paste. Flavour the mixture lightly with powdered cloves. The final consistency should be similar to that of marzipan. This confection may be stored in a small jar and is said to improve on keeping. The sugar and butter are mildly laxative, and the cloves are valuable as a carminative. Some hawks acquire a taste for this medicine and will take it from the fingers. The dose is a pellet the size of an average casting.

Mustard seeds* and cardamom seeds are useful stomachics and are used in mild cases of croaks. Generally speaking, sick hawks appreciate warmth even to the extent of being put in a box in a linen cupboard. Convalescent hawks should be turned loose in a loft. Weak hawks are best fed a small feed three times daily.

Feathers may be pulled out or broken either by some act of clumsiness and inattention of the falconer or when the hawk flies into a wire fence or struggles on the ground with her quarry. If a tail feather is pulled out it may grow again in about six weeks and it may be distorted. If an eyas loses a tail feather the replacement will be the colour

---

* If a hawk appears to retain her casting an emetic can be made of 20 grs. of black mustard seeds crushed to a powder and made into a bolus with a little saliva. Administer by hand.

and length of an adult feather. Flight feathers which are pulled out are rarely replaced. It is believed that if the falconer can plug the hole from which the primary was pulled with grease or wax to prevent it closing, a new feather may grow down. I have not had the opportunity to try this.

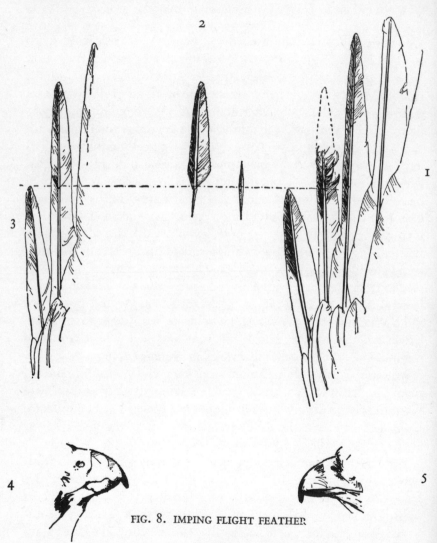

FIG. 8. IMPING FLIGHT FEATHER

1. Damaged flight feather.
3. Imped flight feather.   2. New feather cut and imping needle pushed in.
4. Beak and cere of long-winged hawk.   5. Beak and cere of short-winged hawk.

A bent or frayed feather may be straightened and freshed up by steeping in hot, not boiling water. This must not be done often, though, for it tends to make the feathers brittle. Soiled train feathers may be washed gently in warm water. When a beam or train feather is badly bent so that the shaft is cracked or broken, then it must be "imped." This is done by cutting the broken feather with a razor blade or scalpel about half-way down the shaft at an angle through the pith sloping from the front edge of the feather obliquely backwards to the rear edge. The cut must be clean and the web on both sides must be intact. A corresponding beam or train feather must be selected from a supply of moulted feathers or from a store of feathers from dead hawks which should always be kept. The new feather is cut so that when it is spliced on to the shaft of the broken feather it will correspond to the original length. The angle of the cut must be the same in both feathers, too. An imping needle of suitable size to go into both the pith of the new and the pith of the damaged feather is now selected. Imping needles for large hawks are about $1\frac{1}{2}$ inches long and those for small hawks more slender and about 1 inch long. Smear one end of the needle with seccotine and push it for half its length into the cut shaft of the new feather, then smear the other protruding half of the needle and push it up into the shaft of the broken feather, taking very great care to keep the new feather in the same plane as the old. When the operation is properly done it is difficult to distinguish the imped feather from its sound neighbour.

If a feather is broken too high up in the shaft to imp it, then it must be cut back to where the shaft is hollow. The exposed cavity is then plugged with a piece of pith, from a larger feather, smeared with seccotine. When, a few hours later, the glue has set, a new feather similarly treated is imped on by inserting the glue-smeared imping needle into the two pith-plugged shafts.

Sometimes a hawk's beak becomes overgrown and may crack and split. In order to prevent this occurrence trained hawks occasionally have to have their beaks coped. The provision of a block with a stone top helps to keep the hawk's beak in good shape, for when she feaks after feeding she will strop her beak upon the stone.

To cope a hawk's beak she first must be cast by an assistant. This is accomplished by laying a silk handkerchief across her back as she sits hooded on the falconer's fist. She is then grasped firmly by the body by the assistant, her wings being pinioned against her sides. His thumbs lie in the channel between her shoulders pointing towards her head and his fingers lap round her breast. Her feet are then drawn back by the leash upon the end of which he places one of his feet to prevent her reaching forward and grasping the cushion upon which she is laid, breast down. If she manages to get a wing free she must instantly be released and allowed to stand up. When she has settled down she may be cast again. When the hawk is safely cast the point of the beak is cut off with nail nippers and the beak itself shaped up with a small sharp file. Care must be taken to preserve the notch or tooth in the beak of the true falcons. Do not cut an overgrown beak too short at the first coping or it may bleed. Better wait a week or two and cope it again. The quick will then recede. The germinal layer from which the beak grows is at the junction of the horn of the beak and the cere. Any injury to this area will result in deformed growth of the beak. Ceres are often damaged when hawks are caught in wire netting traps or shut in cages of wire netting. The talons and pounces of trained hawks may occasionally need shortening and sharpening with nippers and file. Be careful to shorten and blunt the hind talon before the moult. Claws are sometimes torn out and when this occurs the toe may bleed profusely. Wrap the toe in adhesive plaster to cover the injured part. Some hawks, especially Merlins, will pull at and even eat an injured toe if it is not covered. Rat bites should be treated with tincture of iodine.

LOST HAWKS

The falconer or austringer who regularly flies his hawks at quarry will sooner or later be faced with the problem of the lost hawk. There is some difference between the loss of a trained hawk while flying quarry and the loss of a hawk that is partly trained during the training period. I will deal with the latter first.

Losses at any time due to faulty equipment are always to be deprecated for they are a reflection upon the efficiency of the falconer, and as they frequently end up in disaster, with the wretched hawk hanging by her tangled leash from the top of a tall tree, they bring both the individual concerned and the sport of falconry into disrepute. It follows that should a hawk escape with her leash and swivel on, or with a length of broken creance trailing, every possible attempt must be made to recover her. This will be difficult if she is not yet obedient to the lure and her recovery then will be largely a matter of luck.

When the creance is removed for the first time, it is possible that through faulty judgement on the part of the falconer or through some unforeseen circumstance, the hawk may refuse to come to the fist (if a short-wing) or to the lure. If the errant bird is a long-wing she may soar round for a bit and then, if one is available, take stand in a tree. If she refuses to come down to proffered lures after a reasonable interval, several subterfuges may be tried. Most hawks are jealous creatures and the sight of another of their kind feeding on the block may be sufficient to bring them down helter-skelter from the tree. The falconer must be near at hand to separate the two hawks quickly for fear that they may injure one another by "crabbing." This method should not be used for getting a short-wing down for it will surely result in the death of the decoy! If a long-wing has raked away while flying to the lure and seems oblivious to the frantic luring of the falconer, it is a good plan to cast off another hawk of the same species and fly her to the lure in the same vicinity in which the truant was lost. With any luck at all the lost hawk will come racing back, and here it is wise to have two lures handy so that both hawks may be taken down together. Short-wings that suddenly become sulky and refuse to come to the fist or lure are a different problem. They are much more nervous than long-wings, and once upset may take some little time to settle down. The only thing to do is to stay with the hawk and follow it should it move from tree to tree. Her mood may suddenly change after what may seem to the austringer an eternity of waiting, and she may, without warning, descend to the outstretched fist. If the hawk is flown in the evening she will tend to get keener as dusk falls and will often come promptly as soon as the sun has gone down. This may be because she sees the chances of a meal that night receding if she doesn't do something about it, or she may find that as the range of visibility decreases with the failing light, so her interest in her surroundings diminishes and she is able to concentrate more fully on her trainer below. Long-wings are often slow to come to a lure in failing light, especially if the lure is cast down in grass of any length. It may be that their night vision is poor and they are afraid to make a forced landing. I have successfully taken a tiercel down to the lure in bad light by tying a white handkerchief to the lure line just above the lure. If all these devices fail the only thing to do is to follow the hawk until she settles down in some tree to roost for the night. When she does this, stay with her till it is really dark. You are lucky if there is no moon or if such moon as there is rises late.

If the hawk is sitting on a branch near the trunk of a climbable tree, it may be possible to carefully and quietly climb the tree. Speak to her as you approach and using a small torch to locate her jesses, secure them and lift her off the branch. Be careful of her feathers as you climb down rejoicing. Should the hawk choose to roost in an unclimbable tree or should you be unable to locate her roosting-place, then there is nothing for it but to return home and retire to bed. For you must be up and back on the scene before it is light. With any luck at all she will not have moved, and the tinkle of her bell as she occasionally rouses will tell you that she is still there. As the sun comes up and warms her she will remember her hunger, which should by now be considerable. You must be sure that your lure, nicely presented, reminds her of the way in which her hunger may be assuaged. A long lure line is an advantage if the hawk is shy and will not approach while you are standing near. Once she is on the lure make in slowly and carefully, talking to her all the time. If she bolts and you cannot approach her on the lure she must be "wound up." To do this she must be lured in an open place. When she has come down to the lure and is feeding upon it, take from your bag a peg about six inches long and push it into the ground. To this peg attach your creance, and, keeping ten or twelve yards from her, walk slowly round her, keeping the line which you are carrying taut. Allow the line to wind round her legs above her bells. She will take little notice of this provided you do not go in too close. When you have encircled her three or four times and you are sure that she is securely wound up, make in quietly to her, shortening the line as you do so. Proffer your fist garnished with attractive food and speak to her. You may be able to take her up without her knowing that she has been snared, but if she tries to bolt then move in and get her on the glove without delay. If this happens this particular hawk may be shy of being approached on the lure for some time, and she must be very carefully handled so that she regains her confidence.

Hawks lost flying quarry are generally lost for two reasons. Either they kill out of sight or they fly the quarry out of sight, lose it, and then check at some other bird they see. This may quickly take a long-wing right out of the district. It is usually a good, persistent hawk that is lost. When such an occasion arises one of the party must stay on the ground from which the hawk was flown luring continuously from the highest point in the vicinity. Unless she has killed, he is the most likely person to recover her, for once outflown hawks nearly always return to the place from which they were slipped. The other members of the field should scatter downwind in the direction that the hawk was last seen. Lures must be shown on all skylines so that the whole area is commanded. Observation and applied natural history now come into play. The movements and behaviour of all birds in the district should be observed. Flocks of lapwings or rooks that suddenly bunch together and tower up into the sky are a sure sign that a falcon is in the area. Rooks may mob and a crow may sit safe in a tree or on a rick jerking about and cursing uneasily. These are the signs that must be looked for and evaluated. Shepherds, farm workers and roadmen working in the vicinity should be questioned for they may have heard the bells and seen the hawk pass over. If darkness falls then the falconer is forced to trudge wearily home in the certain knowledge that dawn will see him swinging his lure again high on some vantage-point on the downs.

It is possible to recapture a shy hawk which will not permit approach on a lure that has to be offered on ground unsuitable for "winding up" by snaring her with a device known as a "snare harness." This consists of a rectangular piece of leather with a loop at the fore end, a loop of elastic on each side at the front and a loop at the back end. To the surface of the rectangle are attached about twenty nylon or horsehair running nooses about two inches in diameter. A freshly killed pigeon is taken and a line is attached to its legs. The forward loop of the snare is placed over the pigeon's head and round its neck, the wings are pushed through the elastic loops at each side. The rear loop is put round the tail so that the leather lies snugly on the pigeon's back with the nooses all standing out at right angles. The pigeon is now pegged down in the sight of the hawk and the falconer withdraws to a place where he can observe the hawk and yet is inconspicuous. When she comes in to the pigeon he must give her time to break in and become well and truly caught in the snares. Even then he must carefully make in and endeavour to take her up without her knowing that she is trapped. A bow-net can be used under similar circumstances.

When a Goshawk is lost flying a pheasant near a wood or other cover a search must at once be made in the direction in which the hawk was last seen to be flying. Once cover is reached pheasants do not fly far in, especially when pressed by the hawk. So search near

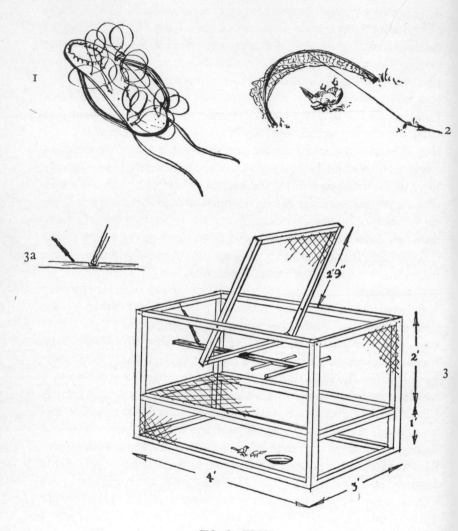

FIG. 9. TRAPS

1. Snare. Horse hair nooses attached to a leather strip which can be fastened to quarry if hawk is difficult to take up.

2. Bow-net with dead bait in centre operated by a single line to pull it over hawk.

3. Cage trap with separate compartment for live bait and spring perch to release. Balanced lid.

3a. Bottom of lid in groove on the perch.

the edge of the cover, both on the ground in case of a kill and in the surrounding trees should the hawk be "at mark" over the pheasant. Goshawks will sometimes drag their kill deep into a bramble thicket or into a ditch and will crouch over it when anyone approaches. A bell on the tail is an absolute necessity when flying quarry in covert. It is my experience that a Goshawk will rarely fly more than a hundred yards into a wood and will usually stop, if outflown, at the first tree that presents a perching-place. She may, of course, from here observe another pheasant or rabbit and start at it. A lost hawk in cover may frequently be located by the persistent alarm notes of blackbirds, wrens and other small birds. Jays and magpies, too, will often take stand in a tree over the place where a Goshawk is crouching on her kill and will proclaim her presence by their harsh cries. In the open, a hawk on a kill may attract heifers grazing in the same field, which will come and stand round in a circle, sniffing enquiringly. Any crows in the area will fly uneasily from tree to tree watching for a chance to humiliate their enemy.

Short-wings, if left out at night, go wild very quickly and must soon be recovered. Once they have been out several days they will be completely feral and impossible to approach. If quarry abounds they will tend to stay in the area in which they were lost and a cage trap, baited with live sparrows for a Sparrowhawk, or a pigeon for a Goshawk, and set in a ride in the wood, will often catch the lost hawk. A cunning German cage trap for Goshawks is baited with a homing pigeon and the trap is so constructed that when the lid comes down after the entry of the hawk, a trap-door opens releasing the bait which wings its way home to inform the austringer that his trap has been sprung!

Eyas long-wings flown in the area in which they were hacked are likely to remain there if lost but passage hawks and haggards who do not know the district so well soon drift away. It is especially dangerous to fly these during the spring and autumn migrations. Peregrines have been taken up on the lure as long as three weeks after being lost and a Merlin as long as six months. Most falconers and austringers will make superhuman efforts to recover a lost hawk, for it is usually those birds which are strong, independent fliers that get lost and their owners know only too well that a lost hawk is often a shot hawk. It is some consolation to those of us who have lost hawks upon which so much time and care has been lavished, to know that some of them,

Goshawks included, successfully return to the wild, find a mate, and in spite of being encumbered by bells and jesses, manage to rear a family.

When flying in a district it is a wise plan to inform as many local countrymen as possible of the fact. A notice in the local pub may help. Many lost hawks have been recovered through information supplied by an observant shepherd or road man. Should a lost hawk be picked up on a kill by a stranger he may, with luck, notice the nameplate and telephone number on the jess. All telephone reports must be investigated even if it seems most likely that they are false alarms. In this way the goodwill of the local populace is maintained and a few words of thanks and explanation to someone who has taken the trouble to ring up and report a strange bird in their garden will ensure a sympathetic reception in the future.

CHAPTER X

CONCLUSION

FALCONRY in Britain has been kept alive during the last two hundred years by successive small bands of enthusiasts who, united in various clubs and as private individuals, have made this most ancient and noble of field sport their main pursuit. That interest in the sport should have waned is obvious enough. The spread of the art of shooting game flying, the enclosure of the great open spaces of England, the Industrial Revolution and especially the preoccupation of the Sovereign and the upper classes with affairs of greater concern than sport, have all played their part in the decline of a pastime which was once indulged in by all ranks of society. Three hundred and fifty years ago the picturesque language of the falconer was commonplace and everyone knew a hawk from a hernshaw. In those more spacious days the noble falcons and the hawks, too, were vigorously protected by the law, administered often by the very ancestors of the modern landowners, who, in ignorance both of natural history and the law, allow their keepers to treat these birds as vermin. Unfortunately this is not all. For racing pigeon enthusiasts, seeking to find a scapegoat for the enormous losses of young pigeons in their first year that they suffer, are endeavouring to lay the entire blame at the door of the Peregrine. These gentlemen are ignoring all other factors, such as bad weather, unprincipled shooters, overhead wires, other predators, and poor quality pigeons insufficiently trained for the races in which they are entered, and are making representations to the Home Secretary with a view to securing the removal of the Peregrine from the Protected List. Peregrines, of course, do occasionally take racing pigeons especially when the flight lines are so sited as to take the flocks of pigeons through mountainous country or along the rocky sea coast. But it should be remembered that many of the pigeon rings found on the legs of freshly killed racing pigeons in Peregrines' eyries come from pigeons which have been missing from their home lofts for months, even years, and have gone completely feral. So the Peregrine may even be doing the pigeon breeder a good turn by weeding out these poorly bred truant birds.

As the numbers of Britain's birds of prey have dwindled over the last century, so they have attracted the attention of the klepto-maniac egg collector who, often posing as some sort of phoney scientist, will rob an eyrie site year after year of both clutches of eggs.

It is these factors that have tended, during the twentieth century, to keep the resident population of our birds of prey at a low ebb. With very few exceptions, modern falconers are bird protectionists first and falconers second. They apply for their licences annually and abide by the advice and decisions of the Home Office Bird Protec-tion Committee. The last thing that any falconer would wish would be for a future generation to point an accusing finger and proclaim that falconers were a factor in the disappearance of a British breeding species. The Merlin, particularly, deserves especial care. As a species it is not by any means as common as it was ten years ago and fal-coners in the future will have to consider very carefully whether they are justified in applying for a licence to take a Merlin, especially as there is no really suitable quarry available at which she may be legally flown.

Unquestionably the biggest blow to falconry in Europe, let alone in Britain, in recent years has been the disappearance of the rabbit as a quarry, due to myxomatosis. Even after the Second World War 90 per cent of *effective* hawking in Europe was practised by those stalwarts who trained and flew Goshawks at rabbits. Here was a ubiquitous quarry, well within the capabilities of even a mediocre austringer, for which permission to hunt could easily be obtained. Now that the rabbit is rarely to be found in hawkable numbers those that live in enclosed country, or in other words, most of us, must try to find alternative quarry. But this is not so easy. Pheasants are jealously guarded. Moorhens in suitable places are really too easy and in unsuitable places are impossible. Wild-duck are never more than a lucky chance quarry. Hares are only taken by one Goshawk in ten. Grey squirrels may provide an answer to the quarry problem for some.

As for long-wings, it is still possible for a favoured few with money and, above all, time, to put up a good show in the field with falcons at rooks or game. It has been suggested that the only hope that those of us of modest means have of seeing hawks flown as they should be at game is for us to combine in a syndicate and rent a moor or partridge shoot. But it is not as easy as that. One of the ways in which the modern enthusiast differs from his forebears is that he insists on training his own hawks. Our ancestors frequently employed professional falconers and were often mere spectators when it came to flying the hawks at quarry. Both hawks and falcons tend to give their best when handled and flown by the person who trained them. To be really successful at game the falcons must be flown daily whenever the weather permits, for six weeks, and few of us can arrange to have a six-weeks' holiday in August and September. So such a syndicate would not show high quality falconry because the hawks would just be getting into their stride when their trainer's holiday came to an end. There are some landowners who might consider flying trained hawks over their moors if they could rid themselves of the misconception that this would drive away the game. Actually, it has many times been proved that the reverse is true and that moors over which hawks have been flown for a season usually have to be shot over at the end of that season in order to thin out the stock. A falconer who flies his hawks daily all through a season will bring to the bag fewer grouse or partridges than three days' shooting by several guns over the same area, and I would venture to suggest that the game would suffer less disturbance from the hawking than the shooting. Falconers of the calibre of the late Colonel Blaine were able to observe that it is possible to fly hawks over the same ground for three times a week and to find the game daily in their familiar haunts. One soon learns the spots which game frequent at any given time of the day and the hawking programme is worked accordingly.

It is a sad thing for falconry that in this age of five-day weeks, shorter working days and longer holidays, the chances of a young man or woman making a success of flying hawks at quarry are so slender. It almost makes one despair when one sees the satellite towns sprawling over good hawking country at a time when through the medium of radio and television the public interest in falconry is probably greater than it has been at any time for the last two hundred years. For falconry is a clean and healthy sport. It demands of its followers the manly virtues of restraint, perseverance, tolerance and skill. Most of all nowadays it requires the exhibition of the will to succeed in the face of greater difficulties than have ever beset the falconers of any other generation.

There has never been any slur cast on falconry on the grounds of cruelty. As a "blood sport," if such an inaccurate phrase must be used, it must be unique. All quarry have sanctuary and frequently outwit or outfly their pursuer. In no other sport are the hunter and hunted so evenly matched. It is not by accident that the lark was the chosen quarry of the trained Merlin in the old days, or the blackbird that of the Sparrowhawk. These two game little birds are well able to take care of themselves when matched against their natural enemy. More often than not the lark ringed up and outflew the Merlin, singing as it did so. The blackbird, less spectacularly, outwitted its fierce pursuer by a show of cunning and manœuvrability that had to be seen to be believed. Game flown by Peregrines may beat the falcon to cover in open flight and rooks similarly gain refuge in trees from which safe retreat they are quick to hurl vocal abuse at their pursuer. In no case is the quarry, be it bird or mammal, ever wounded. Either it is caught and killed outright or it escapes scot free. The flight at quarry is rarely a protracted business with the hunted bird gradually becoming aware of the impossibility of escape. (Cf. the rabbit hunted by a stoat.) The quarry never panics and even at the end may try a stratagem which proves successful. The essence of falconry is the pursuit of a natural quarry (for the species of hawk that is trained) in its natural surroundings. It has been lamented that the Goshawk is not ten miles an hour faster, for if it were it would easily catch pheasants and other game birds. In fact, the evolution of such speedy Goshawks would run parallel with the development of equally swift quarry. Nature never allows a predator such an advantage over its natural prey.

To a layman the most valid criticism of falconry that can be made in modern times is that the returns are often pathetically small for the amount of energy and time expended in training and maintaining a hawk. This is perfectly true, but the fascination of falconry, once it takes hold of a man, is very hard to shake off. It becomes almost a way of life. There is a minority who keep hawks for purposes other than the pursuit of quarry. These persons are not falconers even though they may so label themselves. Others keep hawks in order to attract the attention of the public and so in some peculiar way to boost their personal ego.

I would, from personal experience, advise any young falconer to eschew the Press and avoid undue publicity. He will find that reporters, in their perpetual search for sensation, will twist and distort his words until they are unrecognizable, and he will then be ashamed that he ever agreed to be interviewed. When material is submitted for the Press, broadcasting or television, it is always as well to insist on seeing a proof of the article or script so that inaccuracies and false impressions can be corrected.

It is of the utmost importance that aspiring falconers should know the provisions of the Protection of Birds Act, 1954, for in effect this legislation controls the practice of falconry in the British Isles today.

All the diurnal birds of prey, with the exception of the Sparrowhawk, are hereby protected at all times, but Section 1, paragraph (6) states that—"A licence may be granted to any person by the appropriate authority ... for the purposes of falconry, to take by any means specified in the licence, or to sell or import alive, any number of so specified birds of prey of any description so specified;"

The appropriate authority is given as the Secretary of State after consultation with the appropriate advisory committee.

Quarry, too, are controlled by this Act and perusal of its Schedules is advised.

The following wild birds are of interest to the falconer and are included, with others, in the Second Schedule of the Act it being legal to kill or take them at any time provided one is authorized to do so.

Crow, carrion
Crow, hooded
Domestic pigeon, gone feral
Jackdaw
Jay
Magpie
Rook
House Sparrow
Starling
Stock Dove
Woodpigeon

These birds may be killed or taken at any time except on Sundays in Scotland or on Christmas Day. The following birds, which are

M

possible quarry for the falconer, are listed in the Third Schedule, it being legal to kill or take them *outside* the close season:

> Capercaillie
> Coot
> Curlew (other than Stone Curlew)
> Moorhen
> Snipe, Common
> Snipe, Jack
> Mallard
> Teal
> Woodcock

These birds may not be killed or taken on Sunday in Scotland or on Christmas Day. The expression "close season" means:

"(a) In the case of Capercaillie and (except in Scotland) Wood-cock, the period in any year commencing with the First day of February and ending on the Thirtieth day of September.

(b) In the case of Snipe, the period in any year commencing with the First day of February and ending with the Eleventh day of August.

(c) In the case of Wild Duck and Wild Geese in or over any area below the high water mark of ordinary Spring Tides, the period in any year commencing with the Twenty First day of February and ending with the Thirty First day of August.

(d) In any other case, subject to the provisions of Section Nine of this Act, the period in any year commencing with the First day of February and ending with the Thirty First day of August."

It is also interesting to see that in Section Four of the Act headed General Exceptions " . . . a person shall not be found guilty of an offence against this Act by reason of any act made unlawful by any of the provisions aforesaid if he satisfies the Court before whom he is charged that the act was the incidental result of a lawful operation and could not reasonably have been avoided."

I think this last paragraph makes it clear that the accidental capture or killing of a protected bird by a trained hawk would not necessarily be regarded as an offence against the Act provided it was the "incidental result of a lawful operation."

In Section Five of the Act certain methods of killing or taking wild birds are prohibited. These may be of interest to the falconer who loses his hawk or who contemplates the capture of a wild hawk. He would, of course, in the latter case require a licence and would have to state upon that licence the method of capture he intended using. The use of nets is prohibited and so is the use of any tethered live bird as a decoy. It is also illegal to use an artificial light for the purpose of taking or killing any wild bird other than a bird included in the Second Schedule of the Act.

In certain circumstances licences may be granted to authorized persons to use nets, etc., for taking a wild bird.

Falconers must remember that they must respect the Game (Scotland) Act, 1832; The Game Act, 1831; and the Game Licences Act, 1860.

While the use of bagged quarry is not illegal, all sportsmen will agree that its use is undesirable.

The use of live lures, of course, is forbidden by the Section of the Act which makes illegal the use of any tethered wild bird as a decoy.

Ignorance of the law is no defence—so be warned!

Falconry, due primarily to lack of quarry, is at a low ebb in the British Isles today. Luckily the enthusiasm of the officials and members of the British Falconers Club has not waned over the years in spite of increasing difficulties and disappointments. Contacts have been made with members of other European and foreign Hawking Clubs and the study, if not the practice, of falconry flourishes. British falconers are looking farther afield to other countries which may offer the opportunity to hawk game in more suitable surroundings than are found in the United Kingdom. In Germany, strip cultivation is still practised in many areas and this method of growing crops is especially suited to the flushing of quarry for hawks. In France and Spain there are vast, treeless plains sometimes thickly populated by French partridges, which would be superb places to fly Peregrines. In Southern Ireland the bogs and mosses are suitable places to hawk grouse where they occur—or woodcock, duck and snipe. Magpies, too, can be found here and successfully flown with a cast of Peregrine tiercels.

It is to these places that the falconer of the future, who lives in this overcrowded island, must turn his eyes. For here may lie his best chance to carry on the art and practice of this, our Ancient Occupation.

GLOSSARY

EXPLAINING THE TECHNICAL TERMS EMPLOYED

BY ENGLISH FALCONERS

(Reprinted from Harting's *Bibliotheca Accipitraria*)

ARMS, the legs of a hawk from the thigh to the foot.

AYRE, and EYRIE, *s.*, Fr. *aire*, the aiery, eyrie, or nesting-place.
"Our *aiery* buildeth in the cedar's top."—*Shakespeare.*
The form *eyre* occurs in Reed's *Governance of Hawkes*, 1557 (MS. Bibl. Harl. 676).

BATE, BATING, fluttering or flying off the fist, which an untrained hawk commonly does at the sight of the approaching hood. Literally, to beat the air with the wings, from the French *battre*. "It is calde batyng for she batith with hirselfe, most oftyn causeles."—*Boke of St. Albans*, 1486.

BEAM-FEATHERS, *s.*, the primaries or phalangeal feathers of the wing. See FLAGS.

BECHINS, *s.*, morsels, mouthfuls. Fr. *becquée*, and *bechée*, sixteenth century. "Prend le faulcon et luy donne une *beschie* de char, et luy mets le chaperon."—*Livre du Roy Modus*, 1486. "She bekyth when she sewith; that is to say she wypith her beke."—*Boke of St. Albans*, 1486. The modern French equivalent of *bechins* is *beccades*. Thus Baron Dunoyer de Noirmont, explaining the meaning of the expression "to give tiring" (q.v.), writes "*donner à tirer*, permettre au faucon de prendre quelques *beccades* au tiroir, aileron de volaille préparé," &c.—*Hist. de la Chasse en France*, 1868, iii, p. 85, note.

BEWITS, *s.*, short thin strips of leather by which the bells are fastened to the legs.

BIND, *v.*, to fasten on the quarry in the air.

BLOCK, *s.*, a truncated cone or cylindrical piece of wood having a ring in it for the attachment of the leash, and placed out of doors, whereon the hawk is set to "weather" (q.v.).

BOLT, TO FLY AT, *v.*, said of a short-winged hawk; to fly straight from the fist at the quarry.

BOWISER, *s.*, a young hawk able to fly from bough to bough.

BOWSE, *v.*, to drink; variously spelt "bouse," "boose," "bouze," and "booze." O. Dutch, *buisen*.

All the page numbers given in the glossary and polyglot vocabulary refer to Harting's *Bibliotheca Accipitraria*.

BOWSING, drinking.

BRAIL, s., a narrow slip of thin soft leather, with a long slit in it, used for tying one wing of a restless hawk that bates much.

BRANCHER, s., a young hawk that has lately left the nest. Called also a "ramage-hawk."—Ray, *Summary of Falconry*, 1678.

CADGE, s., the wooden oblong square frame on which hawks are carried hooded to the field.

CADGER, the person who carries the hawk; hence the abbreviated form "cad," a person fit for no other occupation.

CALLING OFF, luring a hawk from an assistant at a distance for exercise. See CREANCE.

CANCELEER, v., Fr. *chevaucher*, to make two or three sharp turns in the descent when stooping.
   "The fierce and eager hawks down thrilling from the skies
   Make sundry *canceleers* ere they the fowl can reach."
        Drayton, *Polyolbion*, 1622, song xx, l. 229.

CARRY, v., to fly away with the quarry.

CAST, s., a "cast of hawks," i.e. two; not necessarily a pair.

CAST, v., "caste her to hode" (1575). When a hawk will not stand to the hood, or requires coping (q.v.), she has to be "cast" or held for the purpose.

CAST GORGE, Fr. *jeter la gorge*, to throw up the meat that is in her crop. See Turbervile's *Booke of Falconrie*, 1575, p. 287.

CASTING, s., fur or feathers given to a hawk with her meat to cleanse the pannel (q.v.), and afterwards cast up in the shape of oblong pellets enveloping the indigestible portions of the food which are thus rejected. Cotgrave gives *Oiseau acuré*, a hawk that hath had "casting" given her. An old proverb says:
   "Wash'd meat and stones maketh a hawk to flie,
   But great *casting* and long fasting maketh her to die."
        Latham's *Falconry*, 1615, p. 23.

CAWKING-TIME, s., pairing time.—Reed, *Governance of Hawkes*, 1557. See Harting, No. 81, Introd., p. xvi.

CERE, s., Fr. *cire*, Lat. *cera*, the bare wax-like skin above the beak.

CHECK, v., whence checking, to fly at; to change the bird in pursuit.

CLUTCHING, seizing the quarry in the feet.

COME TO, v., to begin obeying the falconer.

COPING, cutting off the sharp points of beak and talons. "Let her be short-coped, so I would advise all short-winged hawkes to be used, for the safety of thine owne hands."—Bert, *Treatise of Hawkes*, 1619, p. 67.

COWERING, quivering or shaking the wings, observed in young hawks.

CRABBING, i.e. grabbing; said of hawks when two are flown together, and one seizes the other on the quarry by mistake.

CRAY, s., a disease in hawks, namely, a stoppage of the tewell (q.v.), so that the bird cannot mute (q.v.). "The Cray commyth of washed meete the wich is washed withe hote water in the defawte of hote meete."— *Boke of St. Albans*, 1486.

CREANCE, s., Fr. *créance*, Lat. *credentia*, a long line attached to the swivel, and used when "calling-off" (q.v.); flying a hawk as it were on credit. Bert, in his *Treatise of Hawkes*, 1619, has "cranes" (pp. 20, 21, 24) and "calling-cranes" (p. 54).

CRINES, s., the short hair-like feathers about the cere (q.v.). Nicholas Cox, in *The Gentleman's Recreation*, 1674, has *crinets*.

CROAKS, or KECKS, Fr. *crac*, a disease of the air-passages, analogous to a cough, and so called from the sound the bird makes during any exertion, such as bating, or flying. See PIN.

CROP, s., the dilatation of the gullet which serves as the first receptacle for the food taken by a hawk.

CROSSING FLIGHT, when another bird flies between the hawk and her quarry.

DECK-FEATHERS, s., the two centre feathers of the tail.

DISCLOSED, said of hawks that are just hatched; now obsolete.

DRAW *the hood*, to draw the braces which open and close the hood behind.

DRAWING *from the mew*, i.e. withdrawing a hawk after she has moulted.

ENDEW, v., whence endewing and endewed, to digest the food. "And ye shall say this hauke is fully gorged and hath endewed, or put over."— *Boke of St. Albans*, 1486. The forms *indue* and *induing*, also occur, Fr. *enduire*, and *induire*. See PUT OVER.

ENEW, or INEW, v., the same as PUT IN (q.v.). Drayton has *ineawe*.
"For very fear they instantly *ineawe*."
                    Polyolbion, 1622, song xx, l. 234.

ENSEAM, with old authors ENSAYME, v., whence ensayminge and ensaymed, sc. enseam, from the Fr. *essimer*, to purge a hawk, and rid her of superfluous fat. "Ensayme of an hawke is the grece."—*Boke of St. Albans*, 1486. With a different spelling, "ensaim," the word occurs in a Close Roll of 3 Hen. III (1218). For the context, see Hardy, *Introd. Close Rolls*, p. 170.

ENTER, v., to fly a hawk at quarry for the first time.

EYESS or EYAS, s., a nestling, or young hawk taken from the "eyrie" or nest; from the Fr. *niais*, the initial *n* being dropped, as in many other English words (e.g. adder, from A. S. *nædre*). The terms applied to hawks of different ages are explained by D'Arcussia in his *Fauconnerie*, 1605. He assigns five different names to hawks as they chance to be taken at different seasons—viz. (1) *Niais*, if taken in May; (2) *Gentil*, in June, July, or August; (3) *Pelerin*, or *Passager*, in September, October, November, or December; (4) *Anteneri, Antannaire* (O. Fr. *Antan*, i.e. *l'année passée*), or *Antevere*, in January, February, or March; and (5) *Agar* ("mot Hébreu qui signifie, *estranger*"), if she has once moulted; hence our word "Haggard" (q.v.), applied to a wild-caught old hawk. Tardif, however, had long previously explained these terms in his *L'Art de Faulconnerie*, 1492, thus: "*Nyais* oyseau est celui qui est prins au nid. *Branchier* est celui qui suit sa mère de branche en branche, qui est aussi nommé *rammage*. *Sor* est appellé à sa couleur sorette, celui qui a volé et prins devant qu'il ait mué."

EYRIE, *s*., see AYRE.

FALCON, the female Peregrine *par excellence*, but applied generally to the females of all long-winged hawks.

FALL AT MARK, to alight upon the ground and there await the owner. See Bert, *Treatise of Hawkes*, 1619 (pp. 6, 72).

FEAKE, *v*., feaking; said of a hawk when she wipes her beak on the perch after feeding. It was also said "an hawke snytith or sewith hir beke, and not wipeth hir beke."—*Boke of St. Albans*, 1486.

FILANDERS, *s*., intestinal worms, *filaria. Cf. The Zoologist*, 1881, p. 309.

FLAGS, *s*., the secondary, or cubital feathers of the wing. See BEAM-FEATHERS.

FLY ON HEAD, *v*., to miss the quarry and check.

FOOT, *v*., to clutch. A good footer is said of a hawk that catches well and holds.

FROUNCE, *s*., a canker or sore in the mouth and throat. For modern treatment, see Salvin and Brodrick, *Falconry in the British Isles*, 2nd edit. p. 142.

FULL-SUMMED, *adj*., when a hawk has got all her new feathers after moulting. See SUMMED.

GALBANUM, *s*., a gum resin derived from an umbelliferous plant, *Ferula galbaniflua*; usually obtained by making an incision in the stalks, when a milk-white fluid exudes in tear-like drops, which, after a few hours' exposure to light and air, change to a yellow colour, and become dry and hard enough to gather. It is regarded as an internal remedy in chronic mucous catarrh and rheumatism, and is applied externally in the form of galbanum plaister as a mild stimulant to relieve tumours and chronic pulmonary affections.

GET IN, *v*., to reach the hawk as soon as she has killed.

GLEAM, the substance thrown up after casting gorge.

GORGE, *s*., the crop; GORGED, *adj*., full fed.

GURGITING, choking with too large a mouthful.

HACK, *s.*, the place where the hawk's meat is laid.—Nicholas Cox, *The Gentleman's Recreation*, 1674.

HACK, flying at; Fr. *voler au taquet*; the state of liberty in which eyess falcons are kept for a few weeks before being trained; coming in daily to feed on the hack-board where their meat is cut up for them. Sir John Sebright employs the term: *Observations upon Hawking*, 1826, p. 8. John Dawson Downes, a contemporary falconer of experience, to whom he submitted the MS. of this work for criticism prior to publication, invariably wrote *at heck*, and asserted that the term is not applicable "until the birds have been taken up and trained." See *The Zoologist*, 1890, p. 418.

HACK-BELLS, large heavy bells put on hawks to hinder them from preying for themselves whilst "flying at hack."

HAGGARD, *s.*, a hawk that has been caught after assuming its adult plumage, that is, after having moulted in a wild state. Professor Skeat states (*Etym. Dict.*) that the original sense is living in a hedge (*hag*), hence wild; though Peregrine Falcons do not live in hedges. D'Arcussia derives the word from the Hebrew *agar*, which signifies stranger, and which, in this sense, is synonymous with Passage-hawk. See EYESS. The unknown author of the *Managier de Paris*, 1393, has "Esprevier *hagart* est celluy qui est de mue de haye," ed. Pichon, 1846, vol. ii, p. 317. In a footnote to this remark Baron Pichon observes: 'D'Arcussia (pp. 8 et 36) et Saincte Aulaire (p. 12) disent aussi que le faucon *hagart* (ou mué de champs) est celui qui a déja mué une fois. D'Arcussia fait deriver ce nom du mot hébreu *agar*, signifiant étranger. Il semble qu'il doit plutôt signifier *égaré, sauvage*, a moins qu'attendu l'explication qu'en donne ici notre auteur on ne le fasse venir de *haya*, haie." Selincourt, in his *Parfait Chasseur*, 1683, gives some advice as to the best kinds of hawks to keep according to the sort of country they are to be flown in, and refers to the "fauconniers flamands qui en apportent tous les ans tant de *niais* que de *hagars*."

HALSBAND, *s.*, literally, neck-band; a contrivance of soft twisted silk placed like a collar round the hawk's neck and the end held in the hand; used by Indian falconers, when flying the Sparrowhawk, to steady the bird when cast off.

HAVOCK, to cry, from A.S. *hafoc*, a hawk. See HOO-HA-HA.

HEY and HEYE, *adj.*, in old authors, *sc.* high, i.e. in good condition.

HOOD, *s.*, the leathern cap (Fr. *chaperon*, Dutch huif, and German *haube*) used for blindfolding hawks to tame them. "I never in the house let her sit hooded at all, and when shee is a flying hawke, never unhooded in the field."—Bert, *Treatise of Hawkes*, 1619, p. 23. Before the Crusades the hood was unknown to European falconers; it was introduced by the German Emperor, Frederick II, who adopted the use of it from the Syrian Arabs. The hood proper has a plume of feathers on top; the rufter-hood is without this. See RUFTER-HOOD and SEELING.

HOOD OFF, *v.*, to pull off the hood and slip a hawk at the quarry.

HOOD-SHY, said of a hawk that has been spoilt by clumsy hooding.

HOO-HA-HA. The modern version of an old cry raised by falconers when the quarry is sighted and the hawk is encouraged to pursue. Drayton (No. 23) gives it in a description of hawking by the river, 1622 (*vide anteà*, p. 19). Perhaps the expression, *to cry havock*, meant originally to give the hawking cry before slipping at the quarry, *hafoc* being the A.S. word for hawk. Claude Gauchet, in his *Plaisir des Champs*, 1583, writes: "puis au partir de l'arbre *hoya, hoya*, se crie;" and Dangeau, in his *Etats de la France*, has: "Toutes fois qu'elle part (la Pie) on crie, *houya, houya!*" Baron de Noirmont (No. 206), describing the French method of duck-hawking (vol. iii, p. 184), says: "on mettait les oiseaux, c'est à dire les faucons, *à mont*, puis on faisait partir les canards; au moment où ils prenaient leur vol, on criait *ha, ha!* ou bien encore *hou, hou!* à la mode flamande." The Arab falconers shout "*ha-hou!*" which, according to General Daumas (No. 199), signifies with them "There it is!" The Japanese falconers, when halloaing to a hawk, cry, "*O-ou, O-ou!*" See the *Chinese and Japanese Encyclopædia*, by Simayosi Anko, 1714 (No. 366).

IMPING, from the Lat. *impono*, a method of repairing broken flight or tail feathers. For the *modus operandi*, see Salvin and Brodrick, *Falconry in the British Isles*, 1873, p. 134.

INDUE, INDUING, note to No. 10. See ENDEW.

INKE, *s.*, the neck of the quarry (q.v.), now obsolete.

INTERMEWED is "from her first mewing till she come to be a white hawk." —Latham, 1615. Literally, "between moults." "I have seen divers *entermewers*."—Bert, 1619. This word is now seldom used.

JACK, the male Merlin.

JERKIN, the male Jerfalcon or Gyrfalcon.

JESSES, *s.*, the short narrow straps of leather fastened round a hawk's legs to hold her by. See LEASH.

JOKIN, sleeping; used by old authors; a term now obsolete.

JOKITH, jouketh, i.e. sleepeth. Amongst the "kyndeli termis that belong to hawkis," explained in the *Boke of St. Albans*, 1486, the fifth is that your "hauke *jouketh* and not *slepith*."

LEASH, *s.*, a long narrow thong of leather attached to the jesses with a swivel or varvels (q.v.), and by means of which a hawk is tied to perch or block.

LINES, *s.*, *loynes, lunes*, also *lewnes*. "Lunes for hawks, leashes or long lines to call them."—Phillips, *New World of Words*, 1696. "The jesses were made sufficiently long for the knots [ends] to appear between the middle and the little fingers of the hand that held them, so that the *lunes*, or small thongs of leather, might be fastened to them with tyrrits or rings, and the *lunes* were loosely wound round the little finger."—Strutt,

Sports and Pastimes, p. 32. Hence it would appear that the lunes took the place of the modern leash, which is attached to the jesses with a swivel or varvels. Bert terms them "lines," thus:—"until he hath with her *lines* fastened her *calling-cranes* unto her."—*Treatise of Hawkes*, 1619, p. 54. See CREANCE.

LURE, *s.*, from the O.Fr. *loerre*, modern *leurre*; O. German *Luoder*, a bait. Technically, a bunch of feathers, or couple of wings tied together on a piece of leather, and weighted. Being garnished with raw meat, the hawk is always fed upon it. Hence, when swung aloft, it serves to lure the hawk back to the falconer.

MAIL, *s.*, the breast feathers of a hawk.

MAIL, *v.*, to mail a hawk, i.e. to wrap her up in a sock, or handkerchief (Fr. l'envelopper d'un linge nommé *chemise*), either to tame her, as described by Bert (op. cit., pp. 46–47), or to keep her quiet during an operation, as "coping" or "imping" (q.v.).

MAKE-HAWK, *s.*, an old experienced hawk flown with an eyess, when training, to teach it or encourage it.

MANNING, manned, making a hawk tame by accustoming her to man's presence. See RECLAIM.

MANTLE, *v.*, said of a hawk "when she stretcheth one of her wings after her leg, and so the other."—Nicholas Cox, 1674.

MAR-HAWK, *s.*, one who spoils a hawk by clumsy handling.

MARK, to fly at, *v.*, generally said of a Goshawk when, having "put in" a covey of partridges, she takes stand, marking the spot where they disappeared from view until the falconer arrives to put them out to her.

MARROW, with old authors mary, e.g. mary of beefe; mary of goose; given as a remedy, or to envelope medicine.

MEW, *s.*, the place where hawks are set down to moult. When the royal "mews" at Charing Cross were converted into stables in 1534, the name, confirmed by long usage, remained·to the building, although inapplicable after the hawks were removed. In later times, when the people of London began to build ranges of stables at the back of their houses, they continued the name of the buildings, though appropriated to other uses.—Stow's *Survey of London*, 1598.

MEW, *v.* to moult, from the Fr. *muer*, to change the feathers. In *The Gentleman's Academie*, by Gervase Markham, 1595, will be found special directions for the mewing of hawks, from which we learn that the best time to commence is the beginning of Lent, and, if well kept, the bird will be mewed, that is, moulted, by the beginning of August. French falconers term their hawks "*mués* lorsqu'ils ont fait cette premiere mue en captivité; *mués des bois* ou *de champs*, quand elle a eu lieu en liberté."—Dunoyer de Noirmont. "Pour *les muez des champs*, ils sont du tout infidèles, et vont toujours aux moucherons."—D'Arcussia, *Conférence des Fauconiuers* (11ᵉ journée). This explains the term "*muer de haye*," used in reference to a Goshawk in one of the Paston Letters, November 24, 1472, which seems to have puzzled commentators.

MITES, *s.*, the parasites that infest the head and nares of a hawk.

MOMEY, *s.*, with old authors, *sc.* mummy, Fr. *momie;* formerly, when reduced to powder, used as medicine for hawks: *cf.* Ray, *Summary of Falconry*, 1678, chap. ii. § 9. The old Spanish writers on Falconry refer to it as *momia: cf.* Pero Lopez de Ayala, *Libro de las Aves de Caça*, chap. xxviii. The use of it was probably introduced into Spain by the Moors, as it appears to be derived from the Arabic *moumiya*, from *moum*, wax.— *Cf.* Dozy et Engelmann, *Glossaire des Mots espagnols dérivés de l'arabe*, 2nd edit. Leyde, 1869.

MUER DES CHAMPS, or MUER DE HAYE. See MEW.

MUSKET, *s.*, the male Sparrowhawk; French *mouchet*, Dutch *mosket.*

MUTES, *s.*, the droppings or excrement of hawks. "And ye shall say that your hauke mutith."—*Boke of St. Albans*, 1486. Or, if a short-winged hawk, she "sliceth," op. cit.

NARES, *s.*, the nostrils of a hawk. From the Latin.

NYAS, *s.*, *sc.* an eyas, eyess, Fr. *niais*, a nestling hawk taken from the eyrie or nest.—Dunoyer de Noirmont, *Hist. de la Chasse en France*, iii, p. 120. O.Fr. *nyés*. "*Tu auras faulcons et laniers nyés, ramaiges, sors, muers.*"— Gace de la Bigne, fourteenth century. Turbervile, in his *Booke of Falconrie*, 1575, has a chapter entitled "How to keepe Nyasse Sparow-hawkes." See note to EYESS.

OSTRINGER, *s.*, *sc.* austringer, and astringer (Shakespeare), generally re-stricted to one who keeps short-winged hawks, especially the Goshawk. Fr. *austour* and *autour.* "We usually call a falconer, who keeps that kind of hawk, an *austringer.*"—Cowell, *Law Dict.* Bert employs the term *austringer.*—*Treatise of Hawkes*, 1619. The form *ostreger* also occurs, from *ostercus* or *austercus.*—Ducange, sub voce *Astur.* "A Goshawk is in our records termed by the several names of *osturcum, hostricum, estricium, asturcum,* and *austercum,* all from the Fr. *austour* [mod. *autour*; Lat. *astur*]."—Blount, *Ancient Tenures*, 4to, 1815, p. 266. "A techer or ynstructor of fawkners and ostrigers."—Reed, *Governance of Hawkes*, 1557. Turbervile has "certaine observations for an Ostreger in keeping of a Goshawke."—*Booke of Falconrie*, 1575. Ray also has "Ostreger."— *Summary of Falconry*, 1678.

PANNEL, *s.*, the stomach or lower bowel of a hawk.

PANTAS, *s.*, a disease in hawks akin to asthma.

PASSAGE-HAWK, a wild hawk caught upon the passage or migration.

PASTER, *s.*, plaister; used medicinally; now obsolete.

PELT, *s.*, the dead body of the quarry.

PENDANT FEATHERS, those behind the thighs of a hawk.

PERCH, *s.*, is that whereon you set down your hawk when you put her off your fist.—Ray, *Summary of Falconry*, 1678. The *perch* is used in the house; the *block*, out of doors. See BLOCK.

PETTY SINGLES, the toes of a hawk.

PILL, or PELF, *s.*, what is left of the quarry after the hawk has been fed upon it.

PIN AND WEB, *s.*, a disease of the eye in hawks akin to dimness and film. Bert describes another disease (p. 86) called "pinne in the throat," which from his description resembles what modern falconers term "croaks" (q.v.).

PITCH, *s.*, the height to which a falcon rises in the air by ringing up (q.v.).

PLUMAGE, *s.*, given for "casting" (q.v.).

PLUME, *v.*, to pluck the feathers off the quarry.

POINT, to make her, when a hawk throws herself up in the air above the spot where the quarry has "put in" (q.v.).

POUNCES, *s.*, the claws of a hawk.

PREEN, *v.*, to dress the feathers with the beak.

PRINCIPALS, the two longest feathers in the wing of a hawk.

PUT IN, *v.*, to drive the quarry into covert.

PUT OVER, *v.*, said of a hawk "when she removeth her meat from the gorge into the bowels, by traversing with her body, but chiefly with her neck."—Nicholas Cox, *The Gentleman's Recreation*, 1674. See ENDEW.

QUARRY, *s.*, the game flown at. O.Fr. *curée*, the reward given to hounds when they killed; from the Low Lat. *corata*, the entrails of a slain animal.

QUICK, *adj.*, alive.

RAKE AWAY, *v.*, to take off, instead of pursuing the quarry flown at, or to fly wide of it.

RAMAGE-HAWK. See BRANCHER.

RANGLE, *s.*, small stones given to hawks to aid digestion. If set down on a block where it can reach them, a hawk will pick them up voluntarily.

RECLAIM, *v.*, Fr. *réclamer*, to make a hawk tame, gentle, and familiar. "In the manning and reclaiming, you must by kindness make her gentle and familiar with you."—Nicholas Cox, *The Gentleman's Recreation*, 1674.

RED-HAWK, *s.*, the modern term for a "sore-hawk" (q.v.).

RING-UP, *v.*, to rise spirally to a height.

ROBIN, *s.*, the male Hobby.

ROUSE, *v.*, is when a hawk lifteth herself up and shaketh herself.—Nicholas Cox, op. cit. "Rowse," *Boke of St. Albans*, 1486.

ROUSING; with old authors ROWYSIN. See ROUSE.

RUFF, *v.*, Fr. *buffeter*, to hit the quarry and make the feathers fly, without trussing it. See TRUSS.

RUFTER-HOOD, *s.*, Dutch *ruishuif*, German *rüsthaube*, French *chaperon de rust*, a plain, easy leather hood, through which the hawk can feed, and opening wide behind; used when a hawk is being tamed, and superseded by the hood proper when she is trained. The absence of a plume prevents her from pulling it off. See HOOD.

RYE, *s.*, a disease in hawks which shows itself by a swelling in the head. "For defawte of hote meate this sekenese the Ry commyth."—*The Boke of St. Albans*, 1486.

SAILS, *s.*, the wings of a hawk.

SCOURING, *s.*, purging. See Turbervile's *Booke of Falconrie*, 1575 (pp. 285, 286).

SCREEN-PERCH, *s.*, the form of perch used for hawks when kept in a room. See PERCH and BLOCK.

SEARE, and SERE, *s.*, with old authors, for cere, from Latin *cera*, the waxlike skin above the beak. See CERE.

SEDGE, AT-, a corruption of "at siege;" said of a heron when at the waterside, in contradistinction to being "on passage."

SEELING, an old method of obscuring the sight of the hawk by passing threads through the lower eyelids and tying them behind the head, a practice long superseded in this country by the more humane use of the hood, though still adopted by native falconers in India.

SERVING *a hawk*, helping to put out the quarry from covert.

SET DOWN *to moult*, put into the mew.

SHARP SET, very hungry.

SLOOSE, *s.*, with old authors, for sloes (*Prunus spinosa*, Linn.), used medicinally; A.S. *sla;* O.E. *sle*. For an interesting note on the meaning of this word, see Prior, *Popular Names of British Plants*, 3rd edit. (1879), p. 217.

SNITING, with old authors; an obsolete term for sneezing.

SOCK, German *Falkensack*. See MAIL, *v.*

SORE-HAWK, *s.*, a hawk of the first year. From the French *sor*, or *saure*, reddish-brown; whence sorrel. "A sowyr hawk ys much tenderer than a muyd hawk."—Reed, *Governance of Hawkes*, 1557. A coloured figure of a sore Sparrowhawk is given in Rowley's *Ornithological Miscellany*, 4to, 1875 (vol. i, p. 58).

SPRING, *v.*, to flush the partridge, pheasant, or other bird to be flown at.

STALKE, *s.*, with old authors, the leg (*tarsus*). See Harting, No. 81, pp. 5, 7, 16, 31.

STAVESAKER, *s.*, stavesacre, *Delphinium staphisagriæ*, Linn., a plant formerly in request for destroying lice in a hawk.

STOOP, *s.*, the swift descent of a falcon on the quarry from a height; synonymous with swoop.

STRIKE THE HOOD, *v.*, to half open it, so as to be in readiness to hood off the moment the hawk is to be flown.

SUMMED, *adj*. A hawk is said to be "summed" or "full summed" when, after moulting, she has got all her new feathers, and is fit to be taken out of the mew. See note to No. 10, *anteà*, p. 10.

SWIVEL, *s*., used to prevent the jesses and leash from getting twisted when the hawk is tied upon the perch. See LEASH, TYRRIT, and VARVELS.

TAKE THE AIR, *v*., to mount.

TEWELL, *s*., the lower bowel, affected by the disease termed cray (q.v.).

TIERCEL, TERCEL, TASSEL (Shakespeare), and TARSELL (Bert), the male of any species of hawk, the female being termed a falcon. The tiercel is said by some to be so called from being about one-third smaller in size than the falcon; by others it is derived from the old belief that each nest contained three young birds, of which two were females, and the third and smallest a male. Note the familiar line in *Romeo and Juliet*: "Oh! for a falconer's voice to lure this tassel-gentle back again."

TIRE, *v*., French *tirer*, to pull at a tough piece. See TIRING.

TIRING, *s*., any tough piece (as the leg of a fowl with little on it) given to a hawk when in training to pull at, in order to prolong the meal, and exercise the muscles of the back and neck. "I have knowne many Falconers that never make their hawkes to tyre, saying that it is but a custom, and needelesse; but I say the contrary, for inasmuch as the hawke is exercised by reasonable tyring, shee becommeth the healthier and the lighter both of body and of head by all moderate exercises, yea, and shee is the better in state also as you may perceyve."—Turbervile, *Booke of Falconrie*, 1575.

TOWER, *v*. See RING UP.

TRAIN, *s*., the tail of a hawk. Also the live bird that is given on a line to the hawk when first entered.

TRUSS, *v*., French *trousser*, to clutch the quarry in the air instead of striking it to the ground.

TYRRIT, *s*., a swivel, or turning-ring, from the French *touret*, the use of which is thus explained by Littré: "anneau double qui empêche les jets d'un faucon ou toute autre courroie de s'embrouiller"; and by Baron Dunoyer de Noirmont: "pour empêcher les jets et la longe de s'enrouler, on interposait entre eux un *touret*, composé de deux anneaux de métal, tournant l'un sur l'autre." The word occurs in Chaucer, who describes greyhounds "with mosel fast ybound, colered with gold, and *torretes* filed round." See Warton's note on the passage, *History of English Poetry*, vol. ii, p. 99 (1824). The mode of making a tyrrit or swivel is minutely described and its use explained in the work of the Emperor Frederick II, *De arte venandi cum avibus*, written about 1247, and first printed in 1596. See chapter xl of the second book, entitled *De tornetto, qualiter factum sit, et ad quid sit utile*.

UNRECLAIMED, *adj*., wild.

UNSTRIKE THE HOOD, *v.*, to loosen the braces so that the hood may be easily pulled off.

UNSUMMED, *adj.* A hawk is said to be unsummed while moulting, before her new feathers are grown up.

URINES, *s.*, nets to catch hawks.—Nicholas Cox, 1674. A corruption probably of the French *araigne*, "sorte de filet pour prendre les oiseaux divers et même les oiseaux de proie."—Cerfon, *De la Basse Volerie*, p. 145.

VARVELS, *s.*, small flat rings of silver on which the owner's name was engraved, fastened to the ends of the jesses, and used instead of a swivel, the leash being passed through them. One is figured on the title-page of Bert's *Treatise*, 1619. See also Camden, *Britannia*, i, 329; *Gentleman's Magazine*, vol. 63, p. 101; vol. 65, p. 474; *Archæologia*, vol. xii, p. 410, pl. 51; and Dillon, *Proc. Soc. Antiq.*, 2nd series, vol. iv (1869), p. 353.

WAIT ON, French *tenir à mont*. A hawk is said to "wait on" when she soars in circles over the head of the falconer, waiting for the game to be flushed.

WARBILE, WARBEL, and WARBLE, *v.* A hawk warbleth when after "rousing" and "mantling" (q.v.) she crosses her wings together over her back. "She mantellith and not stretchith when she putteth her leges from her oon after another: and hir wynges follow after hir leggs: then she dooth mantill hir, and when she hath mantilled hir and bryngith booth her wynges togeder ouer hir backe, ye shall say youre hawke 'warbellith hir wynges.' "—*Boke of St. Albans*, 1486.

WATCHING. Part of the old method of taming hawks was to watch them for the first night or two after their capture, to prevent them from sleeping. "I kept them upon the fist that day they came unto me, and that night they were truly watched."—Bert, *Treatise of Hawkes*, 1619 (p. 46). Shakespeare employs the word in this sense, *Taming of the Shrew*, act iv, sc. 1, wherein Petruchio gives a lesson in "reclaiming" a hawk.

WEATHER, *v.*, whence weathering, to place the hawk upon her block in the open air. Simon Latham (who states in the Preface to his book that "the practice and experience of many years is given in a few leaves not drawn from traditions in print, or otherwise taken upon trust, but out of certain and approved conclusions") remarks on the subject of "weathering" that an *eyess* may be set abroad to weather at any time of day unhooded, and better when her gorge is full, for she will then sit quietly upon the block; but a *haggard* should be set down in the morning, or else in the evening before she is fed, and should always be hooded to prevent her from "bating" (as she otherwise would do) and continually striving to be gone, whereby her training would be greatly hindered. See Latham's *Falconry; or the Faulcon's Lure, and Cure*, 1615 (p. 35).

VOCABULARY

IN VARIOUS LANGUAGES, OF THE CHIEF TECHNICAL
TERMS EMPLOYED BY FALCONERS

(Reprinted from Harting's *Bibliotheca Accipitraria*)

ENGLISH	DUTCH	GERMAN	FRENCH
Falconry, *or*	Valkenjagt	Falkenjagd	Fauconnerie
Hawking*	Valkenierderij	Falknerei	Autourserie
"	"	Falkenbeize	Volerie
Falconer	Valkenier	Falkenjäger	Fauconnier
Falcon	Valk	Falke	Faucon
Hawk	Havik	Habicht	Autour
Bag, hawking	Valkenierzak	Falknertasche	Fauconnière
Bate, *v.*	Fladderen	Flattern	Battre; se debattre
Bathe, *v.*	Baden	Baden	Baigner
Bell	Bel; schel	Schelle	Sonnette; grelot
Bewit	Riem (lederen)	Riemen	Porte-grelot
Bind, *or* clutch, *v.*	Binden	Binden	Lier; empiéter
Block	Blok	Block	Bloc
Brail	Breil	Schleife; Flechte	Bride
Brancher	Takling	Flügling	Branchier
Cadge	Cagie	Cage; Trage	Cage; brancard
Cadge-bearer	Cagie-drager	Cage-träger	Cagier; porte-cage
Call off, *v.*	Lokken	Anziehen	Leurrer; réclamer
Carry, *v.*	Trossen	Tragen	Charrier
Cast off, *v.*	Losgooijen	Abwerfen; los-lassen	Jeter; lächer; mettre à mont
Casting, *or* pellet	Uitwerp	Auswurf; Schleimsel	Cure; pelote
Cere	Wassen	Wachshaut; Ring	Cire; couronne
Cope, *v.*	Afsnijden	Abschneiden	Couper; apoltronir
Creance	Vliegdraad	Flugleine; Lockschnur	Créance; filière

* Many of the terms in this Vocabulary are not to be found in the Dictionaries, and have been taken from the most approved and reliable works on Falconry.

SPANISH	ITALIAN	LATIN
Halconería; altanería	Falconeria	Ars falconaria*
Cetrería; caca (caza) de aves	Uccellatura	Ars accipitraria
Volatería	Caccia col falcone	Aucupium, *ex* aucupare
Halconero; cetrero	Falconiere; strozziere; strucciere	Falconarius; accipitrarius
Alcon, halcon, falcon	Falcone	Falco
Açor; azor	Astore	Astur; accipiter; acceptor
Bolsa; O.S. linjavera	Borsa; sacca	Bursa; carneria
Sacudir	Scuotere; debattere	Deverberare, *unde* diverneratio (bating)
Bañar	Bagnare	Balneare; abluere
Campanilla; cascabel	Sonaglio	Campanella; nola
Corréa	Coreggia	Corrigia; corrigiola
Agarrar; empuñar	Attaccare	Arripere; prehendere
Tajo; zoquéte	Tronco; pietra	Sedile; seditorium
Braza	Briglia	Corrigiola; filo ligare alas
Halcon raméro	Ramace; ramengo	Ramalis; ramarius; ramagius
Caja	Gábbia	Portatorium
Portador	Portatore	Falconum portator
Tirar; atraer; Llamar a la tira	Attirare; allettare; chiamare al lodro	Allectare; revocare
Llevar	Portare la preda	Subducere
Arrojar, O.S. desalar; lançar	Lasciare; gettare	Jactare
Curalle; pelotilla; plumada	Pallotolla; O.I. borgature	Pilula; plumata; egestio
Çera	Cera	Cera
Acortar	Tagliare	Ungues aptare
Hilo; O.S. fila; cordél	Fila; credenzia	Credentia; fileria

* The Latin terms given in this Vocabulary are derived from the authoritative work of the Emperor Frederick II, *De arte venandi cum Avibus*, No. 308, in Harting's *Bibliotheca Accipitraria*.

ENGLISH	DUTCH	GERMAN	FRENCH
Crop	Krop	Kropf	Gorge
Drawer, *or* lure	Loer	Lockspeise; Federspiel	Tiroir; leurre
Eagle	Arend	Adler	Aigle
Eagle-owl	Hoornuil	Uhu	Grand-duc
Endew, *v.*	Verduwen	Verdauen	Enduire; *ou* induire
Enseam, *v.*	Zuiveren	Aushungern	Essimer; degraisser
Eyas, Eyess, *or* nestling	Nestling	Nestling	Niais
Eyrie, *or* nest	Horst	Horst	Aire; nid
Feather	Veder	Feder	Plume; penne
Flight feathers	Vleugels	Schwingfedern	Vanneaux
Flight, a	Vlugt	Flug	Vol
Feed up, *v.*	Azen	Füttern; Kröpfen	Faire paître
Fist	Hand	Hand; Faust	Main; poing
Glove	Handschoen	Handschuh	Gant
Gorge	Krop	Kropf	Gorge
Goshawk	Havik; duiven-valk	Habicht; Hühnerhabicht	Autour; *O.F.* austour
Haggard; see "Glossary"	Haggard	Hagard; Alter-falke	Hagard; madré
Hawk	Havik	Habicht	Autour
Hawk of the fist	Hand-valk	Hand-falke	Oiseau de poing
Hawk of the lure	Loer-valk	Lockspeisen-falke	Oiseau de leurre
Hawk-house	Valken-kamer	Falkenkammer	Perchoir
Hawk's meat	Aas	Frass; Fleisch	Pat; nourriture
Heron-hawk	Reiger-valk	Reiher-falke	Heronnier
Heronshaw	Reiger	Reiher	Heronseau
Hobby	Boom-valk	Baum-falke	Hobereau
Hood, *s.*	Huif; kap	Haube; Kappe	Chaperon
Hood, rufter-	Reushuif	Rüst *oder* Rauschhaube	Chaperon de rust
Hood, plume of	Pluimpje	Federbusch	Panache; cornette

SPANISH	ITALIAN	LATIN
Gorja; gola; papo	Gola	Gula; gorgia; ingluvies
Señuelo	Logoro	Tiratoria; lorarium
Aguila	Aquila	Aquila
Buho	Gufo	Bubo
Digerir	Digerire	Induere
Desaynar	Smagrare	Expurgare
Niégo; nidiégo	Niaso; nidiace; nidaso	Nidasius; nidarius; nidularius; clamorosus, *a screamer*
Nido; O.S. ayre	Nido; nidato	Area; nidus
Pluma	Penna	Penna
Cuchillos	Coltelli	Cultellus; vani
Vuelo; volería	Volo; volato	Volatus
Nutrir; alimentar	Nutrire; alimentare	Nutrire
Mano; puño	Mano; pugno	Manus; pugnus
Guante	Guanto	Chirotheca; manica coriacea
Gorja; gola	Gorgia; gola	Gula
Açor; azor	Astore	Astur; austur
Halcon mudado; O.S. çahareño	Falcone mudato	Falco mutatus
Azor; gavilan	Astore	Astur; accipiter; acceptor
Ave de mano	Falcone di pugno	Pugilaris
Ave de señuelo	Falcone di logoro	Loraria, seu pinnaria
Halconera	Camera; muta	Camera; muta; mutatorium
Nutrimento	Nutrimento; alimento	Alimenta; caro
Garçáro	Aironero	Falco ad ardeam
Garça; garza real	Airone	Ardea; ardeola
Alcotán	Lodolaio	Alaudarius
Capiróte	Cappello; cappelleto	Capellus; cucullus
„	„ „	„ „
Penacho; peñola	Pennuccia; pennella	Plumula; pennula

ENGLISH	DUTCH	GERMAN	FRENCH
Hood, *v.*	Ophuiven	Aufhauben	Chaperonner
Unhood, *v.*	Athuiven	Abhauben	Déchaperonner
Hunger traces	Honger-malie	Hungermal; Hungermarke	Pennes affamées
Imp, *v.*	Eene veder aansteken	Anstecken	Enter une penne
Imping needle	Naald	Nadel	Aiguille à enter
Jerfalcon *or* Gyrfalcon	Giervalk	Gierfalke	Gerfaut
Jesses	Schoenen	Schühe; Wurffesseln	Les jets
Kestrel	Torenvalk	Thurmfalke	Cresserelle
Kite	Wouw; milaan	Rother-milan	Milan
Lanner	Lannervalk	Lannerfalke	Lanier
Leash	Langveter	Langfessel	Longe
Short-leash	Kortveter	Kurzfessel	Courtrier
Lure, *s.*	Loer	Lujer; Lockspeise; Federspiel	Leurre; rappel
Lure, *v.*	Lokken	Locken	Leurrer; réclamer
Merlin	Smelleken	Schmerlein, O.G. Smirlin; Merlin-falke	Emerillon
Moult, *s.*	Muite	Mäuser	Mue
Moult, *v.*	Muiten	Mausen	Muer
Mount, soar, *or* ring up, *v.*	Zweven	Auffliegen; Aufsteigen	Prendre l'air; monter à l'essor
Mutes, *s.*	Smettsel	Schmelz	Esmeuts; emeuts; fientes
Mute, *v.*	Smettseln	Schmelzen; Spretzen	Esmutir; emeutir; fienter
Nestling, see Eyess	,,	,,	,,
Passage-hawk, *or* peregrine	Passagier; pelgrim	Dreckfalke; Wanderfalke	Passager; pélerin
Perch, *s.*	Vogelrek; Valkenstang	Das Reck, *oder* Sitzstange	Perche
Quarry	Prooi	Raub; Beute	Curée; proie
Reclaim, *v.*	Verbeteren	Zähmen	Réclamer

SPANISH	ITALIAN	LATIN
Poner el capiróte	Incappellare	Capellum induere
Tirar el capiróte	Discappellare	Capellum deponere
Navajadillas	Penne affamate	Pannæ affamatæ
Enjerir; O.S. enxerir	Inschittire	Imponere
Aguja	Ago; aghetto	Acus
Halcon girifalte	Girifalco	Girofalco; gyrfalco
Pihuélas; O.S. piuélas; pedi-cuélas	Getto; getti	Jactus; jacti sunt laquei de corio facti, imponen di pedibus falconum
Cernicalo	Cristariello; fal-chetto; gheppio	Tinnunculus
Milano	Milano; forceluta	Milvus regalis
Lanero; Alfanéque	Laniere; lanario	Lanerius; lanarius
Lonja	Lunga	Longa
Lonja corta	Corta lunga	Not used; cf. p. 170
Señuelo; O.S. roedero	Logoro; O.I. lodro	Loyrum; logorum; lorarium; tiratorium
Señolear; llamar	Allettare; richia-mare	Allectare; revocare; logorum exhibere vel ostendere
Esmerejón	Smerlo; smeriglio	Smerilio; mirle (Albertus Magnus)
Muda	Muta	Mutatio
Mudar	Mutare	Mutare; plumas exuere
Remontárse; ele-várse	Elevarsi; alzarsi	Altivolare; spiraliter aethera scandere
Excremento; O.S. tulliduras	Smaltitura; calcin-accio	Excrementa; stercora
Tullir; toller	Smaltire	Fimum reddere
” ”	”	”
Peregrino; pelegrin	Pellegrino; pere-grino	Peregrinus; fugitivus
Percha; palo; varal	Pertica; ramo; barra; stanga	Pertica; cf. p. 171
Présa	Préda	Corata; præda
Reducir; amansar	Reclamare	Mansuefacere

ENGLISH	DUTCH	GERMAN	FRENCH
Red-hawk, *or* sore-hawk	Roode-valk	Rotherfalke	Faucon rouge, *ou* sors
Saker	Saker-valk	Saker-falke	Sacre; sacret
Seel, *v.*	Breeuven	Siegeln; Aufbräunen	Ciller; siller
Sock	Valkenzak	Falkensack	Linge; chemise
Sparrowhawk; male, musket	Sperwe; het mannetje mosket	Sperber; Sperlings-habicht	Epervier; *O.F.* espervier, le mâle mouchet
Stoop, *s.*	Aanval; neerschieten	Stos	Choc; attainte; coup; assaut; descente
Stoop, *v.*	Schieten	Stosen; Streichen	Descendre; fondre; donner le coup
Swivel	Draal	Drahle; Wirbel	Vervelle; touret
Talons	Klaaus	Zehen; Krallen	Doigts; serres
Tiercel	Taleken	Terzel	Tiercelet
Tame, *v.*	Spinnen	Abrichten; Zähmen	Apprivoiser
Tire, *v.* to pull at	Afknagen	Nagen	Tirer
Train, *v.*	Treinen; opleiden onderrigten	Unterrichten	Entraîner; affaiter; dresser
Training	Opleiding	Unterrichtung	Affaitage; dressage
Train, *or* tail	Staart	Schwanz	Queue; balai
Varvel	Draal	Wirbel	Vervelle
Wait on, *v.*	Aanwachten	Abwarten; stehen	Tenir à mont; faire la cresserelle
Watch, *v.*	Bewaken	Bewachen	Veiller l'oiseau
Weather, *v.*	In de vrije lucht zetten	Lüften, *oder* in die Luft bringen	Jardiner

SPANISH	ITALIAN	LATIN
Halcon soro	Soro; falcone soro	Falco saurus; sores; p. 154
Alcon sacre	Il sacro	Falco sacer
Sellar	Cigliare	Ciliare; ciliatio (seeling)
Sáco; mála	Sacchetto; maglia	Sacculus; malleolum
Esparvel	Sparviere	Sparverius; spervarius; espervarius; mas *muschetus*, *nisus* autem femina
Golpe; acometida	Colpo	Pulsus
Golpar	Calare	Pulsare; capere prædam
Eslabón	Tornetto; guinzaglio	Tornettum
Garras	Unghioni	Ungues
Terzuélo; O.S. torçuélo	Terzuolo	Tertiarius
Amansar	Domare	Mansuefacere
Roer	Rodere; tirare	Rodere
Hacer; amaestrar; enseñar	Ammaestrare	Instituere; educare
Amaestramento	Ammaestramento	Cura; curatio
Cola	Coda	Cauda
Eslabón	Guinzaglio; tornetto	Tornettum
Esperar	Aspettare; attendere	Expectare
Velar	Vegliare	Advolare
Orear	Mettere sul tronco	Foras portare

FALCONRY CLUBS OF THE WORLD

BRITISH FALCONERS' CLUB
President: J. G. Mavrogordato, C.M.G.
Honorary Secretary: M. H. Woodford, M.R.C.V.S., Summer Lodge, Evershot, Dorchester, Dorset.

NEDERLANDSH VALKENSIERSVERBOND "ADRIAAN MOLLEN"
President: Heer J. W. R. Van de Wall.
Honorary Secretary: Heer G. A. Van Nie, Moormanlaan 11, Knegsel, Post Steensel, Holland.

ASSOCIATION NATIONALE DES FAUCONNIERS ET AUTOURSIERS FRANCAIS
President: M. Christian Antoine de Chamerlet.
Honorary Secretary: M. J. F. Terasse, 60, Rue Sartoris, La Garenne (Seine), France.

DEUTSCHER FALKENORDEN
President: Dr. Heinz Brull, 2359, Hartenholm-Wolfsburg, W. Germany.
Honorary Secretary: D. Gutt, Sundernholz 18, 43 Essen 1, West Germany.

OSTERREICHISCHEN FALKNERBUND
President: Dr. E. Tratnig-Frankl, Aug.-Jaksch-Str., 92, Klagenfurt, Austria.
Secretary: W. Crammer, Osterr. Falknerbund, Postfach 221, Wien, Austria.

CIRCOLO DEI FALCONIERI D'ITALIA
President: Dr. E. Coppaloni, Via Tuscolana 741, Rome.
Honorary Secretary: Signor L. Jarach, ia Academia VAlbertina 37, Turin, Italy.

NORTH AMERICAN FALCONERS' ASSOCIATION
President: G. T. Kotsiopoulos, 7301, N. Hamilton St., Chicago, Illinois.
Secretary: Vacant.

BRITISH COLUMBIA FALCONRY ASSOCIATION
Secretary/Treasurer: Wayne Nelson, 6102 Marine Drive, Vancouver 8, B.C.

CANADIAN FALCONRY ASSOCIATION
Secretary: R. Fyfe, Box 180, Sackville, N.B. Canada.

GAME LICENCES AND SHOOTING-HAWKING SEASONS FOR GAME

Game licences which are necessary under the Game Act of 1831 and the Game Licences Act of 1860, are needed for the shooting and taking of game.

GAME LICENCES	One year	Expiring July 31st	£3
	3 months	Expiring October 31st	£2
	9 months	Expiring July 31st	£2
	Any continuous period of 14 days		£1

SHOOTING–HAWKING SEASONS FOR GAME   All dates inclusive

Grouse   August 12th–December 10th
Ptarmigan   August 12th–December 10th (Scotland only)
Blackgame   August 20th–December 10th
Partridge   September 1st–February 1st
Pheasant   October 1st–February 1st
Hares   No close season

In England and Wales it is illegal to take any of the above on Sundays or on Christmas Day.

BIBLIOGRAPHY

A list of the most important books on Falconry published in the British Isles 1575–1960.

AUTHOR	TITLE	PUBLISHER	DATE	REMARKS
TURBERVILE	*Booke of Faulconrie or Hawking*	Barker Purfoot	1575 1611	Very rare
LATHAM	*Falconry*	Jackson	1615 1618	Rare and expensive
	New and Second Booke of Faulconry	Jackson	1633 1653 1658	One of the classics on long-wings
BERT	*An Approved Treatise of Hawkes and Hawking*	Richard Moore Quaritch	1619 1891	Both editions very rare Reprint Classic on short-wings
CAMPBELL	*Treatise of Modern Faulconry*	Privately printed	1773	
SEBRIGHT	*Observations upon Hawking*	Harding H. Wright	1826 1828	Both editions very rare
BELLANY	*A Treatise upon Falconry*	Privately printed	1841	
BURTON	*Falconry in the Valley of the Indus*	Van Voorst	1852	
SALVIN AND BRODRICK	*Falconry in the British Isles*	Van Voorst	1855 1873	Better illustrations Better text
FREEMAN AND SALVIN	*Falconry; Its claims History and Practice*	Longmans	1859	
FREEMAN	*Practical Falconry*	Cox	1869	
DELMÉ-RADCLIFFE	*Notes on Falconidae used in India in Falconry*	Privately printed	1871	Very useful
HARTING	*Hints on the management of Hawks*	Cox	1884 1898	2nd edition is the better

AUTHOR	TITLE	PUBLISHER	DATE	REMARKS
ANON.	A Perfecte Booke for Kepinge Sparhawkes and Goshawkes	Quaritch	1886	Reprint with introduction by Harting 100 copies
HARTING	Bibliotheca Accipitraria	Quaritch	1891	Most useful
LASCELLES AND COX	Coursing and Falconry, Badminton Library	Longmans, Green	1892⎫ 1899⎭	Good book 4to. Edition
MICHELL	The Art and Practice of Hawking	Methuen	1900	Scarce. Classic on Merlins Excellent book
FISHER	Reminiscences of a Falconer	Nimmo	1901	
PHILLOTT	The Baz-Nama-Yi-Nasiri	Quaritch	1908	Persian Treatise on Falconry
BLAINE	Falconry	Allen	1936	A modern classic
RUTTLEDGE	Falconry for Beginners	British Falconers' Club	1949⎫ 1955⎬ 1965⎭	A short guide for the beginner
STEVENS	Observations on Modern Falconry	Privately printed	1957	
MAVROGORDATO	A Hawk for the Bush	Witherby	1960	A monograph on the Sparrowhawk

This list of books does not pretend to be exhaustive. It only includes those works printed in the British Isles in the last 400 years which the writer considers are useful or interesting to the Bibliophile-Falconer. In actual fact, the beginner in falconry will glean little of use to him from many of these volumes. At first he should confine his attentions to Lascelles, Michell and Blaine (having previously studied *Falconry for Beginners*). Later on, when he has gained some experience he will be able to appreciate the finer points of Latham, Bert and Stevens. The reader of any book published before 1954 must remember to make allowances for the changes in the law on Bird Protection and the change, too, in the climate of public opinion on Blood Sports. Many of the practices advocated twenty years ago would not now be tolerated and in most cases have been since proved to be quite unnecessary.

*　　*　　*

"I would not loose my knowledge of Hawkes, and running Horses for any thing, they are not without use, I meete often with people that understand no other language, and then they make me sociable and not unpleasing to the company."

PROTECTION OF BIRDS ACT, 1954—LICENCES: FALCONRY

1. Section 10(1) (b) of the Act enables the Secretary of State after consultation with the Advisory Committee on the Protection of Birds for England and Wales to grant to any person a licence authorising that person to take by any specified means, any specified number of birds of prey of any specified description for the purposes of falconry.

2. An application for a licence should be made on the official form by the person to whom the licence is to be granted, and should give the information listed below.

3. A licence will authorise the holder to take the birds by himself or with the help of another person. But if the applicant wants someone else, not acting under his immediate supervision, to take the birds for him, that other person must be named in the licence; and his name and address should be stated in the application. If the applicant wishes to ask more than one person to take birds for him, each person should be mentioned.

4. The Secretary of State can grant licences for England and Wales only. Any application for a licence to take birds of prey in Scotland should be addressed to the Under Secretary of State, Scottish Home and Health Department, St. Andrew's House, Edinburgh, 1.

Home Office,
   Whitehall,
      London, S.W.1.

Details required on Form of Application for a licence to take a bird of prey for the purposes of Falconry:

Applicant's name and address.

Applicant's age (if under 21).

Species of bird of prey which it is desired to take.

Means by which bird is to be taken.

Area from which bird is to be taken.

If bird is to be taken by a person other than applicant, agent's full name and address.

Particulars of any club or society concerned with falconry of which applicant is a member, or, if not a member of any such club or society, particulars of the applicants' experience in falconry.

WEIGHTS OF GAME

Game varies in weight according to the season, locality, and age when taken. These weights are the average for adults in a normal season.

Bean Goose .. .. 6 lb.–8 lb.
Bernicle Goose .. 4 lb.–5 lb.
Brent Goose .. .. 3½ lb.–4½ lb.
Blackcock .. .. 3 lb.–4 lb.
Capercaillie .. .. 6 lb.–12 lb.
Common Snipe .. 3½ oz.–4½ oz.
Golden Plover .. 7 oz.–9 oz.
Greylag Goose .. 7 lb.–9 lb.
Grouse (cock).. .. 1¼ lb.–1½ lb.
Grouse (hen) .. .. 1 lb. 1 oz.–1 lb. 5 oz.
Yorkshire grouse are said to be heavier than
   Scottish birds.
Hare (Brown) .. 6½ lb.–7 lb.
Jack Snipe .. .. 1½ oz.–2½ oz.
Mallard .. .. 2½ lb.–2¾ lb.
Partridge (cock) .. 13 oz.–15 oz.
Partridge (hen) .. 12½ oz.–14½ oz.
Pheasant (cock) .. 3 lb.–3½ lb.
Pheasant (hen) .. 2 lb.–2½ lb.
Pink-footed Goose .. 5½ lb.–7½ lb.
Ptarmigan .. .. 1 lb.–1½ lb.
Quail .. .. .. 3 oz.–4 oz.
Rabbit .. .. 2½ lb.–3½ lb.
Teal .. .. .. 11 oz.–13 oz.
White-fronted Goose 4½ lb.–6½ lb.
Widgeon .. .. 1½ lb.–2 lb.
Woodcock .. .. 8 oz.–14 oz.
Woodpigeon 1 lb.–1½

In giving these weights it is not suggested that all these birds and animals are suitable quarry for trained hawks.

FLYING WEIGHTS OF TRAINED HAWKS AND FALCONS

These weights are, of course, only approximate. Great variations will occur with the race of the hawk, the state of manning, the quarry being flown, and the length of time the hawk has been in captivity.

Gyr falcon (*Falco rusticolus* spp. Linn.) 3 lb. to 3 lb. 4 oz.
Jerkin (*Falco rusticolus* spp. Linn.) 2 lb. 8 oz. to 2 lb. 10 oz.
Peregrine falcon (*Falco peregrinus peregrinus* Tunst.) 1 lb. 15 oz. to 2 lb. 2 oz.
Peregrine tiercel (*Falco peregrinus peregrinus* Tunst.) 1 lb. 4 oz. to 1 lb. 7 oz.

Peale's falcon (*Falco peregrinus pealei* Ridgw.) 2 lb. 8 oz. to 2 lb. 13 oz.

Peale's tiercel (*Falco peregrinus pealei* Ridgw.) 1 lb. 6 oz. to 1 lb. 8 oz.

Siberian falcon
Tundra falcon } (*Falco peregrinus calidus* Lath.) 1 lb. 8 oz. to 1 lb. 13 oz.

Siberian tiercel
Tundra tiercel } (*Falco peregrinus calidus* Lath.) 1 lb.

Lanner falcon (*Falco biarmicus* spp. Temm.) 1 lb. 8 oz. to 2 lb.

Lanneret (*Falco biarmicus* spp. Temm.) 15 oz. to 1 lb. 4 oz.

Prairie falcon (*Falco mexicanus* Schleg.) 1 lb. 8 oz. to 2 lb.

Prairie tiercel (*Falco mexicanus* Schleg.) 15 oz. to 1 lb. 4 oz.

Saker falcon (*Falco cherrug cherrug* Gray) 2 lb. 4 oz.

Sakret (*Falco cherrug cherrug* Gray) 1 lb. 11 oz.

Barbary falcon (*Falco pelegrinoides pelegrinoides* Temm.)
Red naped Shahin (*Falco pelegrinoides babylonicus* Sclater) } 1 lb. 6 oz.

Barbary tiercel (*Falco pelegrinoides pelegrinoides* Temm.)
Red naped Shahin tiercel (*Falco pelegrinoides babylonicus* Sclater) } 15 oz.

Sultan falcon
Black Shahin } (*Falco peregrinus peregrinator* Sund.) 1 lb. 9 oz.

Black Shahin tiercel (*Falco peregrinus peregrinator* Sund.) 1 lb. 1 oz.

Kestrel (*Cerchneis tinnunculus tinnunculus* Linn.) 7½ oz. to 8½ oz.

Red-headed Merlin (*Falco chicquera ruficollis* Swains.) 9 oz.

Red-headed Merlin (Male) (*Falco chicquera ruficollis* Swains.) 6 oz. to 7 oz.

Merlin (*Falco columbarius regulus* Pallas) 6¾ oz. to 8 oz.

Merlin (Jack) (*Falco columbarius regulus* Pallas) 5½ oz. to 6½ oz.

Goshawk (*Astur gentilis gentilus* Linn.) 2 lb. to 2 lb. 6 oz.

Goshawk tiercel (*Astur gentilis gentilus* Linn.) 1 lb. 6 oz. to 1 lb. 10 oz.

Sparrowhawk (*Accipiter nisus nisus* Briss.) 8 oz. to 10 oz.

Musket (*Accipiter nisus nisus* Briss.) 5 oz. to 7 oz.

Cooper's Hawk (Eastern) (*Accipiter cooperi cooperi* Bp.) 1 lb. 2 oz.

Cooper's Hawk (Western) (*Accipiter cooperi mexicanus* Swains.) 15 oz.

Cooper's tiercel (Eastern) (*Accipiter cooperi cooperi* Bp.) 12 oz.

Cooper's tiercel (Western) (*Accipiter cooperi mexicanus* Swains.) 10 oz.

Buzzard (*Buteo buteo buteo* Linn.) 1 lb. 15 oz.

Buzzard (Male) (*Buteo buteo buteo* Linn.) 1 lb. 8 oz.

The generic and specific names in this list are taken from *A Synopsis of the Accipitres*, by H. Kirke Swann, London, 1922.

INDEX